Hiking Minnesota

A Guide to the State's Greatest Hiking Adventures

Second Edition

Mary Jo Mosher and Kristine Mosher

FALCONGUIDES

GUILFORD, CONNECTICUT
HELENA, MONTANA

AN IMPRINT OF ROWMAN & LITTLEFIELD

FALCONGUIDES®

Photos by Evan Faltesek, Kristine Mosher, and Mary Jo Mosher.

Library of Congress Cataloging-in-Publication Data is available on file.

ISBN 978-0-7627-4099-4

Printed in the United States of America

♾™The paper used in this publication meets the minimum requirements of American National Standard for Information Sciences—Permanence of Paper for Printed Library Materials, ANSI/NISO Z39.48-1992

Contents

Acknowledgments vi
Introduction 1
    Minnesota Weather 1
    Flora and Fauna 2
    Wilderness Restrictions 5
    Getting around Minnesota 6
    How to Use This Guide 7
Ranking the Hikes 9
Map Legend 11

The Hikes
The Confluence 12
  1 Minnehaha Falls 14
  2 Fort Snelling State Park 20
  3 William O'Brien State Park 25
Honorable Mentions 31

Blufflands 33
  4 Nerstrand Big Woods State Park 35
  5 Barn Bluff 41
  6 Frontenac State Park 46
  7 Whitewater State Park 50
  8 Great River Bluffs State Park 55
  9 Beaver Creek Valley 62

Prairie Lands 68
  10 Camden State Park 70
  11 Pipestone National Monument 76
  12 Blue Mounds State Park 81
Honorable Mention 87

Glacial Lakes and Landforms 88
  13 St. Croix State Park 90
  14 St. Croix State Forest—Tamarack 94
  15 Banning State Park 101
  16 Mille Lacs Kathio State Park 106
  17 Savanna Portage State Park 110
  18 Pillsbury State Forest 116
  19 Lake Maria State Park 121
  20 Minnesota Valley National Wildlife Refuge 125

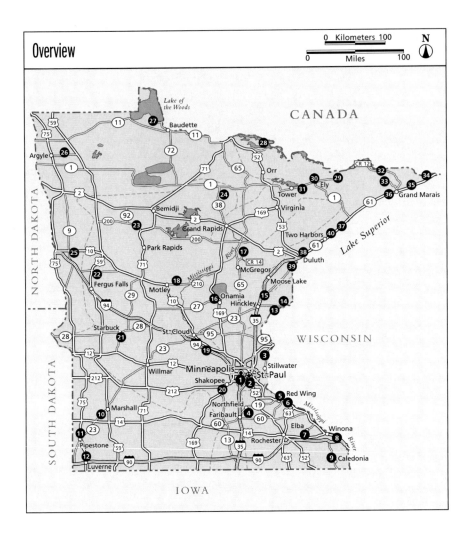

Overview

0 Kilometers 100

0 Miles 100

N

CANADA

Lake of the Woods

Baudette

Argyle

NORTH DAKOTA

Orr

Ely

Tower

Virginia

Bemidji

Grand Rapids

Park Rapids

Two Harbors

Duluth

McGregor

Moose Lake

Fergus Falls

Motley

Onamia

Hinckley

Grand Marais

Lake Superior

Starbuck

St. Cloud

WISCONSIN

Willmar

Minneapolis

St. Paul

Stillwater

Shakopee

Red Wing

Marshall

Northfield

Faribault

Elba

Winona

Pipestone

Rochester

Caledonia

Mississippi River

Luverne

SOUTH DAKOTA

IOWA

21 Glacial Lakes State Park.. 131
22 Maplewood State Park 136
23 Itasca State Park 141
24 Scenic State Park.. 150
Honorable Mentions... 155

Glacial Lake Agassiz Plain.. 156
25 Buffalo River State Park.. 158
26 Old Mill State Park 163
27 Zippel Bay State Park 169

Lake Superior and Border Lakes.. 174
28 Voyageurs National Park 176
29 Secret-Blackstone–Ennis Lake Trail 183
30 Bass Lake Trail... 188
31 Bear Head Lake State Park 193
32 Border Route–Caribou Rock Trail 199
33 Eagle Mountain 205
34 Grand Portage State Park 211
35 Judge C. R. Magney State Park 216
36 Cascade River.. 221
37 Split Rock Lighthouse State Park... 227
38 Park Point.. 234
39 Jay Cooke State Park.. 240
Honorable Mentions... 245

Great Escape—The Superior Hiking Trail 251
40 The Superior Hiking Trail... 253

The Art of Hiking 268
About the Authors... 289

Acknowledgments

There are so many people who were supportive of us during the writing of this book, including the Minnesota Department of Natural Resources, park employees, and others who checked our work for accuracy or who provided us with needed information. We're also indebted to those who helped us with lodging and meals while we were on the road.

We thank our family for their interest and support of this project and Falcon-Guides for providing us with the opportunity to write this book. We would also like to acknowledge Voyageur Press and Constance Jefferson Sansome for permitting us to model our regions of the state after the regions in their book *Minnesota Underfoot*.

HELP US KEEP THIS GUIDE UP TO DATE

Every effort has been made by the authors and editors to make this guide as accurate and useful as possible. However, many things can change after a guide is published—trails are rerouted, regulations change, techniques evolve, facilities come under new management, and so on.

We would appreciate your comments concerning your experiences with this guide and how you feel it could be improved and kept up to date. While we may not be able to respond to all comments and suggestions, we'll take them to heart, and we'll also make certain to share them with the authors. Please send your comments and suggestions to the following address:

GPP
Reader Response/Editorial Department
P.O. Box 480
Guilford, CT 06437

Or you may e-mail us at: editorial@globepequot.com

Thanks for your input, and happy trails!

Introduction

Aptly named from the Lakota word meaning, "water painted blue like the sky," Minnesota's most prominent feature is water. More than 15,000 lakes and ponds, including the largest freshwater lake in the world (Lake Superior), a variety of streams and rivers, and wetlands found in most areas throughout the state provide habitat for wildlife.

Minnesota offers four magnificent seasons to explore. Visit in the spring when the light green forest floor is strewn with all the rainbow's colors as spring flowers emerge from their long, cold sleep. Visit in summer when greens have darkened, prairie flowers are in peak bloom, and farm fields are clothed in tasseling corn, maturing heads of rye, and golden wheat. Fall is the most colorful season for hiking in Minnesota's forests, when the trees offer their awesome artistic display of reds, gold, yellows, greens, and oranges. Many of Minnesota's hiking trails can be explored by ski or snowshoe in the winter, a season of incredible beauty and recreation opportunities.

There's a story behind each place you visit—a history full of drama and colorful individuals that take you back in recorded time. Hike beneath towering pines in the north—the same that Paul Bunyan and his lumbermen left behind. In the western part of the state, visit Blue Mounds State Park and see buffalo that were once part of massive herds grazing on seemingly endless prairies. Walk beside the Pigeon River along the Canadian border and learn about Native Americans gathering berries, fishing the streams, hunting, trapping, trading with the voyageurs, and traveling the rivers in their birch bark canoes. Or step across the mighty Mississippi at its headwaters and imagine Native Americans guiding European explorers to its source.

Like most places, human settlement brought changes to Minnesota's early landscape. Fortunately, as the state's population grew, there were those throughout history who championed the preservation of lands for wildlife and recreation. State and national parks and forests took years of hard work and relentless political lobbying to establish. Organizations and individuals continue to work together in restoration and preservation efforts as a result of growing awareness of the value and importance of beauty and the earth's complex ecosystems.

Hiking is an excellent way to explore Minnesota's scenic landscape. From remote wilderness to city park, you will find in this guidebook a collection of hikes that best represents Minnesota's diversity and beauty.

Minnesota Weather

When hiking in Minnesota, it's important to be prepared for a wide range of conditions. Minnesota is known for its extremes in temperature and for conditions that can vary widely within any given day. Because of its location in the center of the continent, Minnesota has the greatest weather changes in the shortest distances and times in North America, with the exception of mountainous regions. Hot, dry air moves in from the deserts in the southwestern states and collides with cold arctic air flowing south from Canada, creating temperatures that range from 115 degrees to –60 degrees Fahrenheit from summer to winter. Temperatures can vary daily by as much as thirty degrees in one location during spring and fall. For every 100 miles traveled northward, temperatures are two to three degrees cooler and temperature differences from north to south can differ by as much as fourteen degrees.

Prevailing winds come from the south and southwest, bringing relatively dry air. Moist, warm air comes in from the Gulf and cold, dry air from the north. Lake Superior has a moderating effect on weather along its shore as well as occasionally producing its own weather patterns. Temperatures near the lake are cooler in summer and warmer in winter, and east winds bring slow-moving rainstorms and precipitation affecting the northeast part of the state.

Snowmelt comes later in the season in the north and along Lake Superior's North Shore where the warm season is much shorter than in the central and southern portions of the state. Precipitation is moderate and variable statewide with thunderstorms occurring May through September. The most severe storms occur in the southern and central portions of the state, some bringing straight-line winds, tornadoes, and lightning strikes. Most of the time, though, the weather from May through September and even into October is conducive to hiking. The variation in climate from north to south allows the hiker to travel the state to view wildflowers as they emerge from April in the southeast to May and June in the northeast. Prairie wildflowers are in peak bloom in August. Touring the state for fall color viewing is popular in Minnesota, as one can spend five or six weeks enjoying peak colors from north to south.

Flora and Fauna

A drive across Minnesota reveals a great variation in landscape and ecological communities. In the southeast, the Mississippi drainage is a prominent feature with its surrounding limestone and sandstone bluffs—remnants of ancient seas that once covered the area. These blufflands give way to rolling farmland and prairie as one travels toward the state's southwest border. The Red River borders northwestern Minnesota and frames a large expanse of flat land, once a glacial lake bottom. A journey eastward across the northern half of the state traverses both rolling wooded hills left over from glacial deposits and many lakes and wetlands. Deciduous forest gives way to coniferous forest in the north central part of the state and thicker soils give way to exposed bedrock and very thin soils where glaciers scoured the land. The greatest topographic relief occurs in the northeast corner of the state with rugged hills bordering the Lake Superior shoreline.

This diversity is largely due to the convergence in Minnesota of three of North America's largest ecological regions: tallgrass prairie, deciduous forest, and coniferous forest. Called biomes, these ecological regions define the dramatic changes in vegetation and wildlife throughout the state.

Tallgrass prairies, broken up by agriculture and development, stretch from the southeastern to the northwestern edge of the state and extend west to the Rocky

Mountains and south to the edge of northern Mexico. Grasslands once covered one-third of Minnesota, and its prairies remain among the most diverse in North America in spite of their significant reduction.

There are five major types of prairie in the state. Three of these, classified by soil moisture, are dry, mesic (moderate moisture), and wet. Dry prairies exist on sandy and gravelly soils and support shorter grasses and flowering plants, including little bluestem and the beautiful pasque flower. Goat prairies, located on the steep Mississippi River bluffs in southeastern Minnesota, are one of the four sub-types of dry prairie. Mesic prairies support tall grasses, like big bluestem and Indian grass, and are mainly located on nutrient-rich soils of southern and western Minnesota. The wood lily is a common flower of the mesic prairie. Wet prairies occur where there is poor soil drainage, particularly in the northwestern corner of the state, and are dominated by several types of grasses and sedges. Forbs (flowering plants) found in wet prairies include the white lady slipper and New England aster. Dry oak savanna occurs where the frequency and intensity of fires is lower, allowing bur oak and northern pin oak to establish. A unique and rare type of prairie occurring in Minnesota is the calcareous seepage fen, which is dominated by plants adapted to soils saturated with cold groundwater. These fens are found throughout the prairie biome. Prairie restoration has gained momentum in Minnesota where the intricacy and value of prairie ecology is becoming more widespread. Organizations including the Department of Natural Resources, Prairie Passages, and The Nature Conservancy have joined efforts to preserve and re-establish native prairie throughout the state.

Bison and elk were once common mammals of Minnesota's prairies and can still be observed. A bison herd has its home in Blue Mounds State Park and a small herd of elk, remaining after relocation from Wyoming, lives in the northwestern part of the state. Gophers, badgers, and other burrowing small mammals are prominent. They tunnel underground to escape the intense summer heat and harsh winters, feed on prairie plants, and contribute to the nitrogen content in the soils. White-tailed jackrabbit, red fox, and coyote are among mammals that inhabit Minnesota's prairies. Bird life is abundant and includes the red-tailed hawk, northern harrier, and the endangered burrowing owl. The spectacular prairie chicken, protected since 1935 in the state, is a showpiece for avid bird-watchers.

A swath of deciduous forest covers Minnesota diagonally from the northwest corner to the southeast corner. This is the northern and westernmost range for this region, which extends across eastern North America to the Atlantic Ocean. The state's extreme cold temperatures in the northeast and extreme heat in the southwest define the boundaries of this band of deciduous forest in Minnesota.

There are seven types of deciduous forest within this band that provide a wide range of habitats for wildlife. Generally, soil moisture determines three forest communities. Xeric forests, located along the southern and western edges of the biome, grow on dry soils and are composed of drought-tolerant red, white, and black oak, and aspen. Maple-basswood forest, the predominant mesic forest community, once covered more than two million acres west and south of the Twin Cities. Referred to as the Big Woods, this late-succession forest, characterized by sugar maple and basswood, developed in areas that were protected from fires. It has since been reduced by agricultural clearing to a few small remnants found in the south central part of the state. In the spring, ephemerals (wildflowers with a brief lifespan and appearance) color the forest floor, taking advantage of the spring sunlight before the tree canopy emerges. Nerstrand Big Woods State Park is an excellent place to view the display of Dutchman's breeches, spring beauty, bloodroot, trillium and the rare endemic dwarf trout lily.

An isolated band of deciduous forest parallels Lake Superior's North Shore. This northern hardwood forest of maple, basswood, and yellow birch, is mixed with white pine, balsam fir, white spruce, and white cedar. The northern hardwood forest thrives beside the big lake in the area's moderate temperatures. Both the Big Woods and the Northern Hardwood forest are great places for spring ephemerals and fall colors. Lowland forest communities are found in wet areas of river floodplains and swamps. Tree species include cottonwood, elm, willow, and ash. Aspen and birch are found in areas disturbed by logging or clearing.

White-tailed deer are common in the deciduous forest and are found throughout the state. A diversity of mammals inhabits the variety of deciduous forest habitat in Minnesota, including raccoons, cottontail rabbits, bats, and the unique southern flying squirrel. Opossums, intolerant of cold temperatures, are common in the central and southern parts of the state, and the gray fox is found only in deciduous forest (red foxes inhabit all three biomes). Moose and timber wolves are found in the northern reaches of this biome but are more common in the coniferous forest. Black bear inhabit the northern deciduous and coniferous forests.

The deciduous forest supports a vast number of bird species because of the many layers, each of which provides a different type of food and shelter, from the canopy to the forest floor. Bird species include warblers, flycatchers, woodpeckers, owls, and hawks. The great blue heron nests in colonies called rookeries and can be found in large numbers, sometimes exceeding a thousand pairs. The wild turkey is prominent in southeastern Minnesota, which is also home to the largest concentration of amphibians and reptiles in the state, some at the northern edge of their range, due to warmer temperatures. The garter snake is among the most common snake species, including the fox, redbelly, and gopher snakes. Minnesota's only two venomous snakes inhabit the southeastern part of the state, and they are both rare. The Massasauga is listed as endangered in Minnesota and the timber rattlesnake is listed as threatened. Sightings have been rare in recent years.

Minnesota's northeast corner is home to a segment of the coniferous forest biome, which extends northward into Canada and up to the arctic tundra. Covering two-fifths of the state, it is the largest of the state's three biomes. Characterized by a glaciated landscape of lakes, glacial deposits, and bedrock exposed by scouring ice sheets, the coniferous forest covers a variety of terrain. The western edge of the biome is flat lake plain, while moraines and other glacial landforms make up the rolling hills of the central portion. Rugged topography and rocky outcrops are prominent in the northeast along Lake Superior. Trees, plants, and wildlife have adapted to thin soils, cold winters, and cool summers. Most of Minnesota's 15,000 lakes are found in this biome, including the Boundary Waters Canoe Area Wilderness (BWCAW) and Voyageurs National Park. The six forest communities found in the northern coniferous forest are jack pine, white pine, red pine, upland white cedar, spruce-fir, and black spruce-feathermoss. Before European settlement, red and white pines were predominant species. The largest concentration of old-growth forests in Minnesota occurs in this biome, although the majority of the area has been logged at one time. Aspen and birch have established themselves in areas disturbed by logging or fires. Itasca State Park contains about 1,500 acres of 200 to 250-year-old red and white pine forests. The majority of remaining old-growth forests resides within the BWCAW.

Many people associate the "Northwoods" with the timber wolf, black bear, moose, white-tail deer, and beaver. Moose are the largest of Minnesota mammals, weighing as much as 1,200 pounds, and are solitary in nature. They survive winters by browsing on twigs and bark, while their summertime diet consists of aquatic plants. The timber wolf has long been a controversial animal. Once hunted to near extinction, they are thriving today in the northern Rockies and across the Great Lakes with Minnesota containing approximately 2,900 individuals, more than double the number first established for wolf recovery. The United States Fish and Wildlife Service continues to propose federal delisting of the wolf from the endangered species list and transfer management of wolf populations to individual states. The wolf is still listed as a federal threatened species as of this printing. Beavers are historically significant, as they were valued for their quality pelts at the height of felt-hat fashion in Europe in the 1700s. It was because of the demand for this large rodent's fur that Minnesota was mapped and explored. Beaver have great impact on their environment and are essential in maintaining Minnesota's wetlands. Bird life is plentiful and varied in the mosaic of forest types that make up the coniferous forest. Gray jays, ravens, chickadees, and woodpeckers are among year-round residents common in the Northwoods. Ruffed grouse, also year-round residents, practice a unique drumming sound to communicate during courtship and establish territory. This drumming can be heard often when walking through the woods. Several hundred pairs of the majestic bald eagle nest in northern Minnesota each year, and a large number of them winter at Lake Pepin in southern Minnesota. Snowy owls migrate south from the tundra to find food when the lemming population is low, and the boreal owl nests in the coniferous forest of Minnesota.

Wilderness Restrictions

Minnesota has fifty-six state forests covering more than 3.6 million acres and two national forests. The Chippewa National Forest is in the north central part of the state and the Superior National Forest covers the northeast corner, including the

BWCAW. Many of the state's sixty-two state parks lie within the state forests. Regulations are more relaxed in state and national forests than in state parks, national monuments, the national park, and the BWCAW. For example, camping does not have to be at designated campsites on state or national forest land that is outside a park or wilderness area designation.

When trail users are well informed, they can use public lands with minimum impact. For information, rules, and regulations concerning public land, contact the specific land management agency before you hike. Access to sensitive areas can change at any time. Following are some general guidelines applying to all state parks. A complete list is available when you enter the park.

- The park belongs to all Minnesotans. Treat it with respect.
- Familiarize yourself with park rules.
- Some parks have parcels of private property within their boundaries. Please respect and observe signs where posted.
- Build fires only in fire rings provided.
- Hunting is prohibited except in designated areas.
- Daily or annual permits are required for all vehicles entering a state park.
- Protect the environment by staying on designated trails.
- Contact the Minnesota Department of Natural Resources: (800) 646-6367.

Getting around Minnesota

Area Codes
Currently, Minnesota has seven area codes, serving roughly as follows: 612 applies to Minneapolis, Richfield, Fort Snelling, and the airport; 763 applies to the northwest suburbs (north of I-394); and 952 applies to the southwest suburbs (south of I-394). Northern Minnesota is covered by the 218 area code. Just south of that is the 320 area code. The 507 area code applies to an area south of the Twin Cities. The 751 code covers southeastern Minnesota. Maps showing the most current area code locations are available online at www.commerce.state.mn.us.

Transportation
Nearly all modes of transportation in Minnesota fall under the Minnesota Department of Transportation (Mn/DOT). For information, check their Web site at www .dot.state.mn.us. Here, you'll find links that will lead you to road, air travel, and Amtrak information. Mn/DOT's main offices are at 395 John Ireland Boulevard, St. Paul, MN 55155-1899. You may also call them at (800) 657-3774.

By Air: The Minneapolis/St. Paul International Airport (MSP) is Minnesota's largest airport. It, and several smaller airports, fall under the Metropolitan Airport Commission. Information is accessible under Mn/DOT's Web site, or call the Minneapolis/

St. Paul International Airport for general airport information at (612) 726-5555. You can check out the following smaller airports under the same Web site by clicking on Reliever Airports: Airlake, Anoka County Blaine, Crystal, Flying Cloud, Lake Elmo, St. Paul Downtown, and Flying Cloud Expansion.

The Duluth International Airport (DLH) is the second largest airport in Minnesota. For information call (218) 727-2968. There are many other airports throughout the state that have access to the global transportation network. Their flights are provided by major airlines through the commuter network. The following cities have airports: Bemidji (BJI), Brainerd (BRD), Chisolm-Hibbing, Ely, Fairmont (FRM), Grand Rapids (GPZ), International Falls (INL), Rochester, St. Cloud, and Thief River Falls (TVF). Information on all Minnesota airports can be accessed through www.flymn.org.

To book reservations online, check the Web site of a specific airline or search one of the following travel sites for the best price: www.cheaptickets.com, www.expedia .com, www.priceline.com, www.travel.yahoo.com, www.travelocity.com, www.trip .com, or www.orbitz.com.

By Train: Amtrak stations are located in the following Minnesota communities: St. Paul/Minneapolis (MSP), Staples (SPL), St. Cloud (SCD), Red Wing, Detroit Lakes (DLK), and Fargo (FAR). Schedules and fares are available either on the Mn/ DOT Web site, or on www.amtrak.com or by calling (800) USA-RAIL (872-7245).

By Bus: Greyhound serves most cities in Minnesota. Schedules and fares are available online at www.greyhound.com or by phone at (800) 229-9424. Information regarding city buses is available on the Mn/DOT Web site.

Visitor Information

The Minnesota Office of Tourism, also known as Explore Minnesota, has visitor information and travel brochures. Its Web site is www.exploreminnesota.com, and the office may be telephoned at (651) 296-5029 or (800) 657-3700.

How to Use This Guide

Take a look and you'll find that this guide contains just about everything you'll ever need to choose, plan for, and enjoy a hike in Minnesota. Filled with nearly 300 pages of useful Minnesota-specific information, *Hiking Minnesota* features forty mapped and cued hikes, twenty-five honorable mentions, and everything from advice on getting into shape to tips on getting the most out of hiking with your children or your dog. With so much information, the only question you may have is: How do I sift through it all?

We've designed this FalconGuide to be highly visual, for quick reference and ease of use. What this means is that the most pertinent information rises quickly to the top, so you don't have to waste time poring through bulky hike descriptions to get mileage cues or elevation stats. They're set aside for you. And yet, this guide doesn't read like a laundry list. Take the time to dive into a hike description and you'll realize that this guide is not just a good source of information; it's a good read. And so, in the end, you get the best of both worlds: a quick-reference guide and an engaging look at a region. Here's an outline of *Hiking Minnesota*'s major components.

What You'll Find in This Guide

Each region begins with a **Section Introduction,** where you're given a sweeping look at the lay of the land.

Now to the individual chapter. Each hike begins with a short summary. If your interest is piqued, keep reading. If not, flip to the next hike. The hike specs are fairly self-explanatory. Here you'll find the quick, nitty-gritty details of the hike: where the trailhead is located, the nearest town, hike length, approximate hiking time, difficulty rating, best hiking season, type of trail terrain, and what other trail users you may encounter. Our **Finding the trailhead** section gives you dependable directions from a nearby city to where you'll want to park. The section entitled **The Hike** is the meat of the chapter. Detailed and informative, it's the authors' carefully researched impression of the trail. While it's impossible to cover everything, you can rest assured that we won't miss what's important. In our **Miles and Directions** section we provide mileage cues to identify all turns and trail name changes, as well as points of interest. The **More Information** section is a hodgepodge of information. In it you'll find local outdoor retailers (for emergency trail supplies), accommodations, restaurants, and points of interest you may want to visit while hiking in the area.

Lastly, the **Honorable Mentions** section details hikes that weren't featured in the main chapters but are worthwhile hikes to explore. With so many great hikes in Minnesota, we couldn't highlight them all.

Because changes occur so frequently (phone numbers, business ownership, etc.), there is a chance that information in this guide may have changed before this book's publication. Therefore, it is recommended that the hiker check this information before heading out. We don't want anyone to feel restricted to just the routes and trails that are mapped here. We hope you'll have an adventurous spirit and use this guide as a platform to explore Minnesota's hiking trails and discover new routes for yourself. You may wish to copy the directions for our featured hikes onto a small sheet to help you while hiking, or photocopy the map and cue sheet to take with you. Otherwise, just slip the whole book in your backpack and take it all with you. Enjoy your time in the outdoors and remember to pack out what you pack in.

Ranking the Hikes

To help you decide on the type of hike you want, here is a list of hikes in order of difficulty:

Easiest

11	Pipestone National Monument
34	Grand Portage State Park
25	Buffalo River State Park
27	Zippel Bay State Park
9	Beaver Creek Valley
2	Fort Snelling State Park
4	Nerstrand Big Woods State Park
1	Minnehaha Falls
5	Barn Bluff
12	Blue Mounds State Park
26	Old Mill State Park
38	Park Point
13	St. Croix State Park
21	Glacial Lakes State Park
8	Great River Bluffs State Park
23	Itasca State Park
19	Lake Maria State Park
18	Pillsbury State Forest
39	Jay Cooke State Park
16	Mille Lacs Kathio State Park
24	Scenic State Park
15	Banning State Park
22	Maplewood State Park
29	Secret–Blackstone–Ennis Lake Trail
10	Camden State Park
31	Bear Head Lake State Park
30	Bass Lake Trail
17	Savanna Portage State Park
3	William O'Brien State Park
20	Minnesota Valley National Wildlife Refuge
33	Eagle Mountain
28	Voyageurs National Park
6	Frontenac State Park

37   Split Rock Lighthouse State Park
14   St. Croix State Forest—Tamarack
7   Whitewater State Park
35   Judge C. R. Magney State Park
36   Cascade River
32   Border Route–Caribou Rock Trail
40   The Superior Hiking Trail

Most Challenging

Map Legend

Transportation

Interstate Highway	===(15)===
U.S. Highway	==(27)==
State Road	==(19)==
County/Forest Road	=[250]=[FR 13]=
Dirt Road	= = = = =
Railroad	┝━┿━┿━┥

Hiking

Featured Trail	■━■━■━■
Other Trail	- - - - - -
Direction of Travel	→
Turnaround	↺

Hydrology

Lake/Reservoir	
River/Creek	～
Marsh/Swamp	
Waterfall	⫽

Land Use

National Park	
State Park	
Power Line	— · — · —

Symbols

Campsite	▲
Point of Interest	■
Mountain/Peak	▲
Parking	P
Picnic Area	🛆
Restroom	⑪
Tower	🏛
City/Town	○
Trailhead (Start)	❺
Bridge	≍
Boat Launch	🛶
Gate	•—•
Viewpoint	◧
Boardwalk/Steps	▥
Shelter	◩
Visitor Center	❷
Forest HQ	↟
Lighthouse	🕯
Airport	✛
Hostel	🏠
Park	♠
Bench	═
State Border	- · - · - · -

The Confluence

hree great rivers, the Mississippi, St. Croix, and Minnesota, merge in east central Minnesota and are scenic focal points in the state's largest metropolitan area. Portions of all three have been declared wild and scenic or protected waterways. These rivers each carve distinctive valleys through glacial sediment and ancient bedrock, and each one tells a unique geologic story. Located in the deciduous forest and prairie biomes, much of the area surrounding the Twin Cities is either heavily

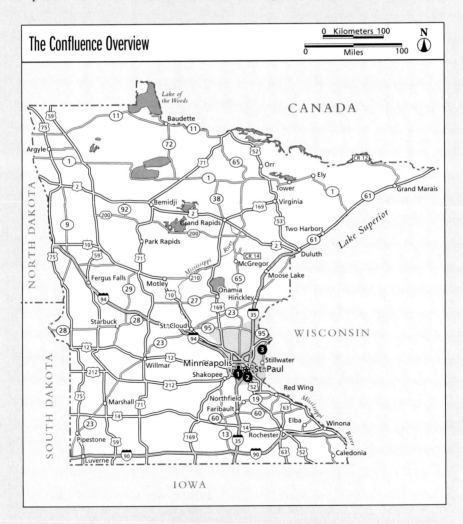

The Confluence Overview

wooded or has been cleared for farmland. An abundance of lakes and rivers, rolling hills, broad river valleys, deciduous forests, small prairie remnants, and sand plain forests of planted red and white pine make this a varied and interesting region. Floodplain forests of willow, cottonwood, and elm thrive along the banks of major rivers and provide habitat for birds and wildlife. This region is bounded to the east by the St. Croix River, to the north by the Anoka sand plain, to the west by the limits of the St. Croix moraine, and to the south by the Bluffland region.

The St. Croix River originated as a path for glacial meltwater and became the Glacial St. Croix River, draining glacial lakes in the Lake Superior basin. As glaciers receded northward, meltwater eventually drained eastward through the Great Lakes to the Atlantic Ocean, causing the St. Croix to shrink to its present size. The river gorge forms a high, rock-bound canyon called a dalles, where the river cuts through a dark basalt flow and layers of siltstone and sandstone that together rise 270 feet above the river. The basalt flow was part of the mid-continental rift that formed 1.1 billion years ago from the Lake Superior region south to Kansas. As plates spread apart along this rift, lava poured out like pancake batter and formed the landscape features of Lake Superior's North Shore and the dalles of the St. Croix.

The Minnesota River is a slow, silt-laden river that occupies the enormous Glacial River Warren valley. Glacial River Warren was a high-volume outlet stream for Glacial Lake Agassiz, which covered northwestern Minnesota and into Canada. As the glacier retreated, Glacial Lake Agassiz drained northward and the river diminished to the present-day Minnesota, which has gradually filled the valley with sediment. The Twin Cities of Minneapolis and St. Paul are located where the Minnesota joins the Mississippi. Originating in the north central part of the state, the Mississippi River cuts a narrow, steep-walled canyon at the confluence through sedimentary sandstone, shale, and limestone deposited in ancient shallow seas. Americans and Europeans traveled north on the Mississippi River, a primary commerce route, to settle in Minnesota near the confluence of the Minnesota and Mississippi rivers. The cities of Minneapolis and St. Paul developed as centers for commerce at the confluence, the northernmost navigable section of the Mississippi River, because of St. Anthony Falls, and became the most populated region of Minnesota.

Despite its size, many people are surprised by the wealth of preserved natural areas within this heavily populated region of east central Minnesota, but Minneapolis and St. Paul contain numerous city parks, regional parks, and nature preserves.

1 Minnehaha Falls

Driving into Minneapolis, you'd never guess that a valuable gem lies hidden deep within the city's maze of freeways and city streets. Unscathed by surrounding development, Minnehaha Creek winds lazily through the city on its way to the Mississippi River. As you hike along the creek—which is surrounded by oak savannas, streams, springs, and marshes—it's easy to imagine yourself far away from city life. This historic hike gives you an idea of what Minneapolis must have looked like during pre-settlement days and later when hundreds of visitors traveled by rail to see these popular falls.

Start: From the parking lot nearest the pavilion
Distance: 3.0-mile loop
Approximate hiking time: 1.5 hours
Difficulty rating: Easy due to well-maintained flat trails along the creek
Trail surface: Dirt trails, stairs that descend to the creek
Lay of the land: Minnehaha Creek valley
Other trail users: Hikers only
Canine compatibility: Leashed dogs permitted
Land status: City park

Nearest town: Minneapolis, MN
Fees/permits: No permits required. Some parking lots require parking fees.
Schedule: Open year round, sunrise to sunset (8:00 a.m. to 10:00 p.m.)
Maps: USGS maps: St. Paul West, MN; state park map
Trail contacts: Minneapolis Park & Recreation Board, Minneapolis, MN; (612) 230-6400 or (612) 722-2220 for Stevens House information, or visit www.minneapolisparks.org

Finding the trailhead: From Minneapolis: If you are coming from north of the Twin Cities, take Interstate 94 to Highway 55 (also Hiawatha Avenue) southeast. The entrance to the park is on your left near the intersection of Highway 55 and Minnehaha Avenue. If you are traveling on Interstate 35E (north or south), head northwest on Highway 55. The park entrance is just before Minnehaha Avenue. *DeLorme: Minnesota Atlas & Gazetteer*. Page 41 D8

The Hike

Minnehaha's "laughing waters" bring to mind the famous poem "Song of Hiawatha," completed and published in 1855 by Henry Wadsworth Longfellow. Inspired by stories and legends of Native American tribes, Longfellow was particularly impressed by descriptions of Minnehaha Creek's dramatic falls. Many of these stories and legends appeared in a book called *Myth of Hiawatha*—the combined effort of famed explorer, historian, and geologist Henry Rowe Schoolcraft, his part-Ojibway wife, Jane, and her mother.

Minnehaha Park, home of the famous Minnehaha Falls, is a precious remnant of undeveloped green landscape that encompasses an area surrounding Minnehaha Creek from just above the falls down to the creek's confluence with the Mississippi

River. The park adjoins a larger green space that follows the Mississippi River Corridor and is now a national park. Embedded in the metropolitan area of Minneapolis and St. Paul, this popular city park is surrounded by skyscrapers no more than 5 miles distant that nearly touch the clouds, busy freeways, and city streets that hum with activity. Here, Minnehaha Park offers a relaxed setting, where one can walk or bike in relative solitude. The park has bike trails that connect to an extensive network of trails that link the Mississippi with area lakes and the Minnesota River down to Fort Snelling at the confluence of the Minnesota and Mississippi Rivers.

The falls is a place where water sparkles as it tumbles over a 53-foot ledge of Platteville Formation, a fossil-bearing, dolomitic limestone structure. Visible under the limestone is a thin layer of grayish-green shale called the Glenwood, under which glaciers formed poorly cemented sand called St. Peter Sandstone. This soft rock that lines the pool is subject to slow erosion and carving by continuously falling water.

Marshes, springs, and a wide, grassy valley flank this touch of wild land near the Mississippi River. Lake Minnetonka, approximately 15 miles away, is the source of Minnehaha Creek, which is considered a small but valuable tributary to the Mississippi. At Lake Minnetonka, the creek begins its short journey to join the great river. St. Anthony Falls played a significant role thousands of years ago in forming the cascade at Minnehaha. St. Anthony Falls originated below Fort Snelling on the Mississippi, but it gradually moved upstream as it eroded the soft rock over which it fell. The mighty Mississippi carved the narrow gorge and was diverted, abandoning the gorge as it moved to its current location. This gorge, and the creek flowing over it, shaped the picturesque Minnehaha Falls. Today, Minnehaha Creek is a beautiful, shallow, gently winding stream flanked by hiking trails.

A couple of nearby historic remnants are worth visiting. One of them is the former home of John H. Stevens (the first European to settle in the area), whose house, built in 1849, was believed to have been the first one built on the west bank of the Mississippi in Minneapolis. The home was moved into Minnehaha Park in 1896, and to its current location by a group of schoolchildren in 1982. Opened to the public as a museum in 1985, the house contains exhibits that reveal the rich history of the home and of the city that surrounds it. The other is the old Milwaukee Road Station, built in the late 1870s to replace a smaller station on the first railroad line from Chicago into the Twin Cities. The first track connecting Minneapolis with Mendota—a small river town—was laid in 1865 by the Minnesota Central Railway. This track was the predecessor of the Chicago, Milwaukee, and St. Paul Railway. Back then, taking the sixteen-minute ride from Minneapolis to Minnehaha Park, the old Longfellow Gardens Zoo, Fort Snelling, and Mendota, was a popular weekend activity. It took three trains making thirteen daily round trips to accommodate traffic in 1910. However, the invention of the streetcar, run locally by the Twin City Rapid Transit Company, eventually reduced the train's usefulness. So, the Milwaukee Road closed the station in August 1963, donating it to the Minnesota Historical Society in 1964. Today, visitors can operate the telegraph key, check the train departure board, and listen to train sounds from the 1920s through the 1950s.

Minnehaha Falls

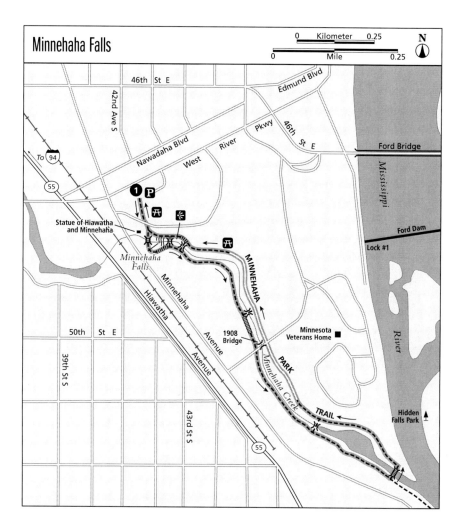

Minnehaha Falls

0   Kilometer   0.25

0   Mile   0.25

N

46th St E

Edmund Blvd

42nd Ave S

Nawadaha Blvd

River Pkwy

46th St E

West

Ford Bridge

To 94

55

Mississippi

Statue of Hiawatha
and Minnehaha

Ford Dam

Minnehaha
Falls

Lock #1

MINNEHAHA

Hiawatha

Minnehaha

50th St E

1908
Bridge

Minnesota
Veterans Home

River

39th St S

Avenue

PARK

Avenue

Minnehaha Creek

43rd St S

TRAIL

Hidden
Falls Park

55

A camera is a must on this picturesque hike for capturing the falls or wildlife along the trail. Watch for bald eagles hunting along the river. You may even spot the rare black-crowned night heron. This stocky, noisy, nocturnal bird feeds on aquatic animals such as frogs, crustaceans, fish, small mammals, and even sometimes the young of other water birds. Its nest is made of reeds, sticks, or twigs constructed in marshes or in trees. Since migration takes place at night, you probably won't be able to see the heron flying over in early spring and fall during migration. The black-crowned night heron is widely distributed in North America, spending winters along the Texas Gulf Coast.

This easily accessible hike follows both sides of Minnehaha Creek, where there are several footbridges crossing from one side to the other. A set of steps will get you to the bottom of the falls, where you will begin your hike. A life-sized bronze by

Jakob Fjelde that depicts Hiawatha and Minnehaha stands at the water's edge above the falls. This piece was an exhibit at the Chicago World's Fair in 1893 and was purchased for the park with pennies donated by schoolchildren. You can also check out other points of interest in the park, including the picnic grounds, Longfellow House, the veterans' home, the flower gardens, and Abandoned Falls Glen, a remnant of the old Mississippi River bed that is the most remote part of the park. The glen is a steep-walled canyon filled with lush vegetation and trees. The forested trail eventually leads to the confluence of Minnehaha Creek and the Mississippi River.

Miles and Directions

0.0   Start from the parking lot near the pavilion. Walk to the south side of the pavilion and look south. There is a wide stairway and bridge that crosses over Minnehaha Creek. (FYI: To the right [upstream] of the bridge is a statue of Hiawatha and Minnehaha.) Walk up the stairway and cross over the creek, then turn left at the first intersection. After a few steps, descend another set of stairs to the base of Minnehaha Falls. You will soon come to an intersection where a stone bridge with a great view of the falls crosses back over the creek and leads to a flight of steps that take you back to the pavilion. After taking a peek at the falls, come back across to the path and follow the creek downstream to the Mississippi. Here you'll see large blocks of limestone that have fallen from the "cap" that forms the lip of Minnehaha Falls. Notice how the fast-moving water quickly carved a steep valley or glen once the cap had fallen away.

0.3   Follow the trail alongside the creek and come to another bridge that crosses it. Stay right to continue downstream along the many large willows lining the bank.

Bridge over the mouth of Minnehaha Creek at its confluence with the Mississippi

0.5 Come to another bridge. A left crosses the creek and leads back toward the pavilion. Continue right and follow the trail, which becomes a wooden walkway. When the boardwalk ends, the path once again becomes dirt with exposed roots and rocks. Small paths lead off the main trail down to gravel bars along the creek.

0.7 A bridge built in 1908 crosses high overhead, leading to the Minnesota Veterans home.

0.8 Come to yet another bridge with a fire circle near it.

1.0 Watch for springs flowing out of the soft sandstone hillside, with colors ranging from rust to white.

1.5 Reach a wooden bridge and the confluence with the Mississippi River. Look up the river to see Ford Dam and lock and dam number 1. Downstream and across the river is the beach at Hidden Falls Park in St. Paul. Cross over the bridge here and return up the creek on the other bank, lined with very large cottonwood trees. At the creek, which is wild and braided, you might see children trying to catch frogs or minnows. The trail merges with a gravel park service road; follow it. Several small footpaths lead left, down to the creek or right, up into the steep wooded glen.

2.8 The service road and trail split. Proceed left and stay near the creek. In a few steps you'll see a small field and picnic area. (FYI: Many years ago when the east and west falls were moving upriver, this was the Mississippi River Valley.)

2.9 Here you are back at the third bridge over the creek. (**Option:** Climb 136 steps up the steep bank for another view of Minnehaha Falls.) Otherwise, stay close to the creek bank, and climb the stairway by the second stone bridge back up to the pavilion area.

3.0 Arrive back at the parking area.

More Information

Local Information

Minnesota Transportation Museum: Minnehaha Depot, St. Paul, MN; (651) 228-0263 or (800) 711-2591; www.mtmuseum.org

Department of Natural Resources, Information Center: St. Paul, MN; (651) 296-6157 or (888) 646-6367(only in MN); www.dnr.state.mn.us/parks

Local Events/Attractions

May Day Celebration: May 1, Powderhorn Park, Minneapolis, MN

Uptown Art Fair: First full weekend in August, (612) 823-4581

Lake Harriet Rose Gardens: Minneapolis, MN; (612) 661-4817 or (612) 370-4900

Mall of America: Bloomington, MN; (952) 883-8800 or www.mallofamerica.com

Minnesota Landscape Arboretum: Chanhassen, MN; (952) 443-1400; www.arboretum.umn.edu

Accommodations

Nicolett Island Inn Hotel: Minneapolis, MN; (612) 331-3035

Restaurants

Sea Salt Eatery: 4825 Minnehaha Ave., Minneapolis, MN; (612) 721-8990; seasalteatery.com

Kincaid's Fish, Chop & Steak House: Bloomington, MN; (952) 921-2255

The Black Forest Inn: Minneapolis, MN; (612) 872-0812

Café Brenda: Minneapolis, MN; (612) 342-9230

REI Recreational Equipment: Bloomington, MN; (952) 884-4315; www.rei.com Midwest Mountaineering: Minneapolis, MN; (888) 999-1077; www.midwestmtn.com

2 Fort Snelling State Park

Fort Snelling sits at the confluence of two great rivers and at the convergence of two great cities as well. Surrounded by the skyscrapers and freeways of Minneapolis and St. Paul, this 3,400-acre state park preserves a portion of wild land for recreation and wildlife. Its wide, easy trails wander through a riverine environment of large cottonwood, silver maple, ash, and willow that shelter you—at least temporarily—from the bustle of city life. The park features many miles of hiking and biking trails that will take you to Minnehaha and a chain of lakes northwest of Fort Snelling. History buffs should take special note of this area, as the region boasts a unique past that is highlighted throughout the park.

Start: From the parking area by the Thomas Savage Interpretive Center
Distance: 3.6-mile loop
Approximate hiking time: 1.25 hours
Difficulty rating: Easy due to wide, flat trails
Trail surface: Paved, crushed gravel, and dirt trails
Lay of the land: River floodplain forest
Other trail users: Hikers only (mountain bikers permitted in other parts of the park)
Canine compatibility: Leashed dogs permitted
Land status: State park

Nearest town: Minneapolis, MN
Fees/permits: State vehicle permit required. There is an admission charge for visiting the historic fort. Contact the park for fee information.
Schedule: Open year-round, day use only
Maps: USGS maps: Saint Paul West, MN; state park map
Trail contacts: Fort Snelling State Park, St. Paul, MN; main office (612) 725-2389, visitor center (612) 725-2724, reservations (866) 857-2757 or www.dnr.state.mn.us/parks

Finding the trailhead: From Interstate 94 in Minneapolis, drive south on Highway 55 to Highway 5. The park entrance is off Highway 5 at Post Road near the Minneapolis/St. Paul International Airport. *DeLorme: Minnesota Atlas & Gazetteer.* Page 41 D8

The Hike

Fort Snelling sits on a bluff that has been shaped and molded by the flow of glaciers, Lake Agassiz and the Glacial River Warren—a long process that began 12,000 years ago when the great Glacial River Warren began draining Lake Agassiz. For the next 3,000 years, tremendous volumes of meltwater poured from Lake Agassiz and thundered across Minnesota, cutting a wide river valley and determining the state's future landscape. Just downstream from present-day St. Paul, the river cut down through layers of sediment in an ancient buried valley, uncovering the Platteville Formation, a hard limestone overlying softer sandstone, and creating River Warren Falls. The falls, which rose 300 feet and spanned a mile, eroded the soft sandstone under the Platteville Formation. This caused the sandstone to break off, moving the falls slowly upstream, where they split at Fort Snelling. Two miles upstream from Fort Snelling, the River Warren Falls dug into another buried channel, and, without the hard capstone, the falls disappeared. When that happened, another set of falls was created. The other falls, now called St. Anthony Falls, continued to move 8 miles up the Mississippi River Valley at an incredible rate of 4.1 feet per year to its present location in downtown Minneapolis. Geologists used the rate of retreat for Warren Falls and St. Anthony Falls to estimate the end of the Ice Age in Minnesota.

St. Anthony Falls played a huge role in the development of Minneapolis and St. Paul. Entrepreneurs harnessed the falls' power to establish mills for flour—the nation's greatest enterprise in the 1880s—and lumber—the world's leading industry in 1890. The falls also were the site of several state "firsts." The first hydroelectric power station in the United States was built here in 1882, and the first permanent bridge over the Mississippi was built here in 1854. Because of its power potential, the falls attracted enterprising people as well as an influx of settlers to Minneapolis and St. Paul.

Minnesota was mainly wilderness at the turn of the nineteenth century when the British ventured down from Canada to trade with the Dakota Indians, who lived in scattered villages along the Minnesota and Mississippi rivers. But the War of 1812 forever changed the territory that was to gain statehood in 1858. Now that America had been wrested from the hands of the British, the government needed another outpost

View from the footbridge over Backwater Channel between the Mississippi and Minnesota Rivers

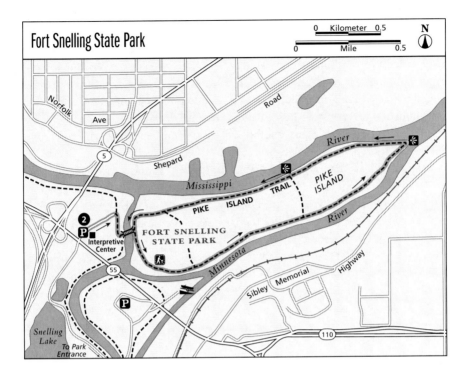

to link a system of forts that already stretched from the East Coast to the Missouri River. What better place than high above the confluence of two important trade waterways to control exploration, trade, and settlement along these rivers?

In 1819, Colonel Josiah Snelling and his 5th Regiment of Infantry arrived in the region to build a fort on the Indian reservation acquired by explorer Lieutenant Zebulon Pike in 1805. Pike successfully negotiated this acquisition for the United States government from the Dakota Indians, which was the first such land deal made between the Dakota and the United States. The fort, situated on a bluff overlooking the Mississippi River, was completed in 1825. Under Snelling's direction, acres of land were put into food production, and a gristmill and sawmill were built at St. Anthony. The area soon became an important gathering place for French, English, Americans, and Dakota, for whom this river confluence had long been considered the sacred center of the world.

Artists such as Seth Eastman, commander of the fort in the 1840s, and John C. Wild, who depicted the fort in the mid-1800s, were inspired by Fort Snelling's unique beauty and visited often to transfer the drama of fort life to canvas. Used as a supply base for the Dakota Territory and a training center for soldiers, the fort survived Indian campaigns, the Spanish American War, World War I, and World War II—after which it was decommissioned in 1945 and turned over to the Veterans Administration. It was designated Minnesota's first National Historic Landmark in 1960 and two years later became a state park.

The fort also served as a neighbor to Minnesota's first governor, Henry Hastings Sibley, who originally came to the Minnesota Territory in 1835 as head of the American Fur Company. He built his house, the first stone dwelling in Minnesota, across the river from Fort Snelling so he could conduct trade with the Dakota and Ojibway tribes. Sibley was a man of involvement, serving in many capacities before becoming Territorial Delegate to Congress and then governor in 1858. His home and the limestone house of Jean Baptiste Faribault remain and are now historic sites open to the public. Faribault was the most prominent French-Canadian in Mendota, which was the center of French-Canadian culture in Minnesota before it became a state in 1858. The Faribault House contains the Bishop Henry Whipple Collection, considered one of the top ten Native American art collections in the United States.

Besides the 18 miles of hiking trails, Fort Snelling State Park offers numerous opportunities to learn about Minnesota's history through conducted tours, demonstrations, and re-enactments of 1820s life. Visitors can watch presentations of candle making, spinning and weaving, soap making, and cooking and baking. Other programs and activities are available through the park's visitor center.

The Pike Island Trail is approximately 3 miles of circular trail sandwiched between the joining points of the Mississippi River and branches of the Minnesota. The island itself was created from sediment carried and deposited by the two great rivers. Prone to flooding, no permanent structures have been established on Pike Island. Tucked into the river valley surrounded by cottonwoods, slow-moving water, and high river bluffs, this hike is a haven from the city, which sits unseen high above on the top of the bluffs.

Miles and Directions

0.0 Start from the parking area by the Thomas Savage Interpretive Center. Walk northeast from the parking area on a paved hiking/bike trail, called Minnehaha Trail.

0.1 Turn right onto a gravel trail and follow signs that direct you to Pike Island.

0.2 Turn left, cross a concrete bridge over a small channel of the Mississippi, and take a right, following Hiking Club Trail signs. Park interpretive signs describe the history of Pike Island.

0.6 A left cuts across the island. Keep right to follow the Minnesota River toward the confluence. (FYI: The forest here has many maples and a dense canopy. It is a cool and shaded place to walk in the heat of summer. During the wet season, mosquitoes can get quite thick, especially on this side of the island.)

1.3 Another crossover trail cuts across to the Mississippi side on the left; continue right.

1.9 Come to the tip of Pike Island and the confluence of the two great rivers. Notice the difference in color and the line where the two rivers converge. Sit on the bench and enjoy the view that remains much the same as it was 200 years ago. Then continue along the trail, walking upstream on the bank of the Mississippi.

2.6 On the left is a crossover trail to the other side of the island. On the right is an overlook of the Mississippi. Continue along the main trail.

3.1 Here is another crossover trail to the left. Keep right. (FYI: There are many gigantic cottonwoods on this side of the island, and the forest is more open.) In another thirty paces there is another trail intersection. Stay left on the main trail, which has widened to the size of a road.

3.4 Return to the Pike Island interpretive signs. Cross the bridge and turn right to retrace your steps back to the parking area.

3.6 Arrive back at the visitor center and parking lot.

More Information

Local Information
Department of Natural Resources, Information Center: St. Paul, MN; (651) 296-6157 or (800) 646-6367 (only in MN); www.dnr.state.mn.us/parks

Local Events/Attractions
Fort Snelling History Center: Open from May through October; (612) 726-1171
Sibley House Historic Site: Mendota, MN; Northeast of the Mendota Bridge. Open May through October; (651) 452-1596; www.mnhs.org
Padelford Riverboat Tours on the Mississippi: April to October; (651) 227-1100; www.riverrides .com
Como Park Zoo and Conservatory: St. Paul, MN; (651) 487-8200

Restaurants
W.A. Frost and Company: St. Paul, MN; (651) 224-5715; www.wafrost.com
Café Latté: St. Paul, MN; (651) 224-5687; www.cafelatte.com
Punch Woodfire Pizza: St. Paul, MN; (651) 696-1066

Hike Tours
Minnesota Historical Society: (888) 727-8386; www.mnhs.org; twenty-five tours including river bluffs, historic mansions, and trails at Fort Snelling

Organizations
James Ford Bell Museum of Natural History: Minneapolis, MN; (612) 624-7083 Dakota County Historical Society and Museum: St. Paul, MN; (651) 552-7548
Minnesota Children's Museum: St. Paul, MN; (651) 225-6001

Other Resources
Wildlife information line: (612) 624-1374

Local Outdoor Retailers
REI Recreational Equipment: Roseville, MN; (651) 635-0211
REI Recreational Equipment: Bloomington, MN; (952) 884-4315
Midwest Mountaineering: Minneapolis, MN; (888) 999-1077; www.midwestmtn.com

3 William O'Brien State Park

William O'Brien State Park is a popular—and easily accessible—recreation area conveniently located just one hour east of the Twin Cities. Here, the St. Croix River, designated a wild and scenic river, stretches for miles until it joins the Mississippi downstream. The featured hiking trail encompasses much of the park, skirting ponds and marshes and traveling through a landscape of rolling meadows, restored prairies and oak savannas, and stands of white and red pines. A trail leading off the main trail crosses Highway 95 to take you to the river and additional recreational options. This park is a favorite among canoeing and boating enthusiasts because of its access to the St. Croix.

Start: From the visitor center
Distance: 5.8-mile circuit
Approximate hiking time: 3 hours
Difficulty rating: Moderate due to wide, easy trails and moderate climbs up and down hills
Trail surface: Wide dirt and mowed grass trails
Lay of the land: A diversity of habitat including St. Croix River floodplain forest, upland forest of oaks, scattered red and white pine, lakes, marshes, and restored prairie and oak savanna
Other trail users: Hikers only
Canine compatibility: Leashed dogs permitted
Land status: State park

Nearest town: Marine on St. Croix, MN
Fees/permits: State park vehicle permit is required; annual or day permits are available at the park office. Camping fees are separate.
Schedule: Open year-round
Maps: USGS maps: Marine on St. Croix, MN; state park map
Trail contacts: William O'Brien State Park, Marine-on-St. Croix, MN; (651) 433-0500; www.dnr.state.mn.us/parks; Department of Natural Resources, Information Center, St. Paul, MN; (651) 296-6157 or (800) 646-6367 (only in MN)

Finding the trailhead: From Stillwater, go north on Highway 95. The park entrance is approximately 2 miles north of Marine on St. Croix. Turn west (left) into the park. *DeLorme: Minnesota Atlas & Gazetteer.* Page 42 B2

The Hike

The St. Croix River Valley forms a scenic border between Minnesota and Wisconsin and is a protected corridor that is part of the National Wild and Scenic River system. Designated a Wild and Scenic River in 1968, development along the St. Croix has been limited to protect the area for wildlife and visitors. Hiking through William O'Brien with its stunning views of the valley and rolling woodlands, it's tough to imagine the area was teeming with development and the river choked with logs on their way to sawmills downriver in 1849.

Once East Coast forests had been cleared of white pine and there were no more of them to feed the logging industry, settlers headed west until they came upon Minnesota's beautiful white pine forests in the St. Croix River Valley. Noting what they determined to be an endless supply of white pine, the Easterners settled near the picturesque St. Croix River, creating the town Marine on St. Croix in 1839. Here, they built a sawmill and set up a logging operation that soon proved profitable. By 1849, the industry had grown considerably, with 75 million feet of logs floating down the river each year. Just 12 miles downstream, business was set up in Stillwater, which quickly grew into a booming logging town that surpassed Marine on St. Croix. By 1854, five sawmills supported 1,000 loggers working feverishly in the forests north of town. Logs rode the Mississippi's currents to mills in Iowa, Illinois, and Missouri. But the logging industry and the wealth it brought were relatively short-lived. In just eighty years, that "endless" supply of timber was gone, and farmers moved in. Thus the American economy in this region transitioned from logging to farming.

The park's namesake, William O'Brien, was one of these early loggers. When the logging industry died out, he purchased a large tract of land from area logging companies. After his death, O'Brien's daughter, Alice, donated 180 acres of her father's land to the state in 1945, and in 1947 the park was dedicated to her father's memory. Thirteen years later, a large island in the St. Croix River was added to the park when David Greenberg donated it to the state in memory of his parents. Named William O'Brien State Park, this beautiful, scenic recreation area has increased to approximately 1,650 acres with 11 miles of hiking and 10 miles of cross-country ski trails. Canoe rentals, winter camping facilities, swimming beaches, and many other amenities are available in the park.

Pond at the southern end of the trail

A notable natural feature within the park is the floodplain forest on Greenberg Island. This floodplain forest, dominated by silver maples mixed with cottonwood and black willow, serves as a refuge for many kinds of birds and animals. Its trees are well adapted to seasonal flooding, severe erosion, and sedimentation.

As you walk, be sure to watch for red-shouldered hawks, which are among the animal species that thrive in floodplain forests. A high density of these migrating birds exists along the St. Croix River, particularly in Washington and Chisago counties.

Hidden in the St. Croix River bottom lies another treasure—the freshwater mussel, which is one of the most endangered groups of animals in North America. Siltation from adjacent eroded lands, pollution, dredging, damming, commercial harvesting, and the influx of exotic species have threatened the freshwater mussel with extinction. One of its greatest enemies is the zebra mussel, which has infested the waters of the Mississippi River and threatens to invade the St. Croix, encroaching on the freshwater mussel's habitat. Biologists are working to eradicate the zebra mussel and to preserve the freshwater mussel, a St. Croix River native that cleans the river bottom and is part of the indigenous food chain.

In addition to unique wildlife, William O'Brien State Park boasts incredible beauty in any season of the year. In May, blooming marsh marigolds highlight the landscape with gold and yellow, while brilliant cardinal flowers and rare cattail sedges show off for late-summer visitors.

Referred to as one of the best canoeing rivers in the nation, the St. Croix was one of the first rivers to be designated wild and scenic. The river is popular for boating and fishing as well. Northern pike, walleye, bass, and brown trout swim its normally placid waters. With no major metropolitan area or industry upstream, the river remains scenic and relatively unpolluted.

The river tends to draw many people, especially in the summer. This park is a popular spot as it's close to the Twin Cities metro area. Away from the crowds, this hike offers a quiet respite, taking you through an upland forest on a trail that winds through a diversity of habitat—including St. Croix River floodplain forest, upland forest of oak, scattered red and white pine, restored prairie, and oak savanna as well as lakes and marshes. Fall is an incredible time to hike this trail, when the spectacular overlooks of the St. Croix River Valley are ablaze with color. Because of the diversity of habitats, you can observe an abundance of bird life, especially because the valley is a flyway during fall and spring migrations.

Miles and Directions

0.0 Start from the west side of the visitor center. Begin at the Hiking Club Trail signs and signs to the upper park area. Go right (north).

0.1 Pass by the maintenance area on your right.

0.2 Cross the paved road that leads to the group camp. Go right, and skirt a large cattail marsh south of the trail and the campground to the north.

0.7 Come to a bench where you can sit and listen to marsh birds.

1.1 Go straight at this four-way intersection and pass through a tunnel under the railroad.

1.6 Stay right at this intersection. A left turn heads south, paralleling the railroad tracks.

1.8 Pass an outhouse and a shelter on the right.

1.9 Come to an intersection on the right with a ski/hiking loop marked difficult off the main trail. Go left to stay on the main trail.

2.3 The ski/hiking loop rejoins the main trail from the right. Continue left through hilly terrain dotted with oaks and maples.

2.7 Pass another shelter and a second outhouse while walking straight ahead. Approach a beautiful overlook of the St. Croix River Valley from open oak savanna.

3.0 A bench for resting and taking in the view marks this trail intersection. Take a right and head south, following the Hiking Club Trail signs, through restored oak savanna. (FYI: Watch for wild turkeys.)

3.3 Pass an outhouse, shelter, and a pond on the left.

3.7 Atop a hill, a picnic table and bench provide another place to enjoy a scenic overlook of the St. Croix River Valley, which is especially spectacular in the fall. The trail turns back north along the railroad tracks.

4.1 Come into view of the outhouse and shelter by the pond on the left.

4.4 At this four-way intersection, turn right, and head east toward the railroad tracks and cross over them.

4.5 Take a right at this intersection to skirt the south side of the marsh that you walked along at the beginning of the hike. (A left heads toward the upper campground.)

4.8 Take a left at this fork and continue east.

5.1 Pass a pond on the right with a bench alongside it. Sit on the bench and enjoy the large beaver lodge in front of you. In the early evening, look for the furry animals that call these lodges their home. Then, come to a jog in the trail. First, stay left, briefly joining a trail that leads north to the group camp and (right) south to Wedge Hill Trail, and then turn right to continue east.

5.3 Take a left at this intersection and enter a shady oak forest, ascending Wedge Hill.

5.5 Descend Wedge Hill and come into an open prairie restoration area and into view of the visitor center to the north. Continue right, and the trail will turn north and head back to the center.

5.8 Arrive back at the visitor center and parking.

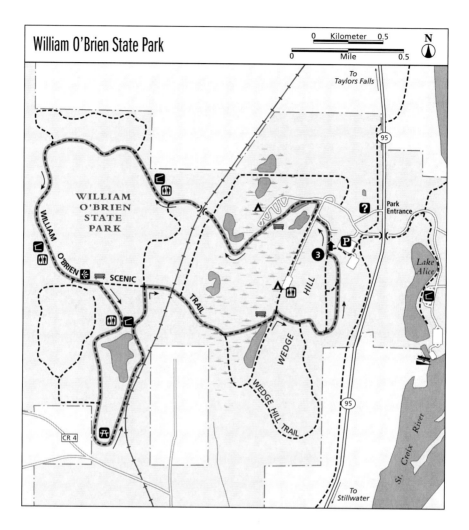

William O'Brien State Park

To Taylors Falls

WILLIAM O'BRIEN STATE PARK

WILLIAM O'BRIEN

SCENIC

TRAIL

HILL

WEDGE

WEDGE HILL TRAIL

CR 4

Park Entrance

Lake Alice

St. Croix River

To Stillwater

More Information

Local Information

Stillwater Area Chamber of Commerce: Stillwater, MN; (651) 439-4001; www.ilovestillwater.com

Local Events/Attractions

Fireman's Dance & Fireworks: July, Marine on St. Croix, MN; (651) 439-4001; www.ilovestillwater.com

Old Fourth of July Parade & Celebration: July, Marine on St. Croix, MN; (651) 439-4001; www.ilovestillwater.com

Marine Art Fair: September, Marine On St. Croix

Stillwater Trolley Narrated Tours: Stillwater, MN; (651) 430-0352

Andiamo Cruises on the St. Croix: Stillwater, MN; (651) 430-1235
Minnesota Zephyr Dinner Train: Stillwater, MN; (651) 430-3000 or (800) 992-6100
Osceola & St. Croix Valley Railway: Osceola, WI; (715) 755-3570

William O'Brien Special Events

Annual Candlelight Ski: January
Marine/O'Brien Ski Race: January
Voyageur Encampment Weekend: September
River of Words, Poetry Weekend: October
Community Halloween Party: October
Call the park for more information: (651) 433-0500 or (651) 433-0506.

Overlook of the St. Croix River Valley

Accommodations

Asa Parker House: Marine on St. Croix, MN; (651) 433-5248 or (888) 857-9969; www.asa
parkerbb.com
Lumber Baron's Hotel: Stillwater, MN; (651) 439-6000; www.lumberbarons.com
William Sauntry Mansion: Stillwater, MN; (800) 828-2653; www.sauntrymansion.com
Historic Afton House Inn: Stillwater, MN; (651) 436-8883; www.aftonhouseinn.com

Restaurants

Gasthaus Bavarian Hunter: Stillwater, MN; (651) 439-7128; www.gasthausbavarianhunter.com
Waterstreet Inn: Lumber Baron's Hotel, Stillwater, MN; (651) 439-6000; www.lumberbarons.com
Mad Capper Saloon & Eatery: Stillwater, MN; (651) 430-3710

Local Outdoor Retailers

St. Croix Outfitters: Stillwater, MN; (651) 439-4891

Honorable Mentions

Compiled here is an index of great hikes in this region that didn't make the A-list
this time around but deserve recognition. Check them out and let us know what you
think. You may decide that one or more of these hikes deserves higher status in future
editions or, perhaps, you may have a hike of your own that merits some attention.

Elm Creek Park Reserve

This park reserve has preserved a remnant of the Big Woods, native prairie, and the
watercourses of Elm and Rush Creeks. Hiking from the Eastman Nature Center on
the Monarch and Creek Trails gives you a pleasant mixture of prairie, lowland forest,
and floodplain marsh without getting your feet wet.

From Osseo, drive northwest on CR 81 for 3 miles to Territorial Road. Turn
right and proceed northwest on Territorial Road for 1 mile to CR 121. Turn right
and drive north 1 mile, then turn right onto Elm Creek Road and proceed for a half
mile. The Eastman Nature Center will be on your right. *DeLorme: Minnesota Atlas and
Gazetteer.* Page 41 B6

Minneapolis City Parks–Lake Harriet Loop

Minneapolis, known as the city of lakes, has several miles of recreational trails to enjoy.
Lake Harriet is an exceptional area for a variety of recreational opportunities right
in the heart of the city, including hiking, biking, rollerblading, sailing, and fishing.
A band shelter houses free concerts all summer, and the Lyndale Rose Gardens, the
second oldest rose garden in the United States, are a main attraction. A considerable
amount of green space adjoins the lake, making this a peaceful place to come when
you're in the big city.

From Minneapolis, take Interstate 35W, exit on 50th Street, and proceed west to Xerxes Avenue. Turn right and proceed to Hennepin Avenue. Turn right and follow the signs to the bandstand parking area. *DeLorme: Minnesota Atlas and Gazetteer.* Page 41 D7

Wood Lake Nature Center

One of the Twin Cities' best birding spots, birders come here to see and hear more than 200 species of birds. The center first opened in the 1960s and has floating board-walks to protect and give humans access to wetland environments. Hike and listen to the sweet songs of warblers, then head over to the Mall of America (the largest shopping mall in the United States) for some shopping.

From Minneapolis exit off Interstate 35W on 66th Street and drive east to Lakeshore Drive (about a half mile). Turn right and the parking area is on the right. *DeLorme: Minnesota Atlas and Gazetteer.* Page 41 E7

Afton State Park

Located in the St. Croix River Valley, Afton State Park is made up of oak savanna, prairie, and river floodplain forest. The river bluffs are steep enough to support a ski resort and the deep ravines give a wild feeling to the area, a prime recreation spot for people living near the Twin Cities metro area. The 3.4-mile River and Bluff Trail follows the western bank of Lake St. Croix, part of the wild and scenic St. Croix River, and climbs onto the top of the river bluff for outstanding views of the beautiful river valley.

From St. Paul drive east on Interstate 94 for 5 miles and go south on Highway 95. Proceed 7 miles to CR 20 and turn left. Proceed for 3 miles to the park entrance. *DeLorme: Minnesota Atlas and Gazetteer.* Page 42 E2

Interstate State Park

The spectacular volcanic and sandstone gorge of the St. Croix River can be viewed from this hike, a 3.5-mile loop trail that links Curtain Falls, Old Railroad, and River Trails to follow the bank of the river and cross Highway 95 to the falls. Numerous potholes near the banks of the St. Croix River are interesting features, including a 60-foot deep pothole that is the world's deepest explored glacial pothole. Established in 1895, Interstate State Park is the first state park in the nation to span two states (Minnesota and Wisconsin).

To get there drive 1 mile south of Taylors Falls on U.S. Highway 8. The park entrance is on the left side of the road. *DeLorme: Minnesota Atlas and Gazetteer.* Page 49 E7

Blufflands

A s you travel south from Minneapolis and St. Paul along roads that hug the picturesque Mississippi River, the landscape changes dramatically from gently rolling farmlands to high, narrow, flat-topped ridges and bluffs separated by broad
river valleys, some of which are as much as 250 feet deep. Numerous springs
percolate through weeping bedrock walls along river gorges. Many of these rivers
in oversized valleys drain the farmlands west of the bluff country and flow into the

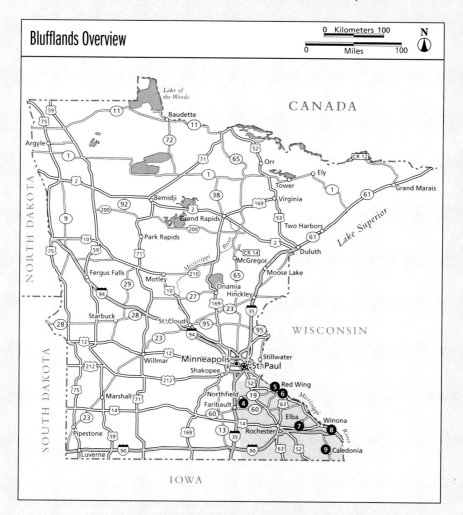

Blufflands Overview

Mississippi. The Blufflands follow the Mississippi south to the Iowa state line and are bordered on the west by hilly moraine country.

The Mississippi River is a main feature in this region and draws many people for boating, fishing, sailing, waterskiing, and birding. The area is well known for its birding as the river is a major flyway for migrating birds. The bluffs and good fishing provide bald eagles with an excellent habitat year-round. Hikes along bluff tops offer spectacular views of the rugged landscape and overlooks of the Mississippi. There are several state parks in the region, many acres of state forest land, and state game and wildlife refuges.

4 Nerstrand Big Woods State Park

Nerstrand Big Woods State Park is home to one of the last remnants of Big Woods and the federally endangered, rare, endemic Minnesota dwarf trout lily—which you can admire and photograph along the featured hike. Rolling hills and valleys, oak savannas, prairie remnants, a meandering creek with its Hidden Falls, lush plant life, and looping trail system, make this a park well worth visiting. The park also encompasses a demonstration dairy farm designed to promote sustainable rotational grazing through cooperative efforts between the Department of Natural Resources, The Nature Conservancy, the Minnesota Department of Agriculture, and the farm family.

Start: From the parking lot next to the picnic area
Distance: 3.2-mile circuit
Approximate hiking time: 1.5 hours
Difficulty rating: Easy due to wide trails and gentle terrain
Trail surface: Wide dirt trails
Lay of the land: Big Woods vegetation with rolling hills and valleys
Other trail users: Hikers only
Canine compatibility: Leashed dogs permitted
Land status: State park
Nearest town: Northfield, MN, and Faribault, MN

Fees/permits: State park vehicle permit required. Annual or day permits are available at the park office. Camping fees are separate.
Schedule: Open year-round, day use from 8:00 a.m. to 10:00 p.m., overnight camping
Maps: USGS maps: Nerstrand, MN; state park map
Trail contacts: Nerstrand Big Woods State Park, Nerstrand, MN; (507) 333-4840; www.dnr.state.mn.us/parks; Department of Natural Resources, Information Center, St. Paul, MN; (651) 296-6157 or (800) 646-6367 (only in MN); www.dnr.state.mn.us/parks

Finding the trailhead: From Northfield: Coming from north of Nerstrand drive south on Highway 246 approximately 11 miles. The park entrance is 1.5 miles west of the town of Nerstrand on County Road 40. Approaching from south of Nerstrand take MN 20 Northeast from MN 60 east out of Faribault. Turn right on MN 27 at Cannon City and follow signs to the park entrance on CR 40. *DeLorme: Minnesota Atlas & Gazetteer*: Page 33 D9

The Hike

Prairies, deciduous woods, pine forests, and oak savannas have been around for thousands of years. But the Big Woods—a maple and basswood forest that once was part of the larger deciduous hardwood forest stretching from southeastern Minnesota to the state's northwestern border—had a relatively short lifetime of approximately 500 years. Now, all that is left of these magnificent tall hardwoods is a stretch of woods that begins in Faribault and ends in St. Cloud. In its infancy, the Big Woods was oak-aspen woodland, savanna, or prairie, and frequent fires prevented the woodland from encroaching on the prairie. Over the years, a cooler, wetter climate and a reduction in

Hidden Falls

fires allowed elm, sugar maple, and basswood to emerge where oak once dominated. The dense forest canopy shaded fallen leaves and other forest litter, thus keeping the forest floor damp and limiting the spread of fire. And since the dampness also hastened leaf decay, there was less debris—or fuel for fires—accumulating from year to year. Thus protected, the big hardwoods thrived and spread. Elm did especially well in the Big Woods, once making up 27 percent of the forest. There were also healthy populations of basswood, sugar maple, ash, and red oak. In the early 1970s, though, the elm population suffered a setback with the onset of Dutch elm disease, which nearly eliminated mature elm trees from all Minnesota forests.

The Big Woods flourished for a few hundred years before farmers discovered the region's rich soil. Historically, what is now Nerstrand Big Woods State Park was an outlying island of Big Woods surrounded by oak savanna and prairie that lay approximately 10 miles from the Big Woods Landscape. Once southern Minnesota was opened to homesteading in the 1850s, the area's fertile soil attracted waves of settlers, who began preparing large tracts of land for the plow. Settlement was on the prairie, which was easy to farm, and the land that is now the park was divided into woodlots varying in size from one to twenty acres for the settlers to use for wood, hunting, and making maple syrup. As more land was homesteaded, the Big Woods grew smaller until the once continuous forest of hardwoods that covered approximately 3,000 square miles was reduced to a handful of scattered green dots on the southern Minnesota landscape. In the 1850s, forests made up 80 percent of the Big Woods ecosystem. Lakes, prairies, and wetlands made up the rest. Today, less than 10 percent of the original forest remains, the landscape having been reconfigured over the years to reflect an agricultural society.

Nerstrand State Park encompasses a small portion of the remaining hardwood forest, which contains a unique ecosystem. Considered one of the state's best and

largest examples of the Big Woods, it consists mostly of maple, basswood, oak, and ironwood. This botanical reserve is home to more than forty mature plant species per sixty square feet that botanists have catalogued or recorded and at least fifty identified varieties of wildflowers, among them Jack-in-the-pulpit, bloodroot, trillium, and yellow lady slipper.

Be sure to watch for the exceptionally rare, endemic Minnesota dwarf trout lily, which only exists in Rice, Goodhue, and Steele Counties and nowhere else in the world. Nerstrand Big Woods State Park is one of two sites where the plant can be observed and photographed. Under a comprehensive park preservation plan, steps are being taken along Prairie Creek to prevent erosion of this plant into the stream.

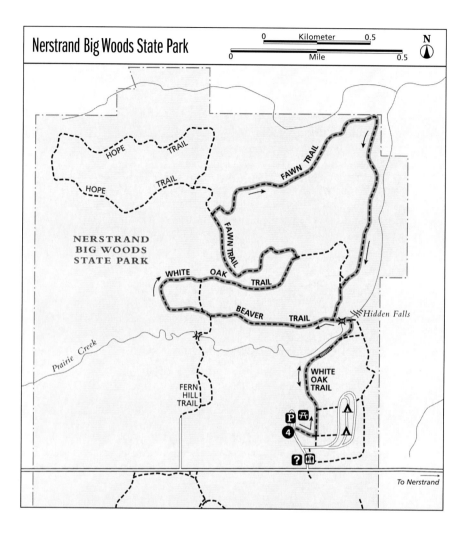

Kilometer

Mile

NERSTRAND
BIG WOODS
STATE PARK

HOPE TRAIL

HOPE TRAIL

FAWN TRAIL

FAWN TRAIL

WHITE OAK TRAIL

BEAVER TRAIL

Hidden Falls

Prairie Creek

WHITE
OAK
TRAIL

FERN
HILL
TRAIL

To Nerstrand

Because of its limited geographic range, this plant is protected by the federal and state Endangered Species acts. Discovered in 1870 by a botany professor at St. Mary's School in Faribault, the trout lily prefers to live on slopes and ravines in maple-basswood forests or floodplain forests adjoining the Straight, Cannon, Little Cannon, and Zumbro Rivers, and Prairie Creek.

Prairie Creek meanders lazily through the park's rolling hills and valleys and is a minor tributary of the 110-mile Canon River, which flows north and east to meet the Mississippi. Prairie Creek's most notable feature is Hidden Falls, where slow-moving water tumbles easily over a 12-foot-high, 90-foot-wide ledge of Platteville limestone. Be sure to notice this limestone, which was previously buried under 150 feet of glacial drift and is only visible in areas where the glacial drift has been eroded away, such as at Hidden Falls and along the creek bottoms.

There are several loops in the park's 13 miles of hiking trails, offering a variety of choices. This loop begins from the picnic area and takes you to Hidden Falls, where the path follows Beaver Trail, White Oak Trail, and Fawn Trail. These trails wind through the Big Woods over rolling terrain and down into the gentle Prairie Creek Valley. Along the trail, you can explore the plant and animal life that inhabits the forest floor under the trees' heavy canopy. Spring and fall are the best times to visit, so you can take in the burst of spring wildflowers or the vibrant fall colors.

Miles and Directions

0.0 Start from the parking lot by the picnic area and pavilion. Walk east from the pavilion toward the campground. Come to a wide trail of crushed gravel and turn left (north). In about 100 feet, come to Hidden Falls/Hiking Club trailhead and sign.

0.3 The park built the boardwalk here to protect a sensitive area from visitors. Here you can see nodding trilliums and hear the slurred whistle and twittering song of the Louisiana water thrush.

0.4 Proceed straight ahead and down a set of stairs to view the cascade of water over the falls from below. Then return to this intersection and turn right (left if you didn't go down the steps to view the falls), cross the bridge over Prairie Creek, and turn left onto Beaver Trail. The wide dirt path meanders through open woods carpeted with flowers in early spring.

0.8 Beaver Trail intersects with White Oak Trail. Take a right to follow White Oak Trail. A left would take you south on Fern Hill Trail.

1.2 The trail climbs a gentle hill and forks. Turn left.

1.4 Take a left onto Fawn Trail. A right continues the White Oak loop, which is an option to shorten the hike.

1.6 Arrive at the intersection with Hope Trail, proceed right and continue on Fawn Trail. The open forest has a spacious feeling with its dense canopy ceiling and green vegetation carpeting the rich soil. The trail descends a gentle hill and turns to parallel Prairie Creek 50 feet below.

2.7 Fawn Trail rejoins White Oak Trail. Take a left and walk downhill toward Hidden Falls.

2.8 Back at the falls, cross the bridge and take a right to retrace your steps to the parking area.

3.2 Arrive back at the parking area.

More Information

Local Information

Northfield Chamber of Commerce: Northfield, MN; (507) 645-5604 or (800) 658-2548; www .northfieldchamber.com

Faribault Chamber of Commerce: Faribault, MN; (800) 658-2354; www.faribaultmn.org

Local Events/Attractions

Jesse James Days: First weekend after Labor Day, Northfield, MN; (507) 645-5604 or (800) 658-2548; www.northfieldchamber.com

Thursday on the Square: Bridge Square, Northfield, MN; (507) 645-6372; www.northfield chamber.com. Concerts, ice-cream socials, pie-baking contests and variety shows

Accommodations

Nerstrand Big Woods State Park: Nerstrand, MN; (507) 333-4840; www.dnr.state.mn.us/parks
The Archer House: Northfield, MN; (800) 247-2235
Another Time Bed & Breakfast: Dundas, MN; (507) 645-6367
Martin Oaks Bed & Breakfast: Dundas, MN; (507) 645-4644

Restaurants

Millersburg Store & Blue Horse: Northfield, MN; (507) 645-6424
Archer House Tavern: Northfield, MN; (800) 247-2235
Ole Store: Northfield, MN; (507) 645-5558
The Depot: Faribault, MN; (507) 332-2825

Local Outdoor Retailers

Cabela's World's Foremost Outfitters: Owatonna, MN; (507) 451-4545

5 Barn Bluff

This is a trail you'll want to take at a slow pace due to its steady climb. Even with the elevation gain and several sets of steps, this hike is worth the effort needed to reach the top of the 340-foot bluff. The cliff showcases a spectacular view of the Mississippi River on one side and Red Wing on the other. It's a pretty trail through a scattering of trees on the south side and, on the north side, a more thickly wooded, rocky trail wedged between the Mississippi and the towering bluff. Wildflowers that begin blooming in mid- to late April are sprinkled along the trail, creating a variety of color. The main highlight of this trail is to experience the view from the top, where miles of Wisconsin and Minnesota urban and rural countryside are visible with the backdrop of the beautiful Mississippi River.

Start: From the top of a flight of stairs across the street, to the east, from the parking area
Distance: 2.1-mile circuit
Approximate hiking time: 1.5 hours with short stops to rest after climbs
Difficulty rating: Easy due to wide, grassy trails, but the trail winds steadily up the bluff
Trail surface: Grass and dirt
Lay of the land: Trails encircle and climb a sandstone-and-dolomite bluff overlooking the Mississippi
Other trail users: Rock climbers

Canine compatibility: Leashed dogs permitted
Land status: City park
Nearest town: Red Wing, MN
Fees/permits: No fees or permits required
Schedule: Hike spring through fall. There are ski trails on Sorin's Bluff.
Map: USGS map: Red Wing, MN
Trail contacts: City of Red Wing, Department of Public Works, Red Wing, MN; (651) 385-3674; www.redwing.net; Red Wing Chamber of Commerce, Red Wing, MN; (651) 388-4719; http://redwingchamber.com

Finding the trailhead: From downtown Red Wing, start from U.S. Highway 61 and take Highway 58, which is also Plum Street, to Fifth Street. Turn left. Continue until you go under the US 61 bridge. There, you will find a small parking area on the right. The trailhead is at the top of the stairs across the street from the parking area. *DeLorme: Minnesota Atlas & Gazetteer.* Page 34 B4

The Hike

Trails that climb the bluffs of southeastern Minnesota may have you puffing and stopping for short breathers along the way, but once you're at the top, the views of the Mississippi River and Red Wing will reward your effort. Be sure to exercise caution on these trails—especially when children accompany you—as some bluff edges drop 600 feet.

Even though the Barn Bluff Trail at the center of Red Wing is only 2 miles long, you'll want to stop often to admire the views. If you have them, take along a pair of binoculars to help you identify the many birds that frequent the area. You may

Barn Bluff overlooking the Mississippi River

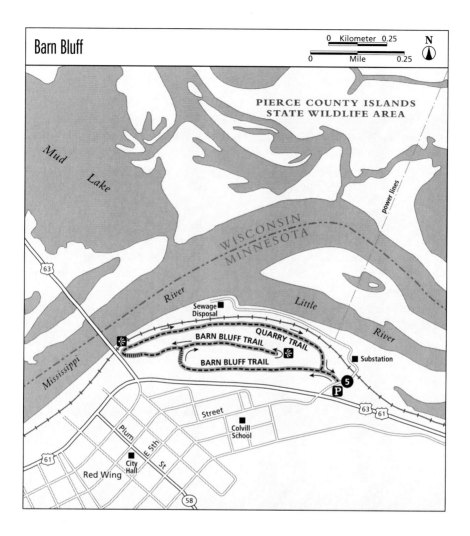

0 Kilometer 0.25

N

0 Mile 0.25

PIERCE COUNTY ISLANDS
STATE WILDLIFE AREA

Mud

Lake

power lines

WISCONSIN
MINNESOTA

63

River

Little

Sewage
Disposal

QUARRY TRAIL

BARN BLUFF TRAIL

River

BARN BLUFF TRAIL

Substation

Mississippi

5

P

63 61

Street

Colvill
School

Plum

E 5th

St

61

City
Hall

58

Red Wing

encounter a bald eagle or turkey vulture gliding along the air currents. Bald eagles were once on the Endangered Species List, but they are now merely protected. The Mississippi is the main migratory path for birds in the central part of the United States, running from Hudson Bay to the Gulf of Mexico, making this an excellent place to watch for migratory birds.

The Mississippi River stretches lazily along the bluff's north side. As you check out the vista from the top, be sure to look for Lake Pepin, a 25-mile-long widening of the Mississippi, and Carlson Island, which sits near the bluff in the middle of the river's divisive waters. Opposite, you'll see Red Wing stretched east to west along the river and nestled against the bluffs. At eye level, you'll see Sorin's Bluff, the home of Soldiers Memorial Park. The bluff was named after a well-known pioneer and

Methodist minister, Mathew Sorin, and set aside as a city park in 1927. The park, which has many footpaths and nine miles of ski trails of varying difficulty, was dedicated to soldiers of all wars.

Barn Bluff—and other bluffs that follow the Mississippi—was once surrounded by the river's swirling waters and cut off from the mainland. Several layers of rock, including Jordan sandstone and dolomite, make up the bluff's foundation and are topped off by a layer of glacial drift. The business district of Red Wing lies on the bed of an old channel of the glacial Mississippi.

This hike begins at a series of concrete stairs, created in the early 1900s and etched with the names of former Kiwanis Club members, who helped develop the trails. The steps take you from the parking lot to the trailhead. There are two main trails that join to encircle Barn Bluff. Head left at the top of the stairs, and you'll gradually climb the bluff's south edge on a dirt and grass trail shaded by a variety of small deciduous trees. This side of the bluff is warmer and drier than the north side. The Quarry Trail follows the north side and leads to an old limestone quarry that is now frequented by rock climbers.

As you approach the west edge of the bluff, you'll see a second set of steps on your right with a historical marker at its base. You may either climb these steps to reach the top of the bluff, where the trail continues in open prairie, or continue along the trail to skirt its west side. Chances are, you won't be alone as this is a popular overlook for relaxing and observing river activity mingled with the bustle of city life. At the top of the stairs, the trail runs east and west along the top of the bluff.

Another long flight of stairs on the bluff's northwest side will take you down to the Quarry Trail, a narrow, rather rugged trail that hugs the bluff facing the Mississippi River. The cool, moist environment on this side of the bluff supports a dense deciduous forest. You'll climb over tree roots on a narrow, hilly dirt path that can be slippery when damp. This wooded trail gradually levels off and widens until the steep cliff face at the bluff's northeast side beckons the adventuresome to hone their climbing skills. Once an old wagon road, this trail was used to haul limestone from the quarry.

Local lore reports that Dakota chief Tatanka-Mami, or Walking Buffalo, established this trail in the early nineteenth century. He is supposedly buried somewhere

BIRTH OF THE WATER SKI

Waterskiing originated at Lake Pepin in 1922 when an avid, eighteen-year-old snow skier turned his thoughts to continuing his sport into the summer—on water. Ralph Samuelson's first water skis looked like narrow toboggans, and, in order to gain the speed needed to pull him to the top of the water, he was towed behind an airplane.

on the bluff. And naturalist Henry David Thoreau studied plants on Barn Bluff in the summer of 1861. The famed *Walden Pond* author later wrote, "Too much could not be said for the grandeur and beauty of the region."

As the trail turns south, it will take you full circle to where you began.

Miles and Directions

0.0   Start from the parking lot and walk north to ascend the first set of concrete stairs.

0.1   Turn left to follow the Barn Bluff Trail and head west along the south side of the bluff.

0.4   Turn right to climb the sets of concrete stairs leading up to the top of Barn Bluff.

0.5   Take a right at the top of the stairs and climb up a short distance on a dirt trail. Take another right to follow the top of the bluff to an overlook on the bluff's east end.

0.8   Come to an overlook of the Mississippi River and an old railroad yard below to the east. Then, retrace your steps to follow the top of the bluff to the far west end.

1.1   Reach the intersection that brought you up to the top of the bluff and stay right to traverse the bluff toward the west.

1.4   Descend a set of stairs and reach an overlook of Mud Lake and Red Wing. Continue to descend to the north side of the bluff and head east along the Mississippi River.

1.8   Come to the old quarry site that is now a popular rock climbing area.

2.0   Trail intersection. Take a left to head back down to the parking area.

2.1   Back to the parking area.

More Information

Local Information
Red Wing Chamber of Commerce: Red Wing, MN; (651) 388-4719; http://redwingchamber.com

Local Events/Attractions
River City Days: First week in August, Red Wing, MN; http://redwingchamber.com. Town festival with entertainment, events, food, a parade, and fireworks

Accommodations
Candlelight Inn: Red Wing, MN; (651) 388-8034 or (800) 254-9194; www.candlelightinn-redwing.com
Golden Lantern Inn: Red Wing, MN; (888) 288-3315; www.goldenlantern.com
The Moondance Inn: Red Wing, MN;(866) 388-8145; www.moondanceinn.com

Restaurants
Port of Red Wing: St. James Hotel, Red Wing, MN; (651) 388-2846
Marie's Casual Dining: Red Wing, MN; (651) 388-1896

Organizations
Goodhue County Historical Society: Red Wing, MN; (651) 388-6024; www.goodhuehistory.mus .mn.us

6 Frontenac State Park

Frontenac State Park encompasses 2,230 beautiful acres that include the 450-foot bluff overlooking Lake Pepin, a widening of the Mississippi. Called Point-No-Point, the 3-mile-long bluff creates an optical illusion to boaters traveling down river. From a distance, it appears to be a point jutting out into the water, but the illusion disappears as boaters approach it. This bluff, which became a state park in 1953, nearly twenty years after its designation was proposed, is a popular birding and recreation site. Here you'll find a diverse wildlife habitat of forests, open meadows, old fields, prairies, and bottomland hardwood marshes.

Start: From the picnic and parking area
Distance: 2.7-mile loop
Approximate hiking time: 2 hours
Difficulty rating: Moderate to difficult due to steep hills and rocky, switchback trails
Trail surface: Dirt and rock trails
Lay of the land: A limestone bluff along the Mississippi River
Other trail users: Hikers only
Canine compatibility: Leashed dogs permitted
Land status: State park
Nearest town: Red Wing, MN, and Lake City, MN
Fees/permits: State park vehicle permit

required. Annual or day permits are available at the park office. Camping fees are separate.
Schedule: Open year-round, day use and campground. Featured hike is open only during the non-snow season.
Maps: USGS maps: Maiden Rock, MN; state park map
Trail contacts: Frontenac State Park, Frontenac, MN; (651) 345-3401; www.dnr.state .mn.us/parks; Department of Natural Resources, Information Center, St. Paul, MN; (651) 296-6157 or (800) 646-6367 (only in MN); www.dnr.state.mn.us/parks

Finding the trailhead: From Lake City, drive 5 miles northwest on U.S. Highway 61. Take a right onto CR 2 and travel 1 mile to the park entrance. From Red Wing, take US 61 approximately 10 miles southeast, turn left on CR 2 and travel 1 mile to the park entrance, which will be on your left. *DeLorme: Minnesota Atlas & Gazetteer.* Page 34 B5

The Hike

Rising 430 feet above Lake Pepin, this 3-mile-long bluff beckons nature lovers to the top for serious bird watching. More than 200 bird species have been identified in this ornithological paradise, including the bald eagle and the peregrine falcon, both of which have been removed from the federal Endangered Species List. Since being taken off the list in 1999, the U.S. Fish and Wildlife Service has been slowly reintroducing these birds of prey to the area. These rare birds aren't the only ones to watch, though. The area is ripe with sanderlings, ruddy turnstones, and prothonotary warblers. Sanderlings and turnstones are small, hardy transient shorebirds that fly between South America and the Arctic each year, feeding on small crustaceans and other invertebrates. But don't let their size fool you: Turnstones have been known to travel as far as 450 miles in one day. The striking prothonotary warbler, with its golden plumage and black markings, received its unusual name from eighteenth-century Louisiana Creoles. To them, the bird's plumage resembled the gilded robes worn by the prothonotarius, a Catholic Church adviser to the Pope. A cavity dweller that makes its home near water of some sort, the prothonotary warbler isn't fussy about choosing a building site—and sometimes settles for the pocket of an old coat or an old tin can. Frontenac's bottomland hardwood forest is one of few areas in Minnesota that provides the right environment for this unusual bird, which often creates trouble for itself by nesting too close to water with flooding potential. However, this bird's numbers are steadily decreasing for other reasons, according to data from the North American Breeding Survey, which shows an annual decline of 1.5 percent. Taking the blame for this decline are wetland losses to logging and development in the bottomland forests of North America and the mangrove swamps of Central and South America, where the warblers winter.

And although they are rare, Frontenac's woods are also home to the 35- to 50-inch long timber rattlesnake, a secretive animal that prefers areas unfrequented by humans. Rarely will you hear it rattle, as it usually doesn't call attention to itself. Adult timber rattlers have a yellow, brown, or orange ground color with black or dark brown crossbands extending along their backs. They lie alongside fallen logs, waiting for small animals to come within striking range. Their habitat includes bluff prairies and oak woodlands in relatively remote areas. In spring and fall, they may be found in rocky outcrops and open grassy areas where it's warm. During the summer, they like deciduous forests and open valleys.

River barge on the Mississippi

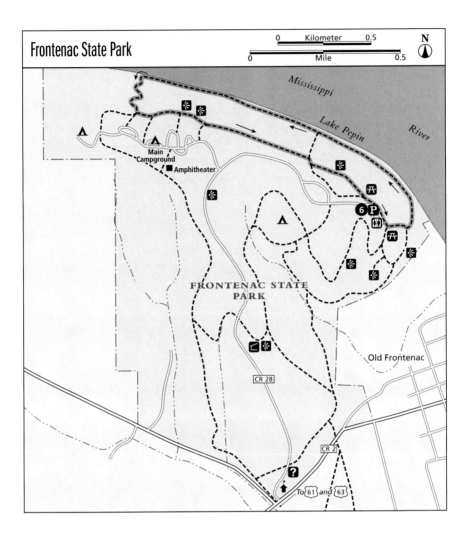

Frontenac State Park

Kilometer 0.5
Mile 0.5

N

Mississippi

Lake Pepin

River

Main Campground

Amphitheater

6 P

FRONTENAC STATE PARK

Old Frontenac

CR 28

CR 2

To 61 and 63

Timber rattlers are slow and infrequent breeders, first reproducing at between seven and eleven years of age and only three to five times during their lives. Litters of ten to fifteen young are born from late August to mid–September, but their mortality rate is high. Raptors, turkeys, badgers, skunks, and raccoons find them a tasty meal. At one time, timber rattler skins were a bounty hunter's income, one hunter boasting a kill of 5,700 in one season. But the snake was listed as a Protected Wild Animal in 1998 and also is listed as a threatened species in Illinois and Minnesota. Conservation and management include education of humans regarding the myths surrounding the snake. For instance, timber rattlesnakes are not a major threat to humans and livestock, and death due to a rattlesnake bite is not likely. This animal is able to control its injection of venom when biting, and up to 60 percent of all bites to humans contain no venom.

Once the home and burial grounds of the Hopewell Indians, Frontenac has a long history—dating back to at least 400 B.C.—of human habitation. Unique in their differences from other Native Americans, the Hopewell Indians were farmers who lived along rivers and other major waterways. Among their major crops were sunflowers, squash, chenopodium (a type of herb), knotweed, marsh elder, little barley and maygrass. Maize was a minor crop that didn't become a staple until between A.D. 800 and 1000. Hopewellians were industrious people, forming well-established trade routes to places as far away as the Rocky Mountains, the Atlantic Ocean, and the Gulf of Mexico. Carved utensils and pottery found in their massive, well-structured burial mounds have revealed many aspects of their culture, including clues about feasts and religious ceremonies. The Hopewell Indians were also skilled metal workers, using native copper, silver nuggets or iron-rich meteors in their work. But in spite of their proficient craftsmanship and organizational skills, Hopewell culture began to fade after A.D. 400.

One of the most notable features in the park's 13 miles of hiking trails is a dolomite (limestone) quarry, inactive for more than fifty years. The soft, porous rock found here was used to construct part of the Cathedral of St. John the Divine in New York City. Limestone was a popular and abundant building material at the time the cathedral was constructed.

The featured hike takes you from the top of the bluff on a switchback trail down to the river's edge, where you can watch the passing ships and view the bluffs on the Wisconsin side. A trail paralleling the river just above the water, takes you to two other switchback trails back to the top again. The shaded bluff provides a cool retreat on a hot summer day and spectacular color in the fall.

Miles and Directions

0.0 Start from the large kiosk near the end of the picnic area parking lot. Follow the dirt trail to the edge of the bluff and descend a switchback trail to a small wood platform overlook. Then continue down the main trail until you reach a fork.

0.2 There is a bench and a YOU ARE HERE sign at the fork. A right at this fork completes the interpretive trail loop back up to the top. Turn left here and continue down the switchback trail.

0.4 The right fork here is a stub trail that dead-ends at the river. Take the left fork, which roughly parallels the river a short distance above the water.

0.7 There is a YOU ARE HERE sign at this intersection. Continue straight ahead. The trail to the right is a short dead-end trail to the water. The left trail is a vertical switchback trail to the top of the bluff.

1.7 At this fork, note the YOU ARE HERE sign. Straight ahead will take you to the campground and group camp. Turn left and follow this trail along the edge of the bluff toward the picnic area. The trail has a number of platform overlooks along the way.

2.4 At this T turn right and proceed the short distance to a junction with a paved trail where you will see another YOU ARE HERE sign. Turn left and follow the paved trail back to the beginning.

2.7 Arrive back at the parking area.

More Information

Local Information
Lake City Area Chamber of Commerce: Lake City, MN; (800) 369-4123; www.lakecity.org
Red Wing Chamber of Commerce: Red Wing, MN; (651) 388-4719 or (800) 762-9516; http://redwingchamber.com

Local Events/Attractions
Water Ski Days: June, Lake City Chamber of Commerce; (800) 369-4123; www.lakecity.org
Johnny Appleseed Days: October, Lake City Chamber of Commerce; (800) 369-4123; www.lake city.org; Tourism Bureau, Lake City; (877) 525-3248 or info@lakecitymn.org

Accommodations
Red Gables Inn B & B: Lake, City, MN; (651) 345-2605; www.redgablesinn.com
Sunset Motel: Lake City, MN; (800) 945-0192
Lake Country Inn: Lake City, MN; (651) 345-5351 or (877) 299-8103
John Hall's Alaska Lodge: Lake City, MN; (651) 345-1212 or (866) 753-3725
The Frog and Bear B&B: Lake City, MN; (651) 345-2122 or (800) 753-9431; www.frogandbear.com

Restaurants
The Galley Restaurant: Lake City, MN; (651) 345-9991
Chickadee Cottage, Tea Room & Restaurant: Lake City, MN; (651) 345-5155 or (888) 321-5177
Skyline: Lake City, MN; (651) 345-5353
Marien's Deli: (651) 345-2526
Papa Tronnio's Pizza: (651) 345-3540

Organizations
Goodhue County Historical Society: Red Wing, MN; (651) 388-6024; www.goodhuehistory.mus .mn.us

7 Whitewater State Park

Eroded white clay along the banks of the Whitewater River causes its water to appear milky white in the spring. This white water impressed the Dakota Indians, who were the first to inhabit the area and gave the river its name. Several miles of trails loop through the popular, scenic Whitewater State Park, offering a variety of hike lengths. The Dakota Trail takes you to the top of the bluffs for panoramic views of the surrounding countryside. The Valley Trail follows alongside the river, offering scenic views of the bluffs from below. The Whitewater River Valley is known for its plant and animal diversity and is home to species not found in other sections of Minnesota, among them the shagbark hickory and the timber rattlesnake.

Start: Across the road from the Nature Store
Distance: 2.5-mile loop
Approximate hiking time: 1.5 hours
Difficulty rating: Difficult to moderate due to steep ascents and descents of the limestone bluffs
Trail surface: Rocky and narrow in some places, dirt- or grass-covered and wide in other places
Lay of the land: The Whitewater River Valley and surrounding limestone and clay bluffs in southeastern Minnesota
Other trail users: Hikers and cross country skiers

Canine compatibility: Leashed dogs permitted
Land status: State park
Nearest town: Elba, MN
Fees/permits: State park vehicle permit required. Annual or day permits are available at the park office. Camping fees are separate.
Schedule: Open year-round, day use and campground
Map: USGS map: Elba, MN
Trail contacts: Whitewater State Park Manager, Altura, MN; (507) 932-3007; www.dnr.state.mn.us/parks

Finding the trailhead: The park entrance is 3 miles south of Elba off Highway 74. *DeLorme: Minnesota Atlas and Gazetteer.* Page 26 A3

The Hike

Because the Whitewater River Valley lies in the driftless area of Minnesota, the glacial deposits responsible for most of the state's wet and rolling topography are scarce to nonexistent here, leaving thin easily eroded soils. Settlers moving into the Whitewater River Valley in the mid–1800s used land practices that were not sustainable in this Blufflands topography. These lessons came too late for the benefit of their farms and

Whitewater River

the ecology. The settlers' biggest concern was not for the land, but for eking a living from it. So they set their plows to work (even on the slopes), burned large areas for pasture, grazed livestock on hillsides, and stripped the land of trees for lumber. The result was loss of vegetative cover, which left the soil vulnerable to erosion. Unsightly gullies formed, and flooding became epidemic, with floodwaters depositing rubble and sand on the valley floor and causing mud and logging debris to accumulate in streams. Soon the land was greatly changed, streams were muddied, and whole villages and farms were abandoned, leaving ghost towns such as Beaver and Whitewater Falls buried beneath several feet of mud.

Such was the condition of Whitewater Valley in the 1940s, when Richard J. Dorer began his fight to restore the land to its former healthy condition. Dorer was a man who had a feel for the land, was sensitive to its delicate needs, and knew what had to be done to save it. He had worked on several projects for the Minnesota Department of Conservation and served as supervisor of the Bureau of Game. Beginning in Whitewater Valley, trees, shrubs, and grasses were planted to hold the fragile soil in place. Gullies were blocked and filled, farmers learned sound cultivation practices, and previously abandoned land was turned over to the state. Dorer spoke to clubs and organizations, educating them in proper care of the land and initiating the "Save the Wetlands" movement. It took several years, but through his efforts and those of others, flooding was significantly decreased—though not eliminated—and the land's wounds slowly began to heal.

In order to manage and continue protecting the state's driftless area, the Minnesota Legislature established the Memorial Hardwood State Forest in 1961. The park was renamed the Richard J. Dorer Memorial Hardwood State Forest in 1976. This protected area now includes private as well as public land. For example, the Whitewater Wildlife Management Area adjacent to the park began in the 1930s as a game refuge. Deer, rabbits, squirrels, ruffed grouse, and wild turkeys are hunted in the Wildlife Management Area, and anglers cast their lines in the streams hoping for their limit of trout.

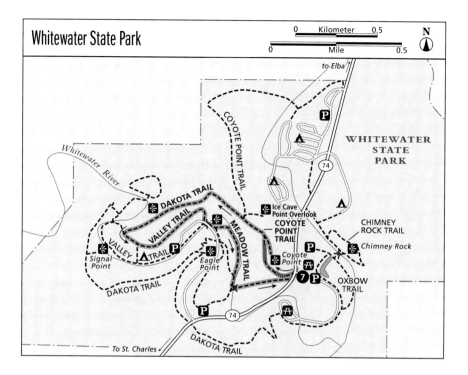

Whitewater State Park is one of the most popular parks in Minnesota due to its scenic value—its rocky, pine-clothed bluffs, deep limestone ravines, and wooded slopes. The park is also well known for its year-round recreational and educational opportunities, drawing school groups and outdoor enthusiasts from around the state. Three forks branch off the Whitewater River, with the park encompassing the middle fork. The river's main stem is approximately 15 miles from the three forks' confluence with the Mississippi. The gradient along this stretch is rather low; however, on the three forks, the gradient is approximately 25 feet per mile. Flooding is still a problem in the Whitewater Valley, and it sometimes floods in spring, causing closure of Highway 74 between Elba and Weaver. The worst floods occurred in 1938 when twenty-eight storms descended on the valley, washing away precious topsoil. Storms of this type are unusual, though, and flooding has decreased due to improved conservation practices. Even when flooding does occur, most hiking trails are not affected. Since conditions change from year to year, it's best to check with park personnel before heading out.

The town of Elba, with its popular antique fire tower whose long stairway takes tourists to the top for a view of the surrounding countryside, sits in the middle of these public lands. A pioneer stone house still stands in the Whitewater Wildlife Management Area, and the old town hall is all that remains of the town of Beaver. Nearby is Weaver Bottoms, part of the Upper Mississippi National Fish and Wildlife Refuge where hundreds of species of migrating birds stop in the spring and fall. Unlike other sections of Minnesota, the Whitewater State Park area is pleasantly void of mosquitoes due to the lack of wetlands and stagnant water that serve as breeding grounds for these annoying insects.

This trail offers a nice overview of the surrounding landscape as it ascends the limestone bluffs for views of the Whitewater River Valley and then descends to follow along the river, offering views from below of the same bluffs.

Note: In the past, flooding has damaged or destroyed Whitewater River bridges. Therefore, we suggest you check with the park manager as to bridge status before you visit the park.

Miles and Directions

0.0 Start from across the road from the Nature Store. Follow the Dakota Trail sign and climb up 238 wooden steps to the top of the limestone bluff.

0.1 Come to the first landing at the bottom of a limestone cliff face about 100 feet up on the left. Continue up another set of 109 wooden steps to reach Coyote Point.

0.2 Walk out to Coyote Point on your right and view the river valley below. Proceed left to continue along the bluff-top on the Dakota Trail. (Note: The trail is narrow here, so be cautious near the edge.)

0.4 Come to a trail that leads to Ice Cave Point overlook. Stay left to follow the Dakota Trail.

0.6 Here, the Coyote Point trail diverges to the right. Stay left to follow the Dakota Trail along the bluff downhill, across a drainage, and back up again. (FYI: Catch a beautiful view of the river on your right from the top.)

0.9 The main trail intersects with an unmarked trail. Continue left.

1.0 Begin the steep descent to the river valley below.

1.2 Reach the bottom, and take a left to follow the Valley Trail back along the spring-fed Whitewater River. A right follows the Dakota Trail.

1.4 Pass the group camp and walk along the edge and across a field to pick up the trail on the other side. Follow this mowed grass trail to the park road.

1.7 Turn left on the park road, and cross the bridge over the Whitewater River. Take in the striking views of the bluffs and river valley from benches along the river's edge.

1.8 Come to the Meadow Trail and take a left toward the river.

2.0 Stay left at this intersection to follow the Meadow Trail.

2.1 Take a left at this intersection and cross a suspension footbridge over the river.

2.4 Cross the road and walk toward the Nature Store.

2.5 Arrive back at the parking area.

More Information

Local Information

Whitewater Valley Visitors Center: In the park, with year-round educational programs; (507) 932-3007

Local Events/Attractions

Gladiolus Days: Last weekend in August, St. Charles, MN; www.stcharlesmn.org

Steamboat Days: June, Winona Area Jaycees, Winona, MN

Outdoor concerts by Winona Municipal Band: Free at 8:00 p.m. each Wednesday, June through August, Lake Park band shell, Winona, MN

Accommodations

White Valley Motel: St. Charles, MN; (507) 932-3142

Victorian Lace Inn: St. Charles, MN; (507) 932-4496; www.bluffcountry.com

Lazy D Campground: St. Charles, MN; (507) 932-3098; www.lazyd-camping-trailrides.com

Restaurants

Del's Café: St. Charles, MN; (507) 932-3098

The Historic Trempealeau Hotel: Trempealeau, WI; (608) 534-6898; www.greatriver.com/hotel.htm

Local Outdoor Retailers

Army/Navy Great Outdoor Store: Winona, MN; (507) 452-1348

8 Great River Bluffs State Park

Hikes in southeastern Minnesota are noted for their spectacular views of the Mississippi River Valley, great expanses of farmland, and nearby cities. Most of the hikes at Great River Bluffs are easy trails the whole family can enjoy. However, watch children closely near bluff edges. Trails can be slippery when wet, and the bluff hikes take you 500 to 600 feet above the river. The Great River Bluffs trails lead you through an interpretive nature trail, to scenic overlooks, and through hardwood forests to the top of King's Bluff for a clear view of green valleys and the Mississippi River far below. You can choose short hikes, take longer loops, or cover all of the 6.5 miles of trails in the park.

Start: From the north end of the parking area

Distance: 4.5-mile circuit

Approximate hiking time: 2 hours

Difficulty rating: Easy due to wide, grassy trails

Trail surface: Grass and dirt

Lay of the land: Blufflands (with mixed hardwood forests), prairies, and overlooks of the Mississippi River

Other trail users: Hikers only. Snowshoeing and cross-country skiing in winter

Canine compatibility: Leashed dogs permitted

Land status: State park

Nearest town: Winona, MN

Fees/permits: State park vehicle permit required. Annual or day permits are available at the park office. Camping fees are separate. There's an additional fee for camping.

Schedule: Open year-round, day use. Campground open seasonally.
Maps: USGS maps: Pickwick, MN; state park map
Trail contacts: Great River Bluffs State Park;

(507) 643-6849; Department of Natural Resources, Information Center, St. Paul, MN; (651) 296-6157 or (800) 646-6367 (only in MN); www.dnr.state.mn.us/parks

Finding the trailhead: From Winona, follow U.S. Highway 61 south approximately 20 miles. Take Interstate 90 west to exit 266. Follow the park signs. An alternate route is to turn right on CR 3 off US 61 (just past mile marker 15). Follow this road for 4 miles to the park entrance. *DeLorme: Minnesota Atlas and Gazetteer.* Page 27 8B

The Hike

Southeastern Minnesota offers a variety of treasures, from picturesque bluffs overlooking the Mississippi River to hardwood forests and fragile ecosystems containing rare plant species. Officially opened in 1976, Great River Bluffs State Park near Winona reveals these highlights and more.

The park, which is within the Richard J. Dorer Memorial Hardwood Forest, is located in Minnesota's driftless area where glacial deposits are thin to nonexistent, as all but one glacial advance missed this area. Ancient seas, wind, and meltwater spent millions of years creating the bluffland landscape encompassed by the 3,000-acre Great

Mississippi River from King's Bluff

River Bluffs State Park. Seas that covered southern Minnesota more than 450 million years ago deposited sediments that formed the distinctive limestone, dolomite, and sandstone bluffs characteristic of the area.

Native stands of northern white cedar found in the park are unique to this area. Common to northeastern Minnesota where the climate is much cooler, these cedars are remnants from glacial times when Glacial River Warren filled the valley to the bluff tops and temperatures were more frigid and damp. You can see the stand of northern white cedar on Queen's Bluff from the overlook at the end of the King's Bluff Trail.

Although the park contains 6.5 miles of trails with several loops from which to choose, you won't want to miss the hike out to King's Bluff. On this trail, you can view Queen's Bluff, gaze down at the sprawling Mississippi River, walk through the bluff prairies, and hike to the western edge of an oak and hickory forest that once stretched from the Atlantic Ocean to southeastern Minnesota. With its wide grass and dirt trails, this is an easy hike—one the whole family can enjoy.

The trail begins in open grassland where you may spot the rare Henslow's sparrow, a small, buff-colored bird that attracts avid bird-watchers. Henslow's sparrow is secretive, so you may have a better chance of spotting the bird by listening for the soft hiccupping *tsi-lick* song. The park is one of several areas in the state that has the right kind of vegetation to support this delicate bird, which requires undisturbed pastures and meadows with tall, dense vegetation. The Henslow's sparrow's nest is made of grass built 2 to 3 inches off the ground. As with many species of wildlife, the Henslow's sparrow is threatened by human intrusion on its habitat, namely, by large-scale conversion of vast historic prairies into agricultural fields and, more recently, increased suburban and rural housing development. The U.S. population of this species declined more than 68 percent from 1966 to 1991. Efforts are being made by the Department of Natural Resources to control habitat in order to prevent further decline in the bird's numbers.

After walking less than a quarter of a mile, you'll come to an interpretive nature loop on your left that leads to an overlook of the picturesque river valley below. This loop will merge into the main trail where an interpretive sign will tell you that you're leaving the pine, mixed oak, and shagbark hickory and entering a beautiful hardwood region that feels like an enchanted forest from a fairy tale. The tall, twisted, gnarled, aging oaks are a reminder of the dry conditions that created this savanna and oak woodland forest.

As you leave this forest, you'll come to another interpretive sign near the end of the trail, which opens to one of southern Minnesota's famous bluff, or goat prairies. These bluffs are called goat prairies because goats were supposedly the only domestic animals capable of grazing on these steep, open hillsides. Prairie grasses and wild-flowers dominated these south-facing slopes because woody plants couldn't gain a foothold due to warm and dry conditions created by the southern exposure, frequent fires, and the almost daily freezing and thawing during spring and fall.

To the northeast is Queen's Bluff, a Scientific and Natural Area and designated educational unit. Because of its fragile ecosystem, it may be used for educational purposes by permit only. Peregrine falcons, an endangered species in Minnesota, have been nesting on Queen's Bluff. King's Bluff, also a Scientific and Natural Area, but open to the public for hiking and bird watching, rises 600 feet above the river. This bluff supports diverse plant growth including fifteen rare plant species, goat prairies, a moist, shaded cliff, oak savanna, oak forest, and second-growth forest. A deciduous forest clothes the northeast face of King's Bluff. This unique mix of plant communities is being preserved and protected by the Department of Natural Resources.

The trail ends before you reach the northern edge of King's Bluff, and, since there is no loop at this point, you'll have to retrace your steps to the interpretive sign that marks the edge of the hardwood forest. Stay to the left, and the trail will take you to the park road near the picnic area. The trail eventually turns eastward and parallels the park road toward the picnic and parking area. During the remainder of the hike, you'll come across many trails that intersect with the featured trail. These are cross-country ski trails that can be hiked, and there are directional signs at each intersection. East of the picnic area are two spectacular overlooks of the Mississippi River. After you check out the views, head south and west through hardwood forest back to the trailhead.

Miles and Directions

0.0 Start from the parking area on the left at the beginning of the King's Bluff trail. Follow the trail going north.

0.1 The trail intersects with a trail that parallels the park road to the picnic area on the right. Continue straight ahead.

0.2 The interpretive loop begins at this trail intersection. Turn left to follow the interpretive trail between stands of ash and white pine.

0.4 This is a four-way intersection and scenic overlook of the Mississippi River Valley. Take a left to continue the interpretive trail. This trail follows the ridge out to King's Bluff and is part of the designated scientific and natural area.

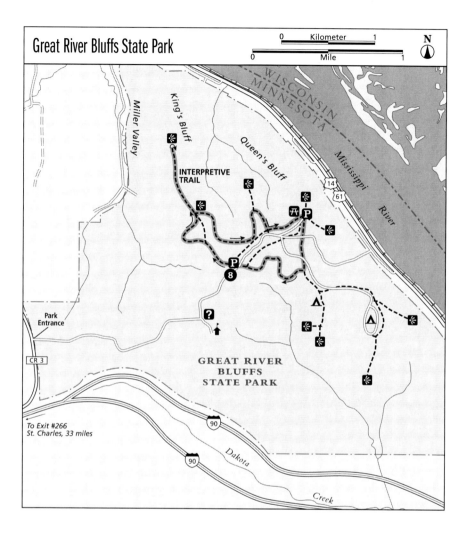

Great River Bluffs State Park

0 —— Kilometer —— 1

0 —— Mile —— 1

N

WISCONSIN
MINNESOTA

Miller Valley

King's Bluff

INTERPRETIVE
TRAIL

Queen's Bluff

Mississippi River

14
61

P

8

Park
Entrance

CR 3

GREAT RIVER
BLUFFS
STATE PARK

To Exit #266
St. Charles, 33 miles

90

90

Dakota

Creek

1.4 You'll reach the end of the trail with a view of the river and Queen's Bluff. Retrace your steps back to the four-way intersection.

2.0 Take a left to head toward the picnic and parking areas. The trail will intersect with many ski trails, most of which are posted.

2.6 The trail intersects with an overlook trail. Go right to stay on the main trail.

3.1 Come to a four-way intersection near the park road. Stay left to continue toward the parking and picnic areas.

3.2 The trail intersects with another ski trail. Continue right and come into view of the parking area. Walk to the north side of the picnic area to pick up the trail.

3.4 There are two overlooks trails at this four-way intersection that lead to views of the river. Take the far right trail to continue on the main trail.

3.7 Cross the campground road and pass a trail on the left that leads to the group camp and two overlooks. Keep to the right to continue on the main trail.

4.1 Pass a ski trail on the right. Proceed left. There may be other ski trails that you will pass; most are marked but some are not.

4.2 Pass another ski trail on the right. Proceed left.

4.3 Pass a trail on the right that parallels the park road and leads to the picnic area. Proceed left.

4.5 Arrive back at the parking area.

More Information

Local Information
Winona Convention & Visitors Bureau: Winona, MN; (507) 452-0735 or (800) 657-4972; www.visitwinona.com

Local Events/Attractions
Steamboat Days: June, Winona, MN
Outdoor concerts by Winona Municipal Band: Free at 8:00 p.m. each Wednesday, June through August, Lake Park band shell, Winona, MN

Accommodations
Great River Bluffs State Park: (507) 643-6849
Windom Park Bed & Breakfast: Winona, MN; (507) 457-9515; www.windompark.com
Winona Farm: Winona, MN; (507) 454-3126; http://members.nbci.com/winfarm. These are rustic country cabins with full kitchens.
The Historic Trempealeau Hotel: Trempealeau, WI; (608) 534-6898; www.greatriver.com/hotel.htm

Restaurants
Bub's Brewing Company Eatery & Saloon: Winona, MN; (507) 457-3121
Acoustic Café: Corner of Second & Lafayette, Winona, MN; (507) 453-0394
The Historic Trempealeau Hotel: Trempealeau, WI; (608) 534-6898; www.greatriver.com/hotel.htm

Local Outdoor Retailers
Army/Navy Great Outdoor Store: Winona, MN; (507) 452-1348

MINNESOTA'S STATE FLOWER

While hiking through the woods in late spring or early summer, watch for the striking pink and white pouch-like blooms of the showy lady's slipper. Among Minnesota's numerous beautiful and unusual species of wildflowers, this is one of the most remarkable. The state flower is easily recognizable when in bloom with its wide, ribbed leaves (up to twelve to a stem) and its distinctive white and pink pouch. Although rare, this orchid is most abundant through the north and north central regions of the state. It is possible to discover one if you're hiking during the right time of year. Watch for it in moist areas such as coniferous swamps, shrub swamps where there are small springs, and even in moist, roadside ditches. Fairly versatile, this plant thrives either in shade or direct sunlight. It's fitting that in the land of 10,000 lakes the state flower is one that can be found in wetland areas.

Hikers may pass by the showy lady's slipper more than once without recognizing it because its most prominent feature, the bloom, is missing. It takes fourteen to sixteen years for these plants to produce their first flower. Additionally, flowering time is limited, lasting roughly from June 7 to July 11. Since the plant remains flowerless for most of its existence, you probably won't recognize it unless you're familiar with the stem and leaves. One would think that the plant's high seed yield would make it a more common flower. Despite the fact that one of this plant's seed capsules normally yields up to 10,000 seeds, at best just ten of them germinate. Once the plant is established, the rhizomes will continue to grow, producing more stems each year. Clumps of stems often found in cedar swamps may be more than one hundred years old.

The state flower is not to be confused with similar orchids of the same genus, such as the small, white lady's slipper, the large, yellow lady's slipper, or the stemless lady's slipper, also called pink lady's slipper or moccasin flower. There are between thirty and fifty species of lady's slipper in North America; eleven of them are in Minnesota. All are recognizable by their unusual, beautifully shaped pouches and brightly colored flowers. However, only the state flower is distinctive, being the largest of Minnesota's native orchids, and the only one with a white and pink pouch. The state flower is unlike the other species, which have a much longer bloom time. Also, most lady's slipper stems rarely have two flowers; the state flower often has two.

Of course, because the showy lady's slipper is the state flower and is rare and difficult to domesticate, this flower is not to be picked should you find one either inside or outside a state park. An attempt to pick the showy lady's slipper or simply touching its leaves may result in a poison ivy–like rash if you're susceptible.

9 Beaver Creek Valley

Beaver Creek, a tributary of the South Fork River in southeastern Minnesota, has been called one of the most beautiful spring brooks in the state's southeastern section. Beginning in large springs and flowing through extensive watercress beds, this stream lies in one of two major trout areas in the state, the other being the North Shore of Lake Superior. Beaver Creek is one of many rivers and creeks cutting their way through forested valleys and deep gorges where wildlife is prolific. The area's beauty, with its many hills and hollows, is much akin to parts of the Appalachians or Ozarks of the South. Cold water and a shaded creek valley make this hike a cool oasis on a hot summer day. And fall is an exceptional time to see spectacular color throughout the park. Most of the park's 8 miles of hiking trails follow the creek, periodically making loops that take you away from the water and up the adjacent bluffs.

Start: From the picnic area parking lot

Distance: 3.5-mile loop

Approximate hiking time: 1.5 hours

Difficulty rating: Easy hike due to wide, flat trails

Trail surface: Dirt/grass trail surface

Lay of the land: A narrow creek valley between two large sandstone and limestone bluffs

Other trail users: Hikers only (though anglers are permitted in the park)

Canine compatibility: Leashed dogs permitted

Land status: State park

Nearest town: Caledonia, MN

Fees/permits: State park vehicle permit is required. Annual or day permits are available at the park office. Camping fees are separate.

Schedule: Open year-round, day use and campground.

Maps: USGS maps: Sheldon, MN; state park map

Trail contacts: Beaver Creek Valley State Park, Caledonia, MN; (507) 724-2107; Department of Natural Resources, Information Center, St. Paul, MN; (651) 296-6157 or (888) 646-6367 (only in MN); www.dnr.state.mn.us/parks. Park maps are available at the Web site.

Finding the trailhead: From Caledonia: From Highway 76 drive west 4 miles on CR 1 to the park entrance. *DeLorme: Minnesota Atlas & Gazetteer.* Page 27 D7

The Hike

Beaver Creek's watershed lies in the small section of Minnesota untouched by the most recent glacial ice. This region is called the driftless area and encompasses approximately 10,000 square miles in Wisconsin, Minnesota, Iowa, and Illinois. Geologists figure that highlands to the northwest and northeast deflected most of the glacial ice, preventing its advance. As a result, the bedrock lies close to the surface and is covered by a thin layer of weathered rock material, soil, loess (a brown, loamy material deposited by the wind), and lake or stream deposits. Small patches of drift found here indicate, however, that earlier glaciers covered this portion of the state but that erosion removed most of the drift.

These geologic processes shaped the rugged topography seen in this region of Minnesota. Here, broad valleys are separated by high, narrow, flat-topped ridges. This landscape was formed when torrents of glacial meltwater flowed through the region, broadening, deepening, and lengthening old stream valleys. The Beaver Creek River Valley is 250 feet deep and exposes porous layers of Oneota dolomite, Jordan sandstone, and St. Lawrence dolomite that were deposited by inland seas approximately 500 million years ago. Dolomite is a type of limestone rich in magnesium carbonate. Jordan sandstone and Oneota dolomite are porous rocks that allow water to percolate through them, creating springs. Some of these natural waters are found in the park along the valley walls near the campground and picnic shelter building. Spring-fed streams run year-round.

This portion of Minnesota was the first to be reached by steamboats traveling upriver along the Mississippi. Passengers fell in love with the area's unique beauty and the rich soil that was perfect for farming. As a result, several towns sprang up by the mid-1800s. Later, settlement picked up on a much larger scale as railroad lines

Bridge over Beaver Creek

expanded westward and steam travel increased. Caledonia, near Beaver Creek Valley State Park, is one of the oldest cities in Minnesota. Named for the ancient capital of Scotland, this town exemplifies early steamer-settled towns that dotted the area in the early 1800s. At that time, early settlers were unable to herd their cattle over the rugged landscape, so they simply went without milk and butter. Caledonia was once a milling town, and its old Schech Grist Mill, built in 1875, still boasts its original millstone and four stone burrs that remain in operating condition. Tours are provided on request, and stone-ground flour is available for purchase. Today, Caledonia is known as the Wild Turkey Capital of Minnesota. Hunters also visit the area for white-tail deer, and anglers come to catch trout from the cold, spring-fed streams.

Here, in the Blufflands Landscape Region of Minnesota, a variety of bottomland hardwoods such as black ash, willow, box elder, cottonwood, and elm grow in the lowlands while maple, walnut, basswood, and oak are found on higher ground above the valley. Patches of native prairie and oak savanna are also found in the park. This mixed vegetation is responsible for the diverse animal life that thrives here, including

Beaver Creek

the Acadian flycatcher and the Louisiana waterthrush. These birds are reportedly on the decline in certain areas where they're losing habitat to human activity.

The Louisiana waterthrush, a small, brown and white ground-dwelling bird, prefers headwater riparian woodlands, rocky streams, swamps, scrub thickets, and ravines near streams. This warbler can be recognized by its constant tail wagging and distinctive song, which differentiates it from the northern waterthrush or the ovenbird. Human pressures, such as agriculture, logging, pollution, and urbanization, are the largest threats to the survival of this species, whose range is from southeastern Minnesota south and east to Texas and Florida. A ground nester, the Louisiana waterthrush breeds along gravel-bottomed streams flowing through hilly deciduous forest.

The Acadian flycatcher is a rare bird in Minnesota, and Beaver Creek Valley is the only place it is regularly reported. The bird is recognizable by its olive-colored back and upper breast, its white lower breast, and its yellow belly. Its wings contain two off-white wing bars. This bird thrives in a similar habitat as the Louisiana waterthrush and is subject to the same pressures—including the bird's main enemy, cowbird parasitism. Cowbirds lay their eggs in the nests of other species and, when those eggs hatch, the larger young cowbirds force the smaller flycatcher chicks out of the nest. While the numbers of both species remain stable, biologists are studying their nesting and migration habits in order to maintain current population levels.

Another critter once common in this area is a small smooth-scaled lizard called the five-lined skink whose numbers declined due to gradual changes in their habitat. Skink survival needs are the availability of bedrock exposure, open sunny areas, abundant cover, and access to water. Over the years, vegetation has encroached on rock outcrops, reducing skink habitat and endangering the species, whose distribution is now reported as patchy. In addition, the area supports several plant species that are of special concern.

The featured hike follows Beaver Creek through the valley, which is surrounded by steep limestone bluffs, and crosses the creek several times. Nestled in the valley, the spring-fed creek soothes hikers with its refreshing sounds. And lowland forests of cottonwood, willow, and elm provide cool respite from the summer sun.

Miles and Directions

0.0 Start from the picnic area parking lot. Go west past Quarry Trail on the right and cross a suspension bridge over Beaver Creek. (FYI: Look for watercress growing along the edges of the creek, a sign that its waters are clean and pure, although you should not drink it without filtering. Also, do not pick the watercress.) Walk along the paved trail, pass the picnic shelter on your right, and look for the Beaver Creek Valley Trail sign.

0.1 Cross a small tributary of Beaver Creek over wooden planks and pass Switch Back Trail on your left. Stay right to follow the creek.

0.2 An overlook trail climbs the bluff on the left for a view of the valley. Continue right to follow Beaver Creek Valley Trail. (Note: During the rainy season areas of the trail may be wet. This area is susceptible to flash flooding, so remember to check weather conditions with the park office.)

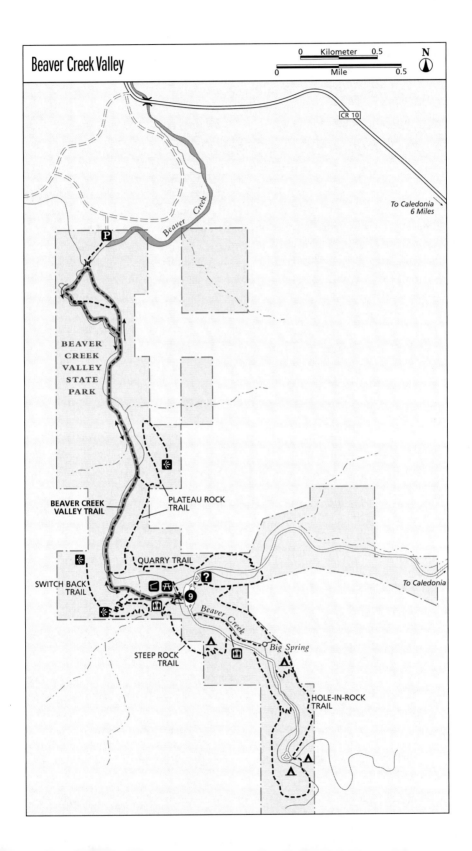

Beaver Creek Valley

0   Kilometer   0.5

0   Mile   0.5

N

CR 10

*To Caledonia
6 Miles*

P

Beaver Creek

BEAVER
CREEK
VALLEY
STATE
PARK

**BEAVER CREEK
VALLEY TRAIL**

PLATEAU ROCK
TRAIL

QUARRY TRAIL

SWITCH BACK
TRAIL

?

9

To Caledonia

Beaver Creek

STEEP ROCK
TRAIL

Big Spring

HOLE-IN-ROCK
TRAIL

0.4 Cross Beaver Creek on wooden planks. Watch your step, as the boards may move. Come to an intersection with Plateau Rock Trail on the right. Go left to follow the east side of the creek. (FYI: You are walking through floodplain forest: elms, oaks, and willows.)

0.8 Pass a spur that leads to Plateau Rock Trail to the right. Go left and once more you will cross Beaver Creek on wooden planks.

1.1 Cross the creek again to follow the east side.

1.4 The trail splits here. You will see a trail sign and an open meadow. Take the right fork hiking away from the creek's edge.

1.5 Pass a crossover trail on the left; stay right.

1.7 A right crosses an iron bridge over Beaver Creek and leads to trail parking. Stay left to follow the creek back south.

1.9 A left follows the crossover trail. Keep right.

2.1 Back at the Hiking Club Trail sign. Continue right to retrace your steps back to the picnic and parking area.

3.5 Arrive back at the picnic and parking area.

More Information

Local Information

Caledonia Chamber of Commerce: Caledonia, MN; (507) 725-5477

Historic Bluff Country: Harmony, MN; (800) 428-2030; www.bluffcountry.com

Local Events/Attractions

Rivers and Bluffs Fall Birding Festival: Lansing, MN; (563) 586-4444

Annual Winona Tundra Swan Watch: First weekend in November, Winona Convention and Visitors Bureau; (507) 452-0735 or (800) 657-4972; www.visitwinona.com

Eagle Watch Weekend: First weekend in March, Winona Convention and Visitors Bureau; (507) 452-2272 or (800) 657-4972; www.visitwinona.com

Fall Foliage Fest: Late September, Harmony, MN; (800) 428-2030; www.bluffcountry.com

Accommodations

Crest Red Carpet Inn: Caledonia, MN; (507) 724-3311 or (800) 845-0904

Eddie's Attic B & B: Houston, MN; (507) 896-3010

The Bunkhouse: Houston, MN; (507) 896-2080

Americinn: Caledonia, MN; (800) 396-5007

Restaurants

Covie's Little Miami: Caledonia, MN; (507) 724-2156

Frankie's Inn: Caledonia, MN; (507) 725-9903

Local Outdoor Retailers

Army/Navy Great Outdoor Store: Winona, MN; (507) 452-1348

Prairie Lands

C alled *Coteau des Prairies* by French explorers, southwestern Minnesota awed early settlers when they emerged from eastern forests to find themselves at the edge of an endless sea of grass. The prairie was capable of swallowing whole teams of oxen and their wagons. Today, although small patches still exist and are being preserved, most of the original prairie and the buffalo that roamed there are gone. They have been replaced by, among other things, fields of corn.

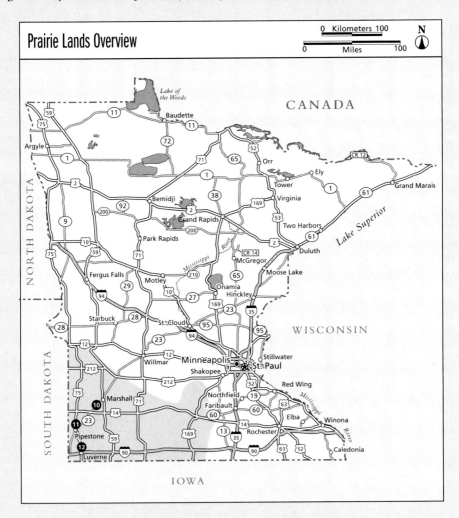

Prairie Lands Overview

Glaciers didn't gouge out lakebeds in this region like so much of Minnesota; many of the few lakes that do exist here are man-made. Glaciers covering this area deposited till and gravel, and even picked up and carried huge boulders, dropping them far from their points of origin. Drumlins and eskers (elongated hills or ridges of glacial drift) so typical in other portions of the state are also scarce here. However, there are some occasional kames (short ridges or mounds of sand and gravel deposited during the melting of glacial ice). Several small rivers and streams drain the nearly level landscape, and it's only where these streams have worn down the topsoil that the bedrock is exposed. Trees, also, are not common in the prairie, although small congregations of maples, basswood, ash, cottonwood, and hackberry are scattered throughout.

This section, which includes Camden, Pipestone, and Blue Mounds State Parks, has a border that runs by Morris on the north, angles southeast to New Ulm, and then heads straight south to the Iowa border before going west to run alongside South Dakota. Three types of bedrock underlie the rich farmland in this region: high-grade igneous metamorphic rock; Sioux quartzite, a descendant of Precambrian sandstone; and marine and continental shales and sandstones.

Much of southwestern Minnesota sits on a high plateau formed by geologic processes that involved a series of glaciations over a period of 500 million years. During the latest glacial period, the Des Moines Lobe crept down from northwestern Minnesota into Iowa, stopping at Des Moines. As it melted, it left behind a thick cover of glacial debris along with occasional outcroppings. The overall lasting effect of this glacier was a mostly level, slightly rolling landscape nearly devoid of lakes. The first vegetation was a spruce forest, which was followed by invasive prairie grasses that prevailed throughout the entire western portion of the state and into the Dakotas. It was this mixture of prairie grasses through repeated ecological cycles that created the rich, dark soils so valuable for sustaining Minnesota's corn belt. Formed by biological processes occurring mostly at root level, this life-sustaining soil, which now feeds America, accumulated at the rate of approximately 1 inch every one hundred years to a depth of 5 feet in some areas. Only in the mid- to latter part of the twenty-first century have people awakened to the importance of this rapidly diminishing ecosystem. Several organizations dedicated to restoration and preservation of the prairies have recently been formed.

10 Camden State Park

This park is part of a geological and biological zone that Joseph Nicollet called the Coteau des Prairies. It is a piece of the high prairie that divides the Mississippi and Missouri River watersheds. Hikers enter the plain of the prairie, then descend into the lush maple-basswood–forested Redwood River Valley. Once a home for bison, elk, and wolves, the park is abundant with springtime wildflowers, bass, trout, songbirds, white-tailed deer, hawks, and coyotes.

Start: From the parking area near the swimming beach
Distance: 6.3 miles
Approximate hiking time: 2.5 hours
Difficulty rating: Moderate due to occasional hills
Trail surface: Dirt and grassy trails
Lay of the land: Wooded Redwood River Valley surrounded by prairie and farmland
Other trail users: Mountain bikers and equestrians
Canine compatibility: Leashed dogs permitted
Land status: State park

Nearest town: Lynd, MN
Fees/permits: State park vehicle permit. Annual or day permits are available at the park office. Camping fees are separate.
Schedule: Open year-round, day use and campground.
Maps: USGS maps: Russell, MN; state park map
Trail contacts: Department of Natural Resources, Information Center, St. Paul, MN; (651) 296-6157 or (888) 646-6367 (only in MN); www.dnr.state.mn.us/parks; Camden State Park, Lynd, MN; (507) 865-4530

Finding the trailhead: From Marshall, take Highway 23 southwest for 10 miles. Turn right at the state park sign onto CR 68. *DeLorme: Minnesota Atlas & Gazetteer.* Page 29 D5

The Hike

As early as 8,000 years ago, when Native Americans first settled in the Redwood River Valley, the valley's beauty and abundant resources have drawn people to it. The Native Americans found they could survive nicely on the plentiful supply of fish and game, fur-bearing animals, and water. An American Fur Company trading post was established in the valley in the middle 1830s. Pioneers pushing west began settling the valley in the mid-1800s, and by the late 1880s, a thriving community had developed. Business by that time included a general store, a hotel, a blacksmith shop, and a sawmill that was later converted to a gristmill—a mill for grinding grain. The town's prosperity continued to grow, but it was short-lived as a result of the railroad's decision to bypass the town in its effort to construct depots along its route. Consequently, business began to fall off, and the settlers moved away. By the early 1930s, the town ceased to exist, but people continued to be drawn to this area they called the Camden Woods for picnics

Redwood River

and family events. In 1934 Veterans Conservation Corps (VCC) Company #2713, all World War I Veterans, part of the Works Progress Administration effort, started to clear trails, build buildings and a swimming pool, develop roads, build bridges over the Redwood River, and create a new state park, which was established in 1935.

Tallgrass prairie is one of the largest ecosystems in North America. More than one hundred years ago, before European settlers discovered the Redwood River Valley, this and other portions of Minnesota were covered with great expanses of tallgrass prairie. As the settlers put down roots and their numbers increased, acres of tallgrass prairie were wiped out as they fell under the plow and mortar. Today, less than one tenth of 1 percent of those original tallgrass prairies remains. A tiny portion of that remnant can be seen in Camden State Park, where preservation and restoration of prairie grasses is underway. Not all of Camden's grasslands are tallgrass prairie, though. Before Camden became a state park in 1935, much of the land in the park had been altered by intense grazing and gravel mining, or converted into cropland. These areas are slowly being replanted with native tallgrass prairie grasses and wildflowers. As you hike you'll see birdsfoot violet, prairie smoke, June grass, wild strawberry, prairie ragwort, puccoon, prairie phlox, and blue-eyed grass.

The Prairie Passages Program—a partnership whose goal is to protect prairie natural areas, cultural sites, and historic sites from Canada to Mexico—implemented the restoration projects at Camden and Blue Mounds State Parks. Partners of the program include any who wish to join including the Department of Natural Resources, The Nature Conservancy, and the departments of Tourism, Transportation, and Natural Resources. Prairie Passages plans to restore and protect natural prairie plants along a network of highways, along roadsides, and in communities throughout the prairie section of North America, and to educate the general public regarding the importance of their prairie heritage.

Camden State Park, consisting of 2,745 acres, is a multiuse park with more than 16 miles of multiuse trails—14.8 of them for hikers. The Bluebird Trail and the Dakota Valley Trail are featured here, with a combined distance of close to 5 miles. Nesting boxes on the bluebird trail attract not only bluebirds but other birds such as tree swallows and house wrens. A new state project, the Minnesota River Valley Birding Trail, has been developed by the Minnesota Audubon Society. The planning phase, completed in 2001, emphasizes the need to protect remaining habitats of birds in southwestern Minnesota and promotes natural recreational opportunities at selected sites, including Camden State Park. The trail spans the Minnesota River watershed from its headwaters near the South Dakota border to its confluence with the Mississippi River in the Twin Cities. Today, illustrated maps, birding trail guides, and interpretive signs are available to birders and hikers.

The spring-fed Indian Creek and an overlook with an excellent view of the river valley are the main features of the Dakota Valley Trail, named for the Dakota Indians who once lived in this area. The Sisseton Dakota was the last Native American group to live in the area that is now Camden State Park.

Autumn is a particularly beautiful time to visit the park as the maples, basswood, ash, cottonwood, and hackberry exchange their greens for yellow, red, orange, and gold and display a rainbow of color. Prairies are most colorful in spring and late summer with their variety of flowers and grasses.

Miles and Directions

0.0   Start from the swimming area. Walk toward the beach house from the parking area and turn left before the beach house. There is a sign indicating the hiking club trail.

0.4   Come to a bench alongside the creek, sit in the cool shade, and enjoy the lively sound of the water. Climb a gradual hill.

0.6   This is a three-way trail intersection with a horseback/hiking trail. Turn left to stay on the hiking only trail and go to a scenic overlook of the Redwood River. (FYI: The first right turn heads south toward Bluebird Trail. A second right heads east and drops down into the Redwood River valley.)

0.7   Return to the intersection with the horseback/hiking trail. Take the first left to follow the trail east toward the river.

0.8   The trail splits here. A left takes you back toward the picnic area along the horseback/hiking trail. Turn right to get back on the hiking-only trail and head south toward the river.

1.1   Come to the Redwood River and cross the bridge. Pick up the trail on the other side of the bridge, and head south along the wooded, shady river.

1.3   Come to the parking area near the group camp. Take a right to cross over the river and follow the hiking/biking trail for a short distance.

1.4   The group camp is on the right near the trail intersection. Take a left at the trail intersection to follow the river trail.

1.9   Take a right to follow a spur trail, climbing out of the river valley toward Prairie Bluff Trail.

2.1   Here, take a right to proceed north along Prairie Bluff Trail, a hiking/horseback trail. (FYI: A

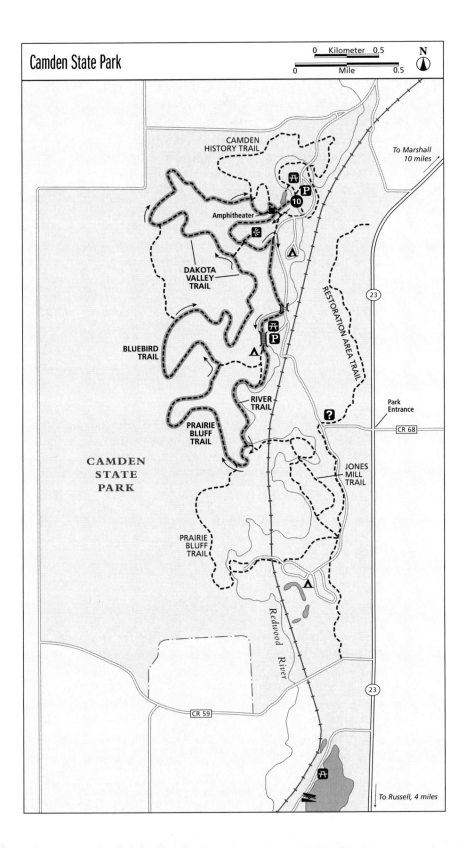

Camden State Park

0 Kilometer 0.5
0 Mile 0.5

N

CAMDEN
HISTORY TRAIL

To Marshall
10 miles

10

Amphitheater

DAKOTA
VALLEY
TRAIL

23

RESTORATION AREA TRAIL

BLUEBIRD
TRAIL

RIVER
TRAIL

Park
Entrance

PRAIRIE
BLUFF
TRAIL

CR 68

CAMDEN
STATE
PARK

JONES
MILL
TRAIL

PRAIRIE
BLUFF
TRAIL

Redwood River

23

CR 59

To Russell, 4 miles

left will take you south toward the horse camp.) Prairie Bluff Trail follows the border of the Oak Forest with the open prairie and farmland.

2.9 Prairie Bluff Trail meets the Bluebird Trail, a mountain bike/hiking/horseback trail. A right heads back toward the group camp, but stay left following Bluebird Trail around the prairie.

3.6 Take a right to stay on Bluebird Trail. (FYI: A left cuts north across the prairie toward Dakota Valley Trail.)

4.5 The trail intersects with the horseback/hiking spur that leads to the overlook above the lower campground. Turn left to follow the Dakota Valley Trail.

5.1 Here the trail meets with the trail that cuts south back to the Bluebird Trail. Stay right to follow the Dakota Valley Trail.

5.9 Come to a four-way trail intersection. Take an immediate right to head back toward the picnic area.

6.1 Take a right toward the picnic area and a left in less than 0.1 mile. This will take you back to the swimming beach/picnic area.

6.3 Arrive back at the parking area.

More Information

Local Information

Marshall Area Chamber of Commerce: Marshall, MN; (507) 532-4484; www.marshall-mn.org

Local Events/Attractions

Lyon County Fair: Second weekend in August, Marshall, MN

International Rolle Bolle Tournament: Second weekend in August, Marshall, MN; A Belgian game that is similar to croquet, bocce ball, and curling. Fun for all ages!

Shades of the Past: Collector cars, dance, and special events, first weekend in June, conducted in conjunction with Sounds of Summer Festival third weekend in August; Marshall, MN

Festival of Kites: July 4, Marshall, MN; Includes a big kite fly, fishing contest, and entertainment

Pursuit of Excellence Marching Band Contest: Third weekend of September, Marshall, MN

Camden Classic Bike Festival/Mountain Bike Race: Same weekend as Marshall's Sounds of Summer Festival, Camden State Park

Accommodations

Arbor Inn: Marshall, MN; (507) 532-2457; www.starpoint.net/~arborinnbb
Delux Motel: Marshall, MN; (507) 532-4441; www.mntrader.com/delux
Travelers Lodge: Marshall, MN; (507) 532-5721; www.mntrader.com/tlodge
Americinn: Marshall, MN; (507) 537-9424
Super 8: Marshall, MN; (507) 537-1461

Restaurants

The Daily Grind: Marshall, MN; (507) 537-9565
Mike's Café: Marshall, MN; (507) 532-5477
Wooden Nickel Saloon: Marshall, MN; (507) 532-3875; www.starpoint.net/~thenickel

Local Outdoor Retailers

Borch's Sporting Goods: Marshall, MN; (507) 532-4880

11 Pipestone National Monument

The Pipestone National Monument interpretive hike has much to offer, with a focus on the famous pipestone quarries that have drawn thousands of visitors over the past 400 years. A stop at the visitor center will educate you on the remarkable history of the region, Native American pipe making, and how pipestone carving and quarrying lives on today. Pipestone National Monument lies in prairie country where more than 300 plant species live, including prairie cordgrass and lanceleaf sage. The hike wanders through oak and ash woodland, along Lake Hiawatha and Pipestone Creek, and through remnants of tallgrass prairie past the quarrying site and large blocks of red quartzite that stand like sculptures along the trail.

Start: From the parking area outside the visitor center
Distance: 0.75-mile loop, the Circle Trail
Approximate hiking time: 45 minutes to stop and absorb the interpretive information
Difficulty rating: Easy. This is a short interpretive trail that is flat and wide.
Trail surface: Paved trail
Lay of the land: Tallgrass prairie, oak and ash woodland, and Sioux quartzite ledge
Other trail users: None
Canine compatibility: Dogs on a leash are allowed on the Circle Trail and in parking lots. Dogs and other pets are not allowed in the monument visitor center with the exception of service animals accompanying handicapped visitors.

Land status: National Park Service
Nearest town: Pipestone
Fees/permits: Free to Native Americans and children younger than 16. Others may contact Pipestone National Monument or the chamber of commerce for fee information.
Schedule: Open year-round. Summer hours Memorial Day to Labor Day: Monday through Friday 8:00 a.m. to 5:00 p.m. and Saturday and Sunday 8:00 a.m. to 6:00 p.m. Winter hours: Every day from 8:00 a.m. to 5:00 p.m.
Maps: USGS maps: Pipestone North, MN; national park map and guide
Trail contacts: Pipestone National Monument, Reservation Avenue adjacent to the pageant grounds, Pipestone, MN; (507) 825-5464; www.nps.gov/pipe

Finding the trailhead: It's 200 miles from the Twin Cities. Depending on the direction from which you're traveling, take U.S. Highway 75, Highway 23, or Highway 30, and follow the signs to Pipestone. Once in Pipestone, take Main Street to Hiawatha Avenue. Follow Hiawatha Avenue north to Reservation Avenue. Turn west onto Reservation Avenue to enter the monument. *DeLorme: Minnesota Atlas & Gazetteer.* Page 19 A2

The Hike

Located on the west slope of a high plateau ranging 1,700 to 2,000 feet above sea level that divides the Mississippi and Missouri Rivers, Pipestone National Monument is a must see not only for hikers but for anyone visiting or living in Minnesota. The story of this stone and the pipes made from it spans four centuries of Plains Indian life. Inseparable from the traditions that structured daily routine and honored the spirit world, pipes figured prominently in the ways of the village and in dealings between tribes. The story parallels that of a culture in transition. The evolution of the pipes influenced, and was influenced by, the white explorers, traders, soldiers, and settlers with whom their makers associated. Plains Indian culture has undergone radical change since the era of the free-ranging buffalo herds, yet pipe carving is by no means a lost art. Carvings today are appreciated as art as well as for ceremonial use. Once again, as commanded by the spirit bird in the Sioux story of its creation, the pipestone here is quarried by anyone of Indian ancestry. An age-old tradition continues in the modern world, ever changing yet firmly rooted in the past.

This unique stone, called Catlinite, was named after George Catlin, an author and artist whose curiosity about the unusual stone inspired him to visit the area in the early 1800s. Native American folklore dictates that the quarry is a place of peace and sacred ground. Native tribe members traveled great distances to the quarry to obtain catlinite, known today as pipestone. Soft as a human fingernail, pipestone is used to make peace pipes and art objects. For the Native Americans in this area, the pipe is culturally significant, viewed as the primary medium for communication with spiritual powers.

Sandwiched between layers of hard quartzite, the valued pipestone, according to scientists, was created billions of years ago by geologic forces. Ancient seas deposited a layer of muddy clay on top of which stream action later deposited sand and sediment. The sand was compressed into sandstone and the red clay under it into clay stone. Glaciers advancing into the area scraped off the sediment down to the sandstone. This

Winnewissa Falls of Pipestone Creek

sandstone was transformed to quartzite, and the red clay 4 to 12 feet beneath the earth's surface metamorphosed into pipestone due to high temperatures and pressure from the extreme weight of glaciers.

While the Native Americans value the soft pipestone for pipes and art objects, early European settlers valued the hard quartzite as an exterior building material. Quartzite was mined during early European settlement in Pipestone, producing exterior building blocks shipped to cities as far away as Chicago. The Pipestone County Museum in downtown Pipestone and the front of the monument's visitor center were constructed of quartzite, much of it containing hand-hewn Sioux quartzite block. By law, only Native Americans of a tribe federally recognized by the U.S. government may quarry pipestone, a process that normally occurs from late May to late October and may take three to six weeks to complete. No power tools are allowed in this process, which involves setting a wedge in cracks in the quartzite and driving it in with a sledgehammer. Chisels and shovels are also used in the process to loosen and pry away the quartzite to get at the valued red stone layer. In past years the park has issued quarrying permits to Native Americans from as far away as the Northwest Territories and Canada as long as they are enrolled in tribes federally recognized by the U.S. government. Interest in quarrying pipestone continues to grow, with a current waiting list of approximately three to four years.

Early pipes were tube shaped but evolved into elbow and disk shapes with elaborate carvings of animals and humans. A popular T-shaped pipe is called a "plains" pipe. Pipes are often called calumet after the French name *le calumet de la paix*. Pipe stems are made of hardwood, the most abundant of which was ash. The ceremonial tobacco is kinnikinick, which often consists of the dried inner bark of the red alder, red dogwood, willow, sumac, or any combination of these and other plant materials.

The Circle Trail, which begins and ends at the visitor center, is a ¾-mile-long family walk that takes the hiker back in time to pre-settlement days and early Native American history. Here, you'll not only see the pipestone quarries but also the initials of Joseph N. Nicollet, which were chiseled into quartzite rock in 1838. Nicollet was a mathematician and scientist whose expedition was the first United States government exploration party to visit the pipestone quarries. It was Catlin's writings about the quarries that also inspired author Henry Wadsworth Longfellow to mention the quarries in his famous poem "The Song of Hiawatha," written in 1855.

Another unusual feature of the park is the three maidens—three large granite boulders believed to have once been a single huge boulder 50 to 60 feet in circumference. Glaciers carried and deposited the boulder near the quarry, which explains how granite, a non-indigenous rock, was introduced to the area. Frost action eventually split the gigantic rock into three fragments. Native American lore took care of the rest. Legend says that two maidens sought shelter under the rocks and that their spirits remained there to guard the quarries.

Once a great expanse of open tallgrass prairie with no trees for many miles, the Pipestone National Monument contains remnants of that prairie—including a variety

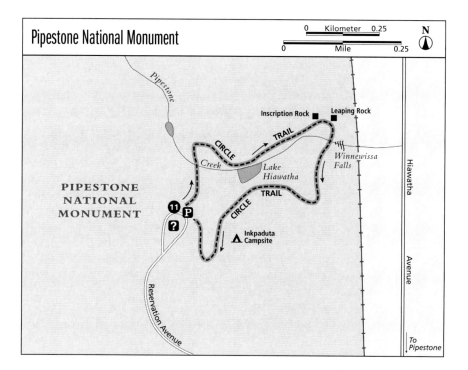

Pipestone National Monument

0   Kilometer   0.25
0   Mile   0.25
N

Inscription Rock   Leaping Rock
Pipestone
CIRCLE TRAIL
Creek
Lake Hiawatha
Winnewissa Falls
CIRCLE TRAIL
PIPESTONE NATIONAL MONUMENT
11 P
?
Inkpaduta Campsite
Reservation Avenue
Hiawatha Avenue
To Pipestone

of grasses, such as big bluestem, prairie cordgrass, western yarrow, blue gramma, and buffalo grass. These pieces of original prairie survived because the ground is too rocky to plow, but it was actively grazed by livestock. Several species of animals can also be found within park boundaries. Other areas of interest are: Winnewissa Falls; Pipestone Creek and Lake Hiawatha (near the visitor center); a red quartzite ledge to the east; and an outcropping of flat, red rock to the south.

Stop at the visitor center before you begin your hike, and pick up the trail guide called *Circle Trail*. It will explain the historical significance and natural resources of areas marked throughout the hike. The quarry site, designated a national monument in 1937, is managed by the National Park Service whose purpose is to develop a broad public understanding of the Indians and their history in this area.

The Nature Conservancy has identified the Sioux quartzite prairie plant community as a globally threatened habitat. Protective measures include prohibiting rock climbing and asking hikers to stay on the trail. It is illegal to collect pipestone without a permit or to collect anything, plants or otherwise, from a national park.

Miles and Directions

0.0   Start from the parking lot outside the visitor center. Walk into the visitor center and look for signs indicating the start of Circle Trail. A *Circle Trail* guide can be borrowed at the front desk or purchased inside. Turn left and exit the side door of the center to begin the interpretive trail.

0.1 Walk along the trail surrounded by trees, shrubs, and grasses. (FYI: Of the approximately 300 plant species found here, roughly seventy were introduced by European expansion.) Cross Pipestone Creek and view the spotted pipestone quarry. Please do not enter the quarry.

0.3 Walk by Lake Hiawatha and watch for signs of beaver and muskrat.

0.4 Climb the natural quartzite stairway and take note of the rippled surface created 1.6 billion years ago when this was seashore. (FYI: View the inscription rock carved in 1838 by a U.S. government exploration party led by Joseph Nicollet. Leaping Rock is to the right of Inscription Rock. See the chasm between Leaping Rock and another large quartzite rock. Legend has it young warriors would leap across to place an arrow in the crack, proving their valor.) The trail then turns south, and a few steps farther will bring you to Winnewissa Falls. Cross Pipestone Creek and walk along a Sioux quartzite ridge. The soft Pipestone is more than 100 feet below. You are now walking through restored tallgrass prairie.

0.6 The trail turns west (and you are now walking through remnant tall grass prairie) and passes the location used by Inkpaduta and a band of Dakota Indians as they fled west with white captives from the Spirit Lake Massacre in 1857.

0.7 Enter the pipestone quarry area.

0.75 Arrive back at the visitor center where you can watch pipestone carving demonstrations or purchase a pipe.

More Information

Local Information

Pipestone Chamber of Commerce, Convention & Visitor Bureau: Pipestone, MN; (507) 825-3316 or (800) 336-6125; www.pipestoneminnesota.com

Pipestone County Museum: Pipestone, MN; (507) 825-2563; www.pipestoneminnesota.com/Museum

Local Events/Attractions

(Note: dates are likely to change year to year. For more information on any of these events, contact the chamber of commerce.)

Song of Hiawatha Pageant: Late July through early August, Pipestone, MN

Pipestone County Fair: End of first week in August, Pipestone, MN

Pow-Wow and Annual Blessing of the Quarries: Same dates as Song of Hiawatha Pageant, Pipestone, MN

Civil War Festival: Even-numbered years, middle of August

Accommodations

Arrow Motel: Pipestone, MN; (507) 825-3331

Calumet Inn: Pipestone, MN; (507) 825-5871 or (800) 535-7610

Pipestone RV Campground: Pipestone, MN; (507) 825-2455; www.pipestonervcampground.com

The Villager: Highway 75 North, Pipestone, MN; (507) 825-5242
Calumet Inn: Pipestone, MN; (507) 825-5871 or (800) 535-7610
Rock Island Espresso & Coffee Shop: Pipestone, MN; (507) 825-3734 or (888) 550-8675; www.pipekeepers.org; also gift shop and gallery

Local Outdoor Retailers

M – M: Pipestone, MN; (507) 825-4133

12 Blue Mounds State Park

Beautiful prairie, blue mounds that are actually pink sandstone cliffs rising 100 feet off the flat prairie landscape, and a sizeable bison herd are points of interest at Blue Mounds State Park in southwestern Minnesota where annual park attendance is more than 93,000 visits. This is one of many areas where the Plains Indians of the 1800s depended on bison for survival. Bison were plentiful then as they roamed the endless prairies where food was abundant. Wolves, elk, and prairie chickens shared this ecosystem more than 200 years ago. Today, bison, a few coyotes, and some white-tailed deer roam the park. The hike follows Upper Cliffline Trail to Lower Mound Lake, and then cuts over to Mound Trail, which returns to the interpretive center. You'll see the bison herd as you hike the Mound Trail. There's also a viewing platform not far from Lower Mound Lake from which you can observe the herd.

Start: From the parking/picnic area at Lower Mound Lake
Distance: 4.1-mile circuit
Approximate hiking time: 2 hours
Difficulty rating: Easy due to wide, flat trails
Trail surface: Wide, mowed grass trails
Lay of the land: Prairie ecosystem on top of Sioux quartzite outcrops
Other trail users: None
Canine compatibility: Leashed dogs permitted
Land status: State park
Nearest town: Luverne, MN

Fees/permits: State park vehicle permit required. Annual or day permits are available at the park office. Camping fees are separate.
Schedule: Open year-round, day use and campground
Maps: USGS maps: Luverne, MN; state park map
Trail contacts: Blue Mounds State Park, Luverne, MN; (507) 283-1307; Department of Natural Resources, Information Center, St. Paul, MN; (651) 296-6157 or (888) 646-6367 (only in MN); www.dnr.state.mn.us/parks

Finding the trailhead: From Luverne and Interstate 90, head north on U.S. Highway 75 approximately 6 miles. Take a right onto CR 20 at the park entrance, and park at the picnic area and swimming beach on Lower Mound Lake. *DeLorme: Minnesota Atlas & Gazetteer:* Page 19 D3

The Hike

As the early settlers headed west across Minnesota's flatland, an unusual sight unfolded before them. A huge rock outcrop a mile and a half long and, in some places, 90 feet high broke the flat contour of the prairie. From a distance, in the afternoon sun, this "mound" appeared blue in color. They called it the Blue Mound.

Quartzite is abundant in this section of Minnesota, where glacial pressure and heat compressed sandstone deposits billions of years ago. Estimated at 3.5 billion years old, it is one of the oldest rocks in the United States. Iron oxide in the rock gives it a pink, red, or purple color. An interesting feature on the rock outcroppings is the scratches made by glaciers as they dragged loose chunks of rock across the bedrock. The quartzite was quarried for constructing stone buildings as far away as Chicago. Although quarrying has ceased at Blue Mounds, you can still see the quarry (which is shaped like an amphitheater) from Lower Cliffline Trail.

The park is a place of mystery as well as a place of beauty—with its colorful mounds, bountiful lakes, and open prairies. Some people believe that bison, once plentiful in the area, were run off the cliff in a huge stampede, possibly by the Plains

Indians, but experts say there's no evidence to support that theory. Another mystery is that of a 1,250-foot man-made line of small rocks aligned east to west low to the ground. It appears to have a solar significance, for on the first day of spring and fall, the sunrise and sunset line up with those rocks.

The featured hiking trail, which begins at the picnic area at Lower Mounds Lake, skirts the buffalo range and heads south across the prairie at the top of the mounds. The path then swings around to skirt the cliff mounds heading north. Spur trails off the main trail descend along the cliff, where you can get a panoramic view of farmland and prairie below. Blue Mounds State Park contains approximately 1,500 acres of prairie and is one of the largest prairie parks in the state. A sizeable fenced-off area allows a small herd of seventy-five to one hundred park bison plenty of grazing. The herd consists mostly of females, a few breeding bulls, and several yearlings and two-year-olds.

Although lakes are scarce in the southwestern part of the state, several rivers and creeks drain the area, including the nearby Rock River—the only major river in Minnesota that is a tributary of the Missouri. The two lakes in the 1,800-acre park were created in 1937, when two dams were constructed on Mound Creek by the federal government for watering livestock. The prairie is a complete, thriving ecosystem, supporting a great variety of wildlife in huge numbers. Each component feeds the other in a well-planned balancing act disturbed only by humans. Food is abundant here in plant seeds and insects sought by birds, nectar from flowers, small animals that nest and scurry about in the tall grasses, and the grasses themselves. In addition to the variety of prairie grasses, patches of prickly pear cactus grow in the shallow soils on top of the quartzite outcrops. Overgrazing by domestic livestock through the years has destroyed much of Minnesota's natural prairies, but the colorful beauty of 7-foot-high bluestem grasses and the hundreds of flowers mixed in with them are still alive at Blue Mounds State Park. Programs designed to restore and preserve native species (including controlled burns necessary to maintaining this ecosystem) are proving effective in prairie management/maintenance.

It was here, among this prairie beauty, that Jim Brandenburg, Minnesota photographer and Luverne native, got his start in photography. Colorful prairie sunsets, prairie wildflowers, bison, and other wildlife offered themselves to his developing artistry with the camera. His grandparents, who farmed in the area, have since donated their property to the park.

Hikers may also want to try the 6-mile Blue Mounds hiking and biking trail that opened in 2004. This trail begins in downtown Luverne and travels along the cliffline of Blue Mounds State Park ending at the park.

Miles and Directions

0.0 Start from the beach area parking lot on the right side of the park road. Follow the Hiking Club Trail that follows Mound Trail south alongside the East Buffalo Range enclosure.

0.8 Reach the end of the enclosure and take a right, heading west along the end of the enclosure. (FYI: In early evening the setting sun is spectacular.)

1.0 Mound Trail splits into Upper and Lower Mound Trails. Turn left and follow the Hiking Club signs on Upper Mound Trail. There is a bench here to watch the sunset and the buffalo.

1.6 A short spur heads left to shortcut over to Upper Cliffline Trail. Stay right to continue on Upper Mound Trail.

1.9 Eagle Rock is on the right. From this point, the highest on the mound (300 feet above the city of Luverne), take in the panoramic vista of Iowa, South Dakota, and Minnesota farmland. A right takes you on the Western Loop Trail. Stay left and head south toward the interpretive center.

View from Upper Cliffline Trail

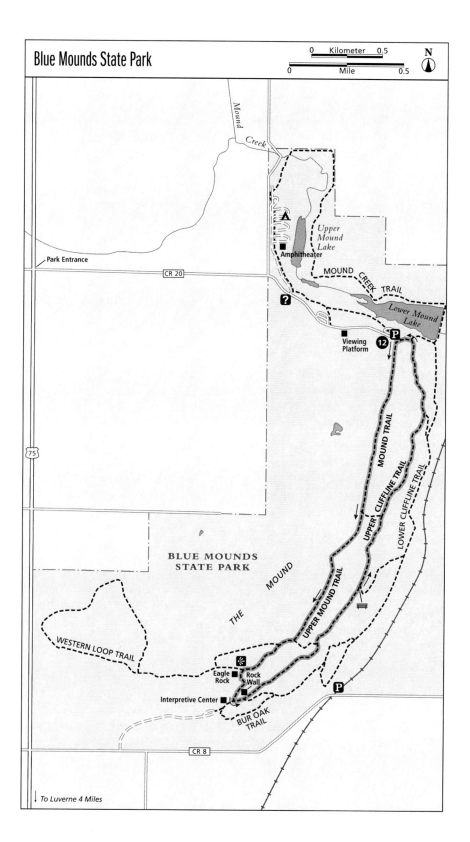

Blue Mounds State Park

Park Entrance

CR 20

Mound Creek

Upper Mound Lake

Amphitheater

MOUND CREEK TRAIL

Lower Mound Lake

Viewing Platform

P

12

75

MOUND TRAIL

UPPER CLIFFLINE TRAIL

LOWER CLIFFLINE TRAIL

BLUE MOUNDS STATE PARK

THE MOUND

UPPER MOUND TRAIL

WESTERN LOOP TRAIL

Eagle Rock

Rock Wall

Interpretive Center

P

BUR OAK TRAIL

CR 8

To Luverne 4 Miles

2.1 Come to the interpretive center and take a left to follow Upper Cliffline Trail north. Pass Bur Oak trail immediately on the right. Continue left. Here you will pass by the remnants of the 1250-foot rock wall built from surface-collected Sioux quartzite.

2.5 Come to a spur trail on the left; this leads back to Upper Mound Trail. Continue right.

2.8 A spur trail to the right leads down to Lower Cliffline Trail. Continue left. There is a bench at this intersection for taking in the view.

3.1 Another spur trail cuts left over to Upper Mound Trail by the buffalo enclosure. Continue right.

3.6 Come to a spur trail leading down to Lower Cliffline Trail to the right. Stay left.

4.0 Reach Lower Mound Lake and Mound Creek Trail. Take a left back to the start and the parking area.

4.1 Arrive back at the parking area and swimming beach.

More Information

Local Information
Luverne Chamber of Commerce: Luverne, MN; (507) 283-4061 or (888) 283-4061; www.luvernechamber.org

Local Events/Attractions
Buffalo Days and Arts in the Park: First weekend in June, Luverne, MN; community festival
Rock County Fair: First weekend in August, Luverne, MN
Winterfest: First weekend in December, Luverne, MN
Tri-State Band Fest: Last Saturday in September

Accommodations:
Cozy Rest Motel: Luverne, MN; (507) 283-4461
Sunrise Motel: Luverne, MN; (507) 283-2347 or (877) 641-2345; www.sunrisem.com
Our House Bed & Breakfast: Luverne, MN; (507) 283-9340 or (888) 283-9340

Restaurants
Coffey Haus: Luverne, MN; (507) 283-8676
JJ's Tasty Drive Inn: Luverne, MN; (507) 283-8317
Magnolia Steak House & Bar: Luverne, MN; (507) 283-9161
Sharkee's Sports Bar & Grill: Luverne, MN; (507) 283-4942

Other Resources
The Brandenburg Gallery: Luverne, MN; (507) 283-1884

Honorable Mention

Here is a great hike in the Prairie Lands region that didn't make the A-list this time but deserves recognition. Check it out and let us know what you think. You may decide that it deserves higher status in future editions or, perhaps, you may have a hike of your own that merits attention.

Kilen Woods

The 1.5-mile circuit around the perimeter of Kilen Woods State Park's hiking trails winds through rolling glacial-formed hills of oak-savanna and follows the edge of restored prairie. The trail begins at the parking and picnic area and follows the perimeter trails along the west bank of the Des Moines River south to Dinosaur Ridge Overlook, then heads east and follows the perimeter trails back to the picnic area.

To get there from Lakefield, drive north on Highway 86 for 4 miles. Turn right on CR 24 and proceed 5 miles to the park entrance. *DeLorme: Minnesota Atlas and Gazetteer:* Page 21 D7

West central Minnesota is an area of hilly land formations (some as high as 1,800 feet), farmland, forest and thousands of lakes. This large region covers most of the central part of the state and is flanked by Precambrian rock to the northeast, flat Glacial Lake Agassiz plain to the northwest, the Minnesota River Valley to the southwest, and the Bluffland region to the southeast. Glacial debris, many hundreds of feet thick in places, covers most of the bedrock in the region. All three of Minnesota's vegetation zones, called biomes, are represented in this diverse region. A prairie/deciduous forest boundary cuts through the western part of the region, noticeable at Glacial Lakes State Park. Here, miles of colorful, sun-bathed western prairie offer a sudden contrast to the protective shade of eastern deciduous forests. Scattered stands of twisted bur oak grow in open savannas. The northeastern third of the region is covered with coniferous forests of pine, spruce, fir, cedar, and tamarack. Hilly topography dotted with lake-filled depressions is the common feature throughout. The Mississippi, Minnesota, and St. Croix Rivers are the region's major waterways with hundreds of smaller rivers and streams emptying into them. A small area in the west drains into the Red River of the North while the majority of the area drains south into the Mississippi, including the famous headwaters located in Itasca State Park.

The first European explorers visited the area in the late 1600s to claim land for their country and to convert Native Americans to Christianity. Fur traders had established a network of posts by the 1700s and were exchanging goods for furs to ship back to Europe to meet the demand for the felt hat industry.

In the 1800s, the search for the Mississippi River's headwaters brought many more explorers. Henry Schoolcraft was led by Ojibwe leader, Ozawindib in 1832 to what is now called Lake Itasca, the source of the Mississippi. By the mid-1800s, logging was a major industry and logs were being transported via waterway to St. Paul and Minneapolis for building. Settlers moved into the cleared areas to farm and homestead as early as the 1890s. The rural population in agricultural areas peaked in the early 1900s and showed dramatic decline in the 1940s as productivity and farm size increased. Today forestry, farming, and recreation are the main industries, and the area is well-known resort country.

Many people visit the area for fishing, boating, horseback riding, hunting, snow-mobiling, hiking, and other outdoor recreation. Numerous lakes and marshes as well as the Mississippi River provide a major flyway for waterfowl migrating north and south. In addition to several state parks, the region contains the Chippewa National Forest, national and state wildlife refuges, and many state forests. High ridges of glacial landforms make excellent places to hike and view the surrounding countryside in this diverse region of grassland, deciduous forest, wetlands, and conifers. Most hikes involve lakes and travel over hilly terrain. A section of the North Country National Trail, which will eventually stretch across the northern United States from New York to North Dakota, traverses the northern part of the region.

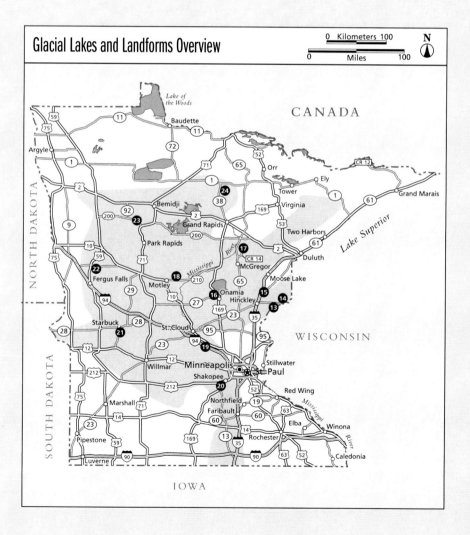

13 St. Croix State Park

The confluence of two designated wild and scenic rivers sets the stage for Minnesota's largest state park. The park's popularity is due not only to its the beauty, but also to its recreational diversity. Possible activities range from camping, horseback riding, hiking, and fishing to snowmobiling and cross-country skiing. Of the park's 127 miles of hiking trails, the Two Rivers Trail is perhaps the most scenic, particularly near the confluence of the Kettle and the St. Croix.

Start: From the parking area near the Kettle River overlook at gate 23

Distance: 4.9-mile loop

Approximate hiking time: 2 hours

Difficulty rating: Easy due to wide, flat trails. The trail does have some exposed rocks and roots.

Trail surface: Dirt, grass, and pine needle-covered trails

Lay of the land: The confluence of the St. Croix and Kettle Rivers

Other trail users: Hikers only

Canine compatibility: Leashed dogs permitted

Land status: State park

Nearest town: Hinckley, MN

Fees/permits: State park vehicle permit. Annual or day permits are available at the park office. Camping fees are separate.

Schedule: Open year-round

Maps: USGS maps: Lake Clayton, MN; state park map

Trail contacts: St. Croix State Park, Hinckley, MN; (320) 384-6591; www.dnr.state.mn.us/parks

Finding the trailhead: From Hinckley, drive east 15 miles on Highway 48 (the Hinckley exit off Interstate 35). Turn right (south) on CR 22 at the park entrance, and drive 5 miles to the park headquarters. Turn right and follow the signs for Head of the Rapids. Drive 9 miles to gate 23 and park. *DeLorme: Minnesota Atlas & Gazetteer.* Page 49 A7

The Hike

Two wild and scenic rivers converge in east central Minnesota where the more turbulent Kettle empties its water into the larger, calmer St. Croix. Thousands of years ago, the St. Croix was a major outlet that drained the ancient Glacial Lake Duluth (now Lake Superior) of meltwaters from retreating glaciers. As glaciers melted and retreated and their resulting glacial lakes drained, leaving a significantly altered earth beneath them, present-day pooling and drainage patterns emerged that were much different than those in pre-glacial times. For instance, glaciers descending from the northeast left a water-filled hole 360 miles long, 160 miles across at its widest point, and 1,302 feet at its deepest, which we now call Lake Superior. Tons of resulting scooped-out debris were carried off and deposited throughout the state. Another glacier advancing from the south called the Grantsburg Sublobe crossed Minnesota and extended into Wisconsin, creating Glacial Lake Grantsburg (now nonexistent), and depositing the layers of sand and red and yellow clay found in St. Croix State Park.

Bordering the St. Croix River to the southeast and the Kettle River to the west and north, the 34,000-acre St. Croix State Park encompasses a varied landscape consisting of uplands, bogs, swamps, marshes, ponds, and a second-growth mixed forest. Along the final reaches of the Kettle River, Minnesota's first wild and scenic river, basalt lava flows—of the same period as those found along the north shore of Lake Superior (1.1 billion years old)—and a younger sandstone are exposed, scoured clean of glacial debris by the abrasive action of fast-moving water. In its last 5 miles to the St. Croix, the river drops 13 feet every mile in picturesque whitewater spray confined within high riverbanks. Long before automobile travel and road construction came to this area, when Minnesota's lush, impenetrable wilderness made overland travel nearly impassable, rivers were the highways connecting settlements, making trade and, later, industry possible. The Dakota and Ojibwe Indians were among the first to travel the St. Croix River highway, followed by European fur traders. Industry followed industry and soon logging camps mushroomed along the river, using the current to carry the once-abundant red and white pine logs to mills downstream. Once the forests were exhausted, farmers moved in, hoping to make a living off the cleared land. Farming was successful in areas such as Hinckley, where corn and clover were the main crops; however, poor soil conditions east toward Wisconsin forced many farmers to sell their land to the government. The land was set aside as a recreational demonstration area in 1935, run by the national park system, until it was designated a state park in 1943.

During the Depression years, government work programs—such as the Civilian Conservation Corps (CCC), Veterans Conservation Corps (VCC), and the Works Progress Administration (WPA)—were largely responsible for developing the parks. Camps were built on site to house the workers, and remnants of many of them are still intact. More than 120 buildings in St. Croix State Park were built during this era. Four of the original seven cabins built by the CCC remain and are available for summer use, and three were moved to make room for the interpretive trail center.

Kettle River

Because of its overall layout and design, the park has been designated a National Historic Landmark. Included in the park's 127 miles of hiking trails are several miles of the Willard Munger State Trail, a multi-use trail within the park not to be confused with the famous Willard Munger paved multi-use trail connecting St. Paul with Duluth. This hike features the beauty and contrast of the two rivers that meet at its midpoint. Along the Kettle, you'll be walking above the river on a sand and mud bank lined with red pine. You can hear the sound of rapids and the swift current as the Kettle drops to meet the St. Croix. At the confluence, the St. Croix is much larger and slower moving than the Kettle. The return hike upriver on the St. Croix is through a mixed floodplain forest that's colorful in the fall when the leaves are at their peak.

Miles and Directions

0.0 Start from the parking area near the Kettle overlook and numbered gate 23. The hike begins on a high bank above the Kettle, which is on your right. (FYI: You can hear the sound of rapids drifting up through the large pines.)

0.3 The trail descends to the river's edge through a mixed hardwood forest.

1.1 Walk through an area of large red pine.

1.2 The trail intersects with a shortcut trail to the St. Croix on the left. Stay right to continue along the Kettle. The trail crosses a an old beaver dam. As there are no lodges visible, it is possible the beavers are using lodges built into the riverbank.

1.4 The Kettle River joins the St. Croix River. Here, the vegetation changes to floodplain. A fire ring and picnic table make a nice spot to sit and enjoy the serenity. Two Rivers Trail continues north from this point, following a braid of the larger St. Croix River.

2.2 Cross a small stream draining into the St. Croix. The larger St. Croix moves more slowly than the Kettle, and you can see many large islands with very large trees.

2.8 Come to Pine Ridge campsite, a canoe campsite near a gentle rapid. The trail widens to a 10-foot mowed trail, and you'll enter an older hardwood forest of maple, oak, basswood, and elm.

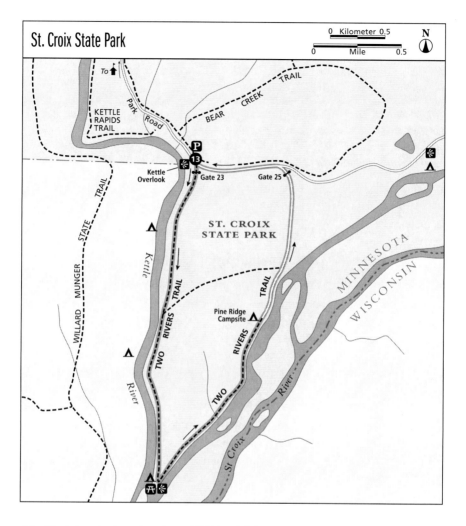

St. Croix State Park

4.0 The trail ends at numbered gate 25. Take a left here onto the park road and walk back to the parking area.

4.9 Arrive back at the parking area.

More Information

Local Information
Hinckley Convention & Visitor Center: Hinckley, MN; (800) 952-4282; www.hinckleymn.com

Local Events/Attractions
Corn and Clover Carnival: First weekend after July 4, Hinckley, MN
Little Britches Rodeo: July, Hinckley, MN
Grand Celebration & Pow Wow: June, Hinckley, MN
Hinckley Fire Museum: Hinckley, MN; (320) 384-7338

Accommodations

St. Croix State Park: Hinckley, MN; (320) 384-6591; www.dnr.state.mn.us/parks
Travelodge: Hinckley, MN; (888) 384-6112; www.travelodge.com
Dakota Lodge Bed & Breakfast: Hinckley, MN; (320) 384-6052; www.dakotalodge.com
Day's Inn: Hinckley, MN; (800) 559-8951

Restaurants

Grand Buffet: At Grand Casino, Hinckley, MN; (800) 472-6321
Cassidy's Restaurant: Hinckley, MN; (320) 384-6129
Tobie's Restaurant: Hinckley, MN; (320) 384-6174

Hike Tours

Interpretive programs are available year-round in the park.

14 St. Croix State Forest–Tamarack

The focal point of the trails within the St. Croix National Forest is the wild and picturesque Tamarack River, a narrow, twisting river that slowly makes its way south to join the much larger St. Croix River. Although often shallow, the Tamarack changes character following a heavy rain and becomes fast, deep, and dangerous. The confluence of the Tamarack and St. Croix is less than half a mile from the south end of the trail at Pine Point. From here, you'll see Wisconsin hills across the St. Croix. The popular but rugged Tamarack Trail is beautiful at any time of the year, but its mixed forests of evergreen and deciduous trees are particularly striking in the fall. The trail hugs the riverbank, crosses the Tamarack several times, ascends the sometimes-steep hills, and, at times, wanders a distance from the river. This gives the hiker a variety of perspectives of the St. Croix State Forest.

Start: From the Boulder Campground at Rock Lake
Distance: 9.7-mile loop
Approximate hiking time: 4–5 hours
Difficulty rating: Moderate to difficult
Trail surface: Narrow dirt trails are often covered with small rocks and are sometimes muddy.
Lay of the land: The land here is by no means flat. Rugged trails wind uphill and downhill, following the river. Some small streams drain across the trail into the river, and, at one point, there is a river crossing (no bridge).

Other trail users: Equestrians
Canine compatibility: Dogs permitted
Land status: State forest
Nearest town: Hinckley, MN
Fees/permits: Per night camping fee
Schedule: Open year-round
Maps: USGS maps: Danbury West, MN; state forest map
Trail contacts: Sandstone State Forest Office, 613 Hwy. 23 South, Sandstone, MN 55072; (320) 245-6789; Trails and Waterways Rt. #2, 701 South Kenwood, Moose Lake, MN 55767; (218) 485-5410

Finding the trailhead: Take Interstate 35W north out of the Twin Cities to Hinckley where you'll exit east onto Highway 48. Proceed 23.6 miles to CR 173, which is just before the St. Croix River crossing. Follow CR 173 north 5.3 miles to the Tamarack Forest Road. Turn right (east) and follow it approximately 4 miles where you'll come to a T-intersection. Turn right and proceed to Boulder Campground to the right. *DeLorme: Minnesota Atlas & Gazetteer.* Page 57 E9

The Hike

It's most likely the beauty of a mixed forest, a gently flowing river, high bluffs and ridges, and the challenge of a somewhat difficult trail system that has made the St. Croix State Forest one of the most popular recreation areas in the state. It's here that the inviting Tamarack River winds its way through a huge forest of maple, basswood, ash, aspen, oak, Norway pine, white pine, and tamarack—in a mix of young and aging timber. Heavily used trails skirt both sides of the Lower Tamarack River crossing twice (there are several informal crossings that are not marked on the map) along the way to Pine Point, which rises 150 to 200 feet above the valley. This popular, Norway pine–covered picnic area offers a 5-mile view of the St. Croix River Valley and of Wisconsin on the St. Croix River's east side.

Footbridge over the Tamarack River

Glaciers that covered much of Minnesota thousands of years ago played a key role in creating the beauty of this state forest. The foundation of its varied landscape was deposited and molded under advancing and retreating ice. The 262,240 acres known as the Duxbury Till Plain, the location of the Lower Tamarack, has sandy loam scattered throughout, deposited by glacial stream water. A hardpan, a compact layer impenetrable by roots located close to the ground surface, slows water percolation, diverting water instead to depressions, creeks, and rivers. Several rivers and creeks empty into the St. Croix including the Grindstone and Kettle Rivers and the Hay, Sand, Bear, and Crooked Creeks. They're all part of the area's drainage system, the main arteries being the Kettle and St. Croix Rivers. The Duxbury Till Plain is made up of 66 percent uplands, 34 percent wetlands, and 1 percent lakes.

Tamarack trees, for which the Tamarack River and trail system are named, are abundant in the forest, thriving in poorly drained soils such as bogs and swamps and on cool, moist, north-facing slopes. This distinctive deciduous conifer is recognizable by its red-brown, thin, scaly bark, and blue-green three-sided needles that grow in clusters of fifteen to twenty-five. Usually found with black spruce, the tamarack is especially beautiful in the fall when its needles turn vivid gold before dropping for the winter.

Horseback groups created the trails along the Lower Tamarack River in the 1960s. Approximately ten years later, the Department of Natural Resources developed and finalized a plan for the creation of trails and a horse camp on the west side of the river. It wasn't long before the fourteen original sites became inadequate for the camp's growing popularity, and, in 1998, the camp was expanded to forty-five sites. An additional 10 miles of trails were created, expanding the system to 25 miles of trails for nonmotorized use.

Although the area experiences heavy use by horseback riders in the spring and fall, hikers are encouraged by the DNR to use the same trails. Terrain in the area is hilly and generally dry. Footbridges have been constructed over wet spots, and a wide, multi-use bridge crosses the river at the north end of the trail system. Some trails hug the Tamarack, while others follow ridges overlooking the river. In addition to Pine Point on the south end of the trail system, a picturesque attraction on the north end is the Tamarack Overlook, a 100-foot-high bluff with a beautiful view of the pine-covered valley below.

You may want to carry an old pair of tennis shoes, sport sandals, or rubber boots as you hike to protect your feet from the river's rocky bottom. While river crossings are generally safe within the trail system, the DNR warns that they may be hazardous during high water, as the current becomes stronger. The St. Croix Bluff trail goes east from Pine Point along the St. Croix River bluff to the Gandy Dancer motorized trail and then across the old railroad bridge high above the St. Croix River into Danbury, Wisconsin. This very scenic trail is worth exploring and is accessible off the Mallard Lake Forest Road.

Several hike-in campsites are located along the river on each side. Campsite 4 at Pine Point and campsite 1 on the west side of the river after you cross the footbridge at the north end of the trail are the most popular sites. Campsite 1 is the most accessible campsite for hikers as it's not far from the road, yet is near the river and trailhead, which is another option for starting your hike. Campsite 5 near the lower end of the river on the west side has the most privacy and is accessible from both the trail and river.

TAMARACK TREES

Tamarack trees were once (and still are) harvested for various uses. Some Native tribes chewed the tree resin to relieve indigestion, while European settlers used the roots in wooden ship construction for joining ribs to deck timbers. Today, the tamarack's heavy, durable wood is used mainly for pulp but also for posts, poles, and fuel.

Miles and Directions

0.0 Start from the parking area at Boulder Campground, past the boat launch. Start hiking from a sign for campsite 18. There is a trail map posted here and a sign that states NO MOTORIZED VEHICLES BEYOND THIS POINT. Walk about 50 feet, and the trail splits from the campsite trail, just before the site. Take the trail to the left (a narrow footpath).

0.5 Cross a boardwalk over a marsh.

1.1 The trail comes to a T-intersection. At this point you'll be above and alongside the edge of the Lower Tamarack River. (**Option:** A left goes north toward the horse camp and bridge [3 miles].) Take a right to proceed south along the river. The trail will initially take you through the woods away from view of the river.

1.3 Cross a small creek.

1.7 Come into view of the river.

1.8 Cross a footbridge over a small creek. (Note: This area can get quite muddy during the wet season.)

1.9 The trail meets the river where you will cross. The river bottom is built up here, creating a shallow spot for ease in crossing. (Note: Exercise caution; the water depth is typically a couple of feet deep, but during the early spring and periods of intense rain it can be much deeper. An old pair of sneakers or sandals could be helpful when crossing.) Pick up the trail on the other side of the river and climb the bank.

2.0 The trail comes to a T-intersection. Take a left to head north toward the bridge.

2.1 Come to Pine Point campsite. (FYI: It is a nice site on a high knob studded with pines. This large campsite features outhouses, picnic tables and a fire pit.)

2.5 The trail intersects with a spur that leads to the Gandy Dancer Trail. Stay left to continue on the Tamarack River Trail.

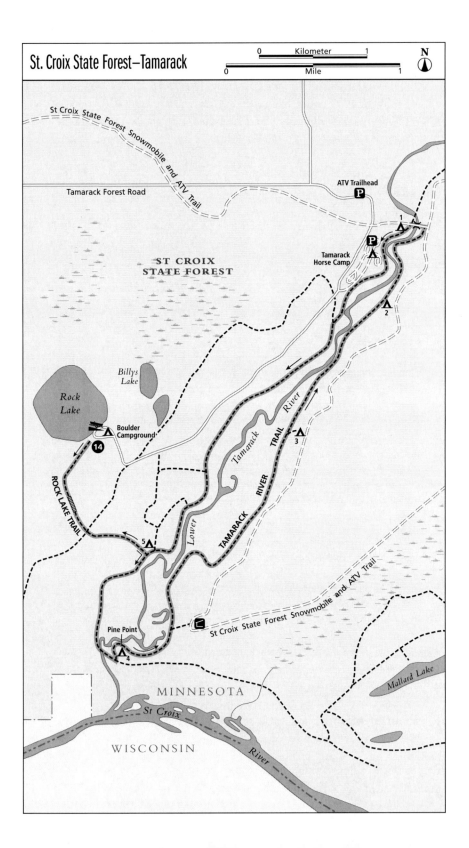

St. Croix State Forest–Tamarack

0   Kilometer   1

0   Mile   1

N

St Croix State Forest Snowmobile and ATV Trail

Tamarack Forest Road

ATV Trailhead

P

P

Tamarack Horse Camp

1

2

ST CROIX STATE FOREST

Billys Lake

Rock Lake

Boulder Campground

14

Tamarack River

3

ROCK LAKE TRAIL

TAMARACK RIVER TRAIL

Lower

5

St Croix State Forest Snowmobile and ATV Trail

Mallard Lake

Pine Point

4

MINNESOTA

St Croix

WISCONSIN

River

2.6 Come to another spur trail that connects with the state forest snowmobile trail and the Gandy Dancer trail. Take a left to continue on the hiking trail, following the sign for Tamarack horse camp.

3.2 Cross a small creek.

3.8 Walk through a red pine plantation area. Notice the signs for a reforestation project.

5.0 Pass the sign for campsite 3 (this campsite is scheduled to be removed, due to proximity to the ATV trail). A short spur trail leads to the campsite. Keep left to stay on the trail.

5.7 The hiking/horseback trail meets the state snowmobile and four-wheeler trail. Take a left to cross the bridge over the Tamarack River.

5.8 After crossing the bridge, take the first left to continue on the horseback/hiking trail toward the horse camp. Here there is another hike-in campsite, campsite 1.

6.1 Pass the horse camp on the right. Stay left to continue along the river.

7.9 Pass a spur trail on the right. Continue left.

8.7 Come to the trail that leads back to Boulder Campground to the right. Take a right to head back to the campground and parking.

9.7 Arrive back at the parking area.

More Information

Local Information

Hinckley Convention & Visitor Center: Hinckley, MN; (800) 952–4282; www.hinckleymn.com

Local Events/Attractions

Great Trail Sled Dog Race: January, Hinckley, MN
Grand Casino Concert Series: June through September, Hinckley, MN
Little Britches Rodeo: July, Hinckley, MN
Grand Celebration & Pow Wow: July, Hinckley, MN
Corn and Clover Carnival: July, Hinckley, MN
Arts and Crafts Festival: August, Hinckley, MN
Hinckley Fire Museum: Hinckley, MN; (320) 384-7338

Accommodations

Boulder Campground: Tamarack Forest Road, St. Croix State Park; (320) 384-6146; www.dnr.state.mn.us/parks; no reservations accepted
Grand Casino Hinckley Chalets: Hinckley, MN; (800) 995-4726; www.grandcasinomn.com; RV resort with fifty chalets

Restaurants

Grand Buffet: At Grand Casino, Hinckley, MN; (800) 472-6321
Tobie's Restaurant: Hinckley, MN; (320) 384-6174
Cassidy's Restaurant: Hinckley, MN; (320) 384-6129

TIPS FOR NOT GETTING LOST

Before beginning a hike on any trail, it's a good idea to pick up a trail map and study it. While most trails are well marked and getting lost is not likely, it could still happen. And, when you're lost in Minnesota's woods, every tree suddenly appears to have an identical twin just to confuse you.

Besides maps, Global Positioning System devices (or GPS as they are more commonly called) are becoming increasingly popular for recreational use as they become more affordable each year. Though the GPS devices' capabilities of programming in landmarks and trail starts and giving exact distances make them appear more useful than a compass, it's still not a good idea to leave your compass at home. The accuracy of the GPS is not always ensured as the system can be affected by poor satellite geometry and periodic adjustments to GPS satellites, which are subject to change by the U.S. government. Therefore, the map and compass should be your companion on every hike.

Using these two instruments together can keep you found, but there's one other aid that will help as well. Found within you, it's called awareness. If you examine your surroundings as you go, you'll soon find that each tree has its own distinct identity, that the landscape changes as well as the foliage, rocks, and even the composition of the trail. Keep track of each turn you make. On some trail systems, it's possible to turn off onto other loops. Make a mental note of which way you turned and any unusual features at the turnoff in case you should have to retrace your steps.

When you go out on a hike, no matter how short, be prepared to spend a night in the woods if it should become necessary, even if you're sure you can't possibly get lost. Take along warm clothing, matches, plenty of water, and some extra food. Keeping warm, hydrated, and dry are most important in surviving a wilderness experience.

With map and compass along and your wits and awareness about you, your chances of having to use your safety kit will be greatly reduced.

15 Banning State Park

People travel great distances to experience the designated wild and scenic Kettle River. One of the most spectacular stretches of the river cuts through Banning State Park, near the small town of Sandstone. The park's 17 miles of intertwining hiking trails allow for several hiking options. Beginning at the picnic area, the featured hike heads into the hardwood forests above the river valley, and then descends to the Quarry Trail along the river where pieces of history are evident in late twentieth century village and quarry remains. As you walk along the river-cut sandstone cliffs you can see where a hard pebble, spinning in a former eddy, has carved one of the infamous kettles into the softer sandstone. Banning's pine, mixed hardwood, and tamarack woods, as well as its wetland areas, make this an excellent area for birding.

Start: From the parking lot at the picnic area off Highway 23
Distance: 2.6-mile loop
Approximate hiking time: 1.5 hours
Difficulty rating: Moderate due to short up- and downhill climbs and wide, pine needle-covered dirt trails that are rocky in places
Trail surface: Dirt and rock
Lay of the land: The pine-forested Kettle River valley cuts through Precambrian sandstone
Other trail users: Canoeists and kayakers who are scouting the rapids
Canine compatibility: Leashed dogs permitted

Land status: State park
Nearest town: Sandstone, MN
Fees/permits: State park vehicle permit required. Annual or day permits are available at the park office. Camping fees are separate.
Schedule: Open year-round
Maps: USGS maps: Sandstone North, MN; state park map
Trail contacts: Banning State Park, Sandstone, MN; (320) 245-2668; Department of Natural Resources, Information Center, St. Paul, MN; (651) 296-6157 or (800) 646-6367 (only in MN); www.dnr.state.mn.us/parks

Finding the trailhead: From Sandstone, take Highway 23/61 north 3 miles. Turn right to continue on Highway 23 as it splits from Highway 61 and proceed 1 mile to the park entrance. *DeLorme: Minnesota Atlas & Gazetteer:* Page 57 D6

The Hike

Remnants of sandstone buildings lie along the banks of the Kettle River in Banning State Park, ghosts of the once-bustling town and the quarry that brought it about. Attractive and strong, this pink stone's abundance and popularity provided a livelihood for 500 workers at the quarry during the late 1800s. But in September 1894, all of that would change. The Hinckley forest fire altered the fate of the quarry, for the business suffered significant financial losses, as did the St. Paul & Duluth Railroad that shipped the stone and brought supplies.

Nature and humans spent several years setting the stage for the most terrifying fire in Minnesota's history, known as the Great Hinckley Fire. For three consecutive years, the St. Paul weather bureau recorded a steady loss of humidity, and, by the summer of 1894, temperatures were averaging 4.2 degrees F above normal with no rainfall. Extensive logging in the area produced massive piles of treetops and branches (called slash piles), which would later provide fuel for the fire. Along with the low humidity and lack of rain came moisture-robbing winds that dried the tinder even more. Still, no one knows for sure what ignited the blaze. At that time, Hinckley, a town within 10 miles of the quarry, had a population of 1,700. More than 400 of those residents would lose their lives in the fire. Those who escaped were taken out by train or found safety in the gravel pit near town. Survivors describe thick smoke, fiery masses, oceans of flame, instant bursts of fire, melting train tracks, and huge fireballs. The fire covered more than 500 square miles, affecting or destroying more communities than just Hinckley.

Recovery soon followed for many of those communities, and a few years later, a new village was platted in the fields above the quarry, which grew to a population of 300 by the turn of the twentieth century. This new village and quarry were named after William L. Banning, banker and president of the St. Paul & Duluth Railroad. As the quarry was reestablished, development of much stronger structural steel in the construction industry began to replace the demand for sandstone, carrying with it the demise of the sandstone quarry by 1905. The town hung on, even after workers left the quarry in search of other employment, but continuing forest fires finally drove its remaining population to safer ground. By 1912, the town was abandoned.

A large kettle hanging over the trail

Kettle River

Today, Banning State Park houses the old quarry, and remnants of the old sandstone buildings that were once part of the business can be seen along the featured hike. All that remains of the town of Banning is its name. The focal point of this wooded 6,237-acre park is the beautiful Kettle River. Named for the large potholes that were carved by harder stones spun round and round by the river's eddies, these kettles are underfoot and overhead (in the sides of the gorge where the younger river cut down through) as you hike. The quarry trail takes you in a loop around the old quarrying site and continues down to the banks of the river. Here the previously placid river, as it cuts down through the hard sandstone, changes into a series of whitewater rapids—the gradient increases from a 6.3-foot-per-mile average to a steep 40 feet per mile. Narrowing to a 100-foot gorge cut through solid sandstone, this portion of the river is where sensible canoeists portage and skilled kayakers congregate.

The Kettle, which with its tributaries drains more than a thousand square miles of watershed, was the first stream designated a component of the state's Wild & Scenic Rivers Act in 1974. From its beginning in Kettle Lake in the Fond Du Lac State Forest, the Kettle River flows approximately 80 miles to empty into the St. Croix River at St. Croix State Park.

Bass, walleye, and northern pike swim the Kettle's waters, and the aspen, berries, and shrubs within the park support a good grouse population. Lake sturgeon spawn in the Kettle, and the state has instituted a sturgeon restoration project to help the struggling species by improving habitat. Despite its struggling status, sturgeon is recognized as a game species that it is still legal to catch. In 1994, a ninety-four-pound, four-ounce fish was taken from the Kettle, creating a state record.

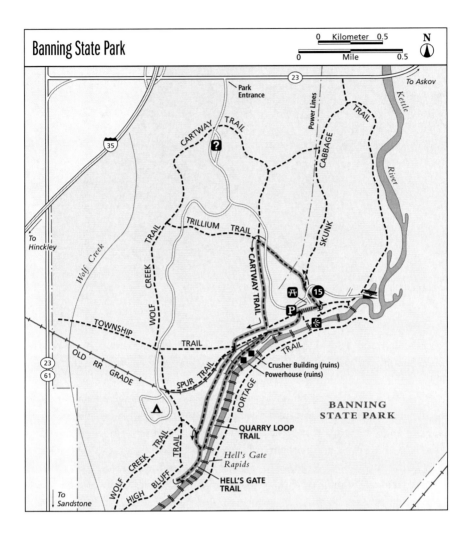

Miles and Directions

0.0   Start from the parking lot at the picnic area and walk north (away from the river) to the start of Trillium Trail. Go left at the fork (a right follows Skunk Cabbage Trail), pass under a power line, and enter a maple/oak forest.

0.3   At a four-way intersection take a left on Cartway Trail.

0.7   Come to the intersection with Quarry Loop Trail and take a right. (FYI: Notice an increasing number of white pines, and hear the river as you near it.) The trail crosses the old railroad grade as it descends in switchbacks down the steep slope to the old quarry.

1.0 Sandstone cliffs appear on the right, striped with colorful mosses and lichens growing on the weeping brown stone.

1.1 A spur trail on the right leads to High Bluff and Wolf Creek Trails. Stay left and follow signs for the self-guided tour and Deadman Trail. The trail will descend to another intersection; stay left and continue on Quarry Loop Trail.

1.3 Diverge from Quarry Loop Trail to follow Hell's Gate Trail for excellent views of many kettles, some 12 feet in diameter. Stop to view the Kettle River, and rest on a large, flat rock alongside the river that has a 3-foot kettle carved into it. Move with caution as you continue along this trail as it becomes rugged with roots, rocks, and boulders to scramble over.

1.5 A rock island appears on the left signaling the end of the trail. Retrace your steps back to Quarry Loop Trail.

1.7 Back at the Quarry Loop Trail intersection, take a right and follow the river amidst large white pine and white spruce trees.

2.1 Pass two old structures from the quarrying days, an old powerhouse and crusher building, which crushed sandstone rocks that were too small to use as building blocks into smaller stones used in cement mix and rail beds.

2.3 A spur trail leads off to the left. Continue right along the river.

2.4 The beginning of Quarry Loop Trail comes in on the left as you climb a stone staircase. Stay right.

2.6 Arrive back at parking lot.

More Information

Local Information

Sandstone Chamber of Commerce: Sandstone, MN; (320) 245-2271
City of Sandstone: Sandstone, MN; www.ci.sandstone.mn.us

Local Events/Attractions

Hinckley Fire Museum: Hinckley, MN; (320) 384-7338
Great Trail Sled Dog Race: January, Hinckley, MN
Grand Casino Concert Series: June through September, Hinckley, MN
Little Britches Rodeo: July, Hinckley, MN
Grand Celebration & Pow Wow: June, Hinckley, MN
Corn and Clover Carnival: July, Hinckley, MN
Arts and Crafts Festival: August, Hinckley, MN

Restaurants

Grand Buffet at Grand Casino: Hinckley, MN; (800) 472-6321
Tobie's Restaurant: Hinckley, MN; (320) 384-6174
Cassidy's Restaurant: Hinckley, MN; (320) 384-6129

16 Mille Lacs Kathio State Park

This winding walk over a large terminal moraine and through a beautiful second-growth hardwood forest has scenic views of wetland areas with lots of potential wildlife viewing. Mille Lacs Kathio State Park is filled with striking geologic features and has a rich archaeological history. This beautifully wooded park, the fourth largest in Minnesota, is especially inviting when the hardwoods and tamaracks don their fall colors. Several miles of trails loop their way through the park, some of them along Ogechie Lake and the Rum River.

Start: From the Landmark Trail parking lot
Distance: 3.2-mile loop
Approximate hiking time: 1.5 hours
Difficulty rating: Moderate due to a few hills
Trail surface: Grass and dirt
Lay of the land: Rolling hills, woods, and meadows adjacent to Ogechie Lake
Other trail users: Equestrians
Canine compatibility: Leashed dogs permitted
Land status: State park
Nearest town: Onamia or Garrison, MN

Fees/permits: State park vehicle permit required. Annual or day permits are available at the park office. Camping fees are separate.
Schedule: Open year-round
Maps: USGS maps: Onamia NW, MN; state park map
Trail contacts: Mille Lacs Kathio State Park, Onamia; (320) 532-3523; Department of Natural Resources, St. Paul, MN; (651) 296-6157 or (888) 646-6367 (only in MN); www .dnr.state.mn.us/parks

Finding the trailhead: From Onamia, take U.S. Highway 169 north approximately 8 miles. Look for a state park sign marking the CR 26 turnoff. Turn left and proceed south approximately 1 mile on CR 26 and turn right at the park entrance. Mille Lacs Kathio State Park is approximately 90 miles north of the Twin Cities. *DeLorme: Minnesota Atlas & Gazetteer*. Page 55 9E

The Hike

Mille Lacs Kathio State Park, designated a National Historic Landmark, is one of the most significant archaeological areas in Minnesota. More than forty known archaeological sites in the park have yielded artifacts dating as far back as 9,000 years. These discoveries have revealed much about the Native Americans' way of life, as well as insight into the lives of European traders and explorers who passed through the area hundreds of years ago. (It was early explorers and fur traders who first referred to the area as Mille Lacs—French for 1,000 lakes.)

The Mille Lacs Indian Museum (north of the park on US 169) tells the story of early settlement, which involves two tribes of Native Americans—the Mdewekanton Dakota and, later, the Ojibwes, a tribe that continues to live in the area. The Dakota, who had settled near the lakes and were harvesting wild rice, waterfowl, and fish, had begun migrating to the southern plains areas in the 1800s in an effort to follow the buffalo when the Ojibwes began moving in from the east.

Nearby Mille Lacs Lake, the most popular fishing lake in this area of Minnesota, formed from glacial debris in the form of a terminal moraine: rocks, boulders, and gravel left behind when a glacier retreated. This debris blocked the natural drainage and caused water to build up, creating the lake. Mille Lacs Lake is the source of the Rum River, which gradually winds its way through 146 miles of Minnesota countryside to join the Mississippi at Anoka.

Logging became an important industry on the Rum River in the mid 1800s. Due to the river's convenient location in the middle of the pinelands of the St. Croix Delta, the Rum River played an important role as a driving stream in delivering pine logs from the St. Croix Delta to the Mississippi River above St. Anthony Falls. The river's attributes were attractive to lumbermen, and the pine harvest was so swift and thorough that this resource was exhausted in less than a half century.

Much of the area's geological and archaeological history is told at the park's interpretive center (follow signs along the park road) located at the start of a self-guided, mile-long nature trail that showcases a variety of trees (among them ash, basswood, maple, aspen, and tamarack), flowers, and wildlife. Interpretive program schedules are posted throughout the park and at the interpretive center.

Rowboats and canoes are available in the park for rental to explore the Rum River, Ogechie Lake, or Shakopee Lake, or just to drop a fishing line near the dam. The park also has a swimming beach where you can cool off during the warmer days of summer.

The featured hike is the Hiking Club Trail and park favorite, giving the hiker a taste of the glacial landscape with its rolling hills, wetland areas, and views of Ogechie Lake. The first half mile follows the historic Landmark Trail, which has interpretive signs describing the surrounding natural and cultural resources. Other highlights of the trail include stops at the Cooper and Wilford archaeological sites. Look for signs of porcupine, beaver, and muskrat along the trail.

Ogechie Lake

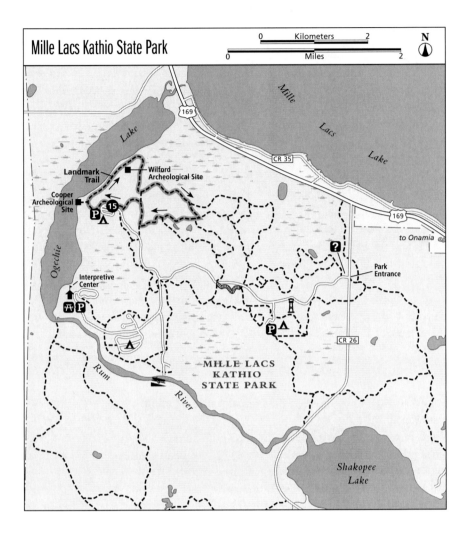

Mille Lacs Kathio State Park

Miles and Directions

0.0 Start from the Landmark Trail parking lot information kiosk. Look for the Hiking Club Trail signs.

0.2 Trail passes the Cooper archaeological site where a Dakota Village once stood. Interpretive signs are located throughout the site. Continue to follow Hiking Club Trail signs as you walk along Ogechie Lake.

0.6 Trail passes through the Wilford archaeological site. At this point the Landmark Trail returns to the parking lot. Continue northeast along Ogechie Lake following Hiking Club Trail signs at trail junction 17.

1.0 At trail junction 16 stay to the left following the Hiking Club signs.

1.6 At trail junction 15 turn right.

1.8 At trail junction 14 turn right.

2.3 At trail junction 24 keep right.

2.5 At trail junction 23 turn right.

2.7 At trail junction 19 turn left.

2.9 At road crossing turn right and follow the road for 0.3 miles back to the Landmark Trail parking lot.

3.2 Arrive back at the Landmark Trail parking lot.

More Information

Local Information
Mill Lacs Area Tourism: (320) 532-5626

Local Events/Attractions
Onamia Days: Early June, Onamia, MN

Accommodations
Mille Lacs Kathio State Park: Onamia, MN; (320) 532-3523
Hunters Point Resort: Isle, MN; (320) 676-3227; www.hunterspointresort.com
South Isle Family Campground: Isle, MN; (320) 676-8538; www.southislecampground.com
Twin Pines Resort and Motel: Garrison, MN; (320) 692-4413 or (800) 450-4682; www.fishand game.com/twin

Restaurants
Chico's Restaurant & Bar: Onamia, MN; (320) 532-3535
Spotlite Family Restaurant: Garrison, MN; (320) 692-4692

Hike Tours
Interpretive programs are available year-round through the state park.

Local Outdoor Retailers
Easy Riders: Brainerd, MN; (218) 829-5516

17 Savanna Portage State Park

Although the featured hike is the most picturesque in the Savanna Portage State Park, there are several other trail options from which to choose. A few of them will take you to Wolf, Savanna, Remote, and Loon Lakes where, if you choose to carry fishing equipment, you may be able to catch your dinner. There are also some walk-in campsites along the trails. The featured trail circles around a pristine lake and travels along Continental Divide Trail to the Old Schoolhouse Trail and ends following the historic Savanna Portage Trail. At the high point of this hike (elevation 1,300 feet), you'll be standing at the line of demarcation that separates the watersheds of the Mississippi River and the Great Lakes.

Start: From Lake Shumway boat landing in the park near the campground
Distance: 7.5-mile loop
Approximate hiking time: 3 hours
Difficulty rating: Moderate
Trail surface: Varies from a narrow path with roots and rocks to wide grass and dirt trails and old roads
Lay of the land: Rolling hills and sandy soil with large bogs and marshes, all remnants of past glacial activity. This height of land divides the Mississippi River and Great Lakes watersheds.
Other trail users: Mountain bikers
Canine compatibility: Leashed dogs permitted

Land status: State park
Nearest town: McGregor, MN
Fees/permits: State park vehicle permit is required. Annual or day permits are available at the park office. Camping fees are separate.
Schedule: Open year-round for day use and camping
Maps: USGS maps: Balsam, MN; state park map
Trail contacts: Savanna Portage State Park, McGregor, MN; (218) 426-3271; Department of Natural Resources, St. Paul, MN; (651) 296-6157 or (888) 646-6367 (only in MN); www .dnr.state.mn.us/parks

Finding the trailhead: From McGregor, take U.S. Highway 65 7 miles north to CR 14 and 36. Turn right and follow this road 10 miles to the park. *DeLorme: Minnesota Atlas & Gazetteer:* Page 64 D3

The Hike

Though it was a difficult portage—with long stretches of muddy swamps filled with thick, tall grass, reeds, wild rice, tangled debris and annoying, biting bugs hindering their progress—Native Americans and French fur traders continued to traverse this rugged land because it was the most efficient way to transport goods from Lake Superior to the Mississippi River. They thought nothing of wading through deep mud when the water was too shallow. Their fragile birch bark canoes often had to be emptied of their heavy loads and guided over rocks, rough branches, and other debris that threatened to rip holes in them. Loads were generally divided into ninety-pound packs that were carried on their backs until it was safe to reload the canoes. In some areas, canoes were pushed ahead by long poles. Traders used this route because along it a chain of lakes, streams, and rivers lay relatively unbroken from Big Sandy Lake to Lake Superior to the east.

The destination for these fur traders was a post on a peninsula on the northwest bank of Big Sandy Lake, which drains into the upper Mississippi River. This post was where William Aitkin, significant in the settlement of this area and manager of the

Portage between East and West Savanna Rivers

Fond du Lac district of the American Fur Company, maintained his headquarters from 1822 to 1840. A Minnesota lake, county, and city are now named for him. Some old buildings and rice pits remain at the post site. Big Sandy Lake, a significant headwater tributary of the Mississippi, was also the point from which many expeditions were launched in the search for the Mississippi River headwaters.

The journey for these traders began along the shores of Lake Superior at the mouth of the St. Louis River. After paddling a few miles up river, the travelers made a 9-mile portage around a set of waterfalls and rapids that were impassable by canoe.

They then headed west and northwest to where the East Savanna River empties into the St. Louis. From Lake Superior, the trader had climbed more than 650 feet in elevation and now faced increased difficulties due to shallow water, marshy conditions, and long portages before reaching the height of land to the West Savanna River. The West Savanna flows into Big Sandy Lake, which drains into the Mississippi River. From this point the journey became much easier, paddling downstream all the way to St. Paul.

A story in the *Superior Chronicle* dated December 11, 1855, gives an account of a birch bark canoe trip from Lake Superior to St. Paul using the Savanna Portage. The 90-mile trip up the St. Louis River, although not easy, was fairly uneventful, but the author describes the East Savanna River as a wide, debris- and grass-clogged swamp for miles, making travel difficult. From there, canoes had to be portaged as much as 16 miles in times of low water, but this distance could shrink considerably in summers of heavy rains to as little as 6 miles. Some of the portage to the West Savanna River was on dry, high ground forested with birch, maple, and pine, which made for easier travel. It typically took five days to portage the 6 miles to the West Savanna River, which was only a few feet wide and barely deep enough to float a canoe. (An alternative for travelers was to head south at Shumway Lake to the Prairie River, which was deeper and wider, although a little longer, to reach Big Sandy Lake and join the Mississippi River.) During the portage to the West Savanna River, the expedition reached a divide at 1,300 feet. Here, the water on one side flows northeast to the Atlantic Ocean via Lake Superior and the St. Lawrence Seaway. The water on the other side flows southwest to the Mississippi River and on to the Gulf of Mexico.

Overlook of a bog on the Continental Divide Trail

This pleasant hike ventures around beautiful Lake Shumway over hilly glacial deposits and easily crosses a marsh along a comfortable boardwalk—travelers never had it so easy! At the highest point, enjoy a view that goes beyond Wolf Lake and over an immense bog that drains into the East Savanna River. The hiker is treated to a diverse walk through mixed forest and marsh environs that echoes historical significance.

Miles and Directions

0.0 Start from the boat launch on Lake Shumway. Facing the lake, walk right along the beach and pass the campground on your right. Continue around the south shore of Lake Shumway on a hiking only trail.

0.2 A bridge crosses a small creek that drains the lake. (FYI: Notice the beaver sign in this area, including felled trees and a small dam. The smells of campfire and cooking waft by as you pass campsites and hundred-year-old white pines.) The trail here is a narrow footpath with roots and rocks.

0.4 The trail moves away from the lakeshore for a short distance. The mixed hardwood forest floor is covered with club mosses here.

0.7 The hiking-only trail intersects with the mountain bike/hiking trail here. Take a left, and in about 200 feet stay left again to continue around the north side of Lake Shumway. The trail is now a wide two-track trail. Follow the boardwalk on the edge of a wide beaver dam and view an active beaver lodge.

1.5 Enter a grassy clearing planted with red pines.

1.7 Return to the parking area and turn right, past the outhouses to the Hiking Club Trail sign.

1.8 Take a right. This trail starts as an old road that passes through previously farmed land that has been replanted with red pines. You will see remnants of farm machinery.

2.0 Pass a snow machine trail on the right that leads to the town of Floodwood, where the East Savanna River empties into the St. Louis River on its way to Lake Superior. Turn right at this intersection and leave the old road to take the trail marked JACOBSON/CONTINENTAL DIVIDE/WOLF LAKE 1.6 MILES. The trail crosses a drainage and climbs onto a small ridge.

2.7 Come down a hill to a five-way intersection (crossing the Savanna Portage Trail) and follow the Continental Divide/Hiking Club Trail signs, ascending a hill.

2.9 Take a right at an unmarked intersection and stay on the Continental Divide Trail.

3.3 Cross a winter ski trail, not marked on the map, and continue straight ahead. You may see mountain bike or deer tracks, or flush a grouse.

4.4 Pass a log shelter, outhouse, and campsite with a fire pit, cooking grate, and picnic table. (FYI: Just beyond the picnic area on the right is an observation platform overlooking the tamarack bog. Here you can read interpretive information on the continental divide and the forest bog community.)

4.5 Continue along rolling hills until you come to a four-way intersection. Go left onto Old Schoolhouse Trail. The trail widens and levels out. Walk through a burned area and a forest with 130-year-old oak trees.

5.5 The trail parallels the park road here.

6.1 Take a left onto the road and walk toward the portage trail. There is a parking lot on the

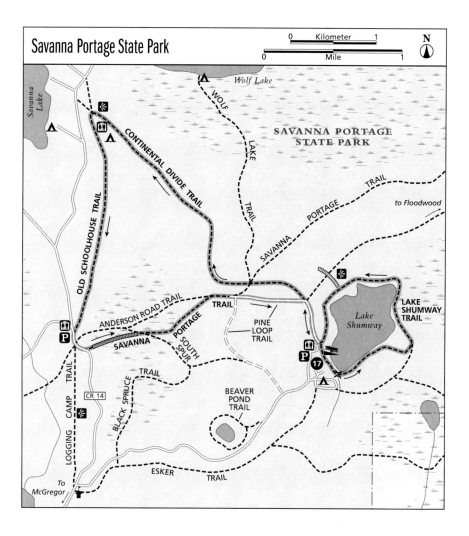

right. Where the Savanna Portage crosses the road, take a left onto it. In 50 feet a long boardwalk crosses a large marsh.

6.4   Take a right here toward Lake Shumway.

6.5   Stay on the portage trail and take a left at this intersection.

6.9   Enter a young forest with many white paper birches. Take a right at this intersection, where Anderson Road Trail joins Savanna Portage Trail, and continue on the portage trail.

7.0   Turn right at this intersection and follow Hiking Club Trail signs through a mature planted red pine forest. The trail is now a dirt two-track road. The portage trail continues to the left. Soon Lake Shumway will come into view.

7.4   Take a right back through the old farm field and back to the parking area.

7.5   Arrive back at the parking area.

More Information

Local Information
McGregor Area Chamber of Commerce: McGregor, MN; (877) 768-3692; www.mcgregor.mn
Tourist Information Booth & Wayside Rest: (218) 768-3692 or (877) 768-3692; open May through October

Local Events/Attractions
Wild Rice Days: Labor Day Weekend, McGregor, MN
McGregor Lions Corn Feed: Sunday of Labor Day weekend, Marty Paquette Pavilion, McGregor, MN
Rice Lake National Wildlife Refuge: McGregor, MN; 5 miles south of McGregor on Highway 65
Sandy Lake Recreation Area: McGregor, MN; on the northwest side of Big Sandy Lake just off Highway 65

Accommodations
Aitkin Lake Resort & Campground: McGregor, MN; (218) 426-3327
Country Meadows Inn: McGregor, MN; (218) 768-7378 or (888) 331-7378
Larson's Barn: McGregor, MN; (218) 426-3648; www.larsonsbarn.com
Town & Country Motel: McGregor, MN; (218) 768-3271
Big Sandy Lodge: McGregor, MN; (218) 426-3333

Restaurants
Bann's Bar & Grill: McGregor, MN; (218) 426-3450
Wilderness Family Restaurant: McGregor, MN; (218) 768-4311
Fireside Inn: McGregor, MN; (218) 768-3818 or (800) 294-6154
Horseshoe Lake Inn: McGregor, MN; (218) 426-3029 or (888) EAT-KRAUT
Big Sandy Lodge: McGregor, MN; (218) 426-3333

Local Outdoor Retailers
Glen's Army Navy: Grand Rapids, MN; (218) 326-1201

18 Pillsbury State Forest

The trails at Pillsbury State Forest meander through a heavy forested area consisting of a variety of deciduous and evergreen trees. The woods are dotted with small lakes and ponds where you're likely to see evidence of beavers and other wildlife. You may also find several varieties of wildflowers, including the yellow lady's slipper. Gently rolling, often cobbled, and sometimes a little muddy, the trails are fairly easy for family hikes. A non-equestrian campground with picnic, swimming, and boating areas, as well as a short nature trail, is located at the west side of Rock Lake to the north and east of the forest's main hiking trail.

Start: East side of Pillager Forest Road at the Stark Assembly Area and equestrian camp
Distance: 8-mile loop
Approximate hiking time: 3.5 hours
Difficulty rating: Easy to moderate due to wide, well-groomed trails
Trail surface: Wide, grassy and sandy, slightly cobbled throughout
Lay of the land: Mixed deciduous and conifer forest dotted with numerous small ponds and lakes. Gently rolling hills.
Other trail users: Equestrians, mountain bikers, and hunters (in season)
Canine compatibility: Dogs permitted

Land status: State forest
Nearest town: Pillager, MN
Fees/permits: No permits required. However, there is a camping fee.
Schedule: Open year-round
Maps: USGS: Pillager, MN, and Wilson Bay, MN; Pillsbury State Forest map
Trail contacts: Department of Natural Resources, St. Paul, MN; (651) 296-6157 or (888) 646-6367 (only in MN); www.dnr.state.mn.us; Brainerd Forestry Field Station, Brainerd, MN; (218) 828-2565; Backus Area Forest Supervisor, Backus, MN; (218) 947-3232

Finding the trailhead: From Brainerd, travel west on Highway 210 for 13 miles. Turn right onto the Pillsbury State Forest Road and proceed north approximately 3 miles to the horse camp. *DeLorme: Minnesota Atlas & Gazetteer.* Page 54 B3.

The Hike

Fall is a great time to hike Minnesota's forests, especially if the forest consists of a mixture of evergreen and deciduous trees. Pillsbury State Forest in central Minnesota has such a mix and is most beautiful in October when the aspen proudly displays its yellow and the maples and oaks their various shades of red against the bright green backdrop of scattered white and jack pines.

In 1900, John Pillsbury (governor of Minnesota from 1876 to 1887) donated 990 acres to the State Forestry Board. This became the core of Minnesota's first state forest, established in 1935 by the state legislature and named after John Pillsbury. Today the forest consists of 14,756 acres of state, county, and private land. Unlike state parks, state forests consist of privately owned and county managed lands within the forest. Different divisions of the state manage the remaining forestland, 8,105 acres of which are managed by the Department of Natural Resources in a reforestation program. Pillsbury is home to the state's first forest tree nursery, begun in 1903.

Look for the beginning trail marker on the east side of the Pillager Forest Road. This also is a camp area used primarily by equestrians. Pillsbury State Forest is a favorite among horseback riders. Unlike state parks, hunting is allowed on state forestlands. In season, you'll also find upland game hunters along the wooded trails trying to scare up ruffed grouse from the thick underbrush. Deer hunting is another popular activity, as evidenced by the many stands seen just off the trails.

This wide hiking trail is a loop trail on the east side of the Pillager Forest Road. Along the way, you'll encounter a number of hills and a spattering of ponds and

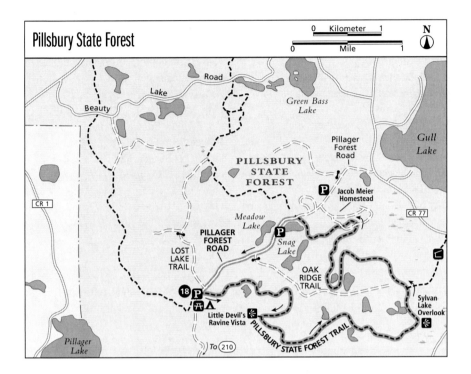

0   Kilometer   1

0   Mile   1

N

Road

Lake

Beauty

Green Bass
Lake

Pillager
Forest
Road

Gull
Lake

PILLSBURY
STATE
FOREST

Jacob Meier
Homestead

CR 1

CR 77

Meadow
Lake

PILLAGER
FOREST
ROAD

Snag
Lake

LOST
LAKE
TRAIL

OAK
RIDGE
TRAIL

Sylvan
Lake
Overlook

18

Little Devil's
Ravine Vista

PILLSBURY STATE FOREST TRAIL

Pillager
Lake

To 210

small lakes—evidence of glacial activity. The hills are part of a long glacial deposit (or moraine) that extends from Camp Ripley, south of Pillager, through the Foothills State Forest in Central Cass County.

Among the wildlife in this area, black bear have been known to roam these woods in search of berries, but it's unlikely you'll see them because they are generally shy and steer clear of humans. The area is also known for its beaver population. Their sometimes-elaborate lodges decorate several of the small lakes and ponds. Beaver activity is also evident in teeth marks on felled or partially felled trees along the trails.

Raspberry bushes line the trail in abundance. Late July through August would be a good time to hike through these woods if you want to pick berries. Among the numerous varieties of wildflowers seen in the woods is the yellow lady's slipper, which blooms from May to mid-July.

Near the end of the first mile, a small lake on the left close to the trail is a favorite watering area for horses as a path through the underbrush meets the water and allows easy access. The grassy but somewhat rocky trail winds east for a while in a mix of flat terrain and gently rolling hills. A little farther on, Little Devil's Ravine Vista offers a beautiful view of the heavily forested valley nearly 200 feet below—especially impressive when the trees have dropped enough of their leaves to expose what lies beyond.

As you begin mile three, you'll reach the Sylvan Lake Overlook, where in the fall you'll see the large lake below. Look for a sign identifying a basswood forest. Basswood or linden trees are typically found mixed with other hardwoods such as sugar maple and red oak. They have distinctive broad, heart-shaped, coarsely toothed leaves and provide a dense canopy, making them excellent shade trees.

Before you come to mile four, you'll see signs letting you know that County Road 77 and Gull Lake are to the right. Gull is a very large, popular recreational and fishing lake with several large bays. Brainerd and Nisswa are to the east of Gull Lake, both of which are well-frequented resort towns.

As you hike, you'll see trail splits, some of which are old logging roads. STAY ON TRAIL signs will tell you which is the main hiking trail. One such road is evident as you cross it in mile five. After you cross it, watch for the Jacob Meier homestead sign on the right. Meier purchased the land in the late 1880s after the area had been initially logged. Homesteaders who had farming in mind didn't stay long, though, as the land, with its sandy soil, was not productive. Tree harvest has been fairly continuous in Pillsbury, although it's not evident along many of the hiking trails. A number of companies harvest timber for pulpwood (which is turned into a variety of paper and wood products) and sawtimber.

The last segment of trail winds around Snag Lake on your left, then turns right. Soon, Burned Camp Lake, which laps at the edge of the forest road, will come into view. Turn left when you reach the road and walk 1.5 miles back to the horse camp. Another option would be to cross the road where there is a YOU ARE HERE sign, and continue hiking north. In 2.2 miles, you'll come to Beauty Lake Road. Here, the trail heads north (4.2 miles) to Shafer Lake where there is a canoe launching, parking, and picnic area. Checking the state forest map, you'll find that there is a network of other hiking trails both to the east and west of Shafer Lake.

Miles and Directions

0.0 The trailhead is on the east side of the road in the Stark assembly area. The Pillsbury State Forest Trail is marked with a snowmobile sign near an outhouse.

0.5 The trail passes a small pond on your left and follows the top of Dahlstrom Ridge.

1.2 You'll come to an intersection for snowmobiles. Continue left on a trail marked RIDING AND HIKING TRAIL. The trail to the right is a snowmobile trail to the town of Pillager.

1.5 Look for a trail on your right that leads to the Little Devil's Ravine Vista Overlook. (This is a high point where you can get a view of a large ravine approximately 200 feet below. This view may be somewhat obstructed when the trees are fully clothed.)

2.2 Pass a marsh and ravine on the left and a pothole lake on the right.

2.3 At this point, you'll come to a logging area.

2.5 While trekking through this forest of basswood trees, look for their large, green leaves.

3.3 Sylvan Lake Overlook will be on your right. In early spring or fall when the trees are not fully clothed, you can see this large lake approximately 130 feet below.

3.4	As you hike down a hill, there will be a lake on your left and a beaver pond on your right.
3.7	Stay left at the trail intersection, as the trail to the right goes to CR 77.
4.1	You'll come to an old forest logging road in an area where large red pines are left standing. Follow the STAY ON TRAIL signs.
4.5	The trail moves into a younger forest with many paper birch trees.
4.8	The trail passes between two lakes.
5.9	You'll see a sign marking the old Jacob Meier Homestead site.
6.5	Snag Lake comes into view on your left (USGS topo map calls this Stump Lake), and in just a short distance you arrive at Burned Camp Lake. When you reach a gravel road, turn left onto the road.
6.6	You'll pass a parking area on your left.
8.0	Arrive back at the assembly area trailhead.

More Information

Local Information

Brainerd Chamber of Commerce: Brainerd, MN; (218) 829-2838 or (800) 450-2838; www.brainerdchamber.com
Pillager City Hall: Pillager, MN; (218) 746-3322
Pillager Trading Post: Pillager, MN; (218) 746-3219

Local Events/Attractions

Cass County Fair: Dates vary year to year, Pillager, MN
Antique sales, Pillager Trading Post: Pillager, MN; (218) 746-3936
Bluegrass Festival: Gull Lake Ski Resort, Labor Day weekend

Restaurants

North Woods Café: Pillager, MN; (218) 746-3186
Stew's Sub Shop & Arcade: Pillager, MN; (218) 746-3305; This is also Stew's Barbecue Friday, Saturday, and Sunday evenings (back side of building).

Accommodations

Rock Lake Campground: Pillsbury State Forest, MN; (218) 828-3075
Auger's Pine View Resort: Motley, MN; (218) 575-2100 or (888) 705-5253; www.augerspine view.com
Don & Mayva's Crow Wing Lake Campground: Brainerd, MN; (218) 829-6468; www.brainerd .net\~cwcamp

Local Outdoor Retailers

Easy Riders: Brainerd, MN; (218) 829-5516
Fleet Farm: Baxter, MN; (218) 829-1565

19 Lake Maria State Park

Fourteen miles of hiking trails exist in this beautiful wooded forest dotted with marshes and lakes—and it's all situated in a place where you'd never expect to find such seclusion. The park's wide, winding trails take you over rolling hills, between marshes and ponds full of wildlife, and end at a campsite of your choice. There are several loops in this park, some of them shared with horseback riders. All trails are easy and the loops fairly short for whole-family enjoyment, but there's much more to do than hike here. Besides camping, fishing, hiking, and horseback riding, there are annual programs such as maple syrup making, bird hikes, bluebird workshops, and candlelight skiing. Because the park is popular, Lake Maria State Park cabins are booked well ahead of the approaching season, so plan ahead.

Start: From the trailhead on the south side of the visitor center off CR 111

Distance: 4.1-mile loop

Approximate hiking time: 2.5 hours

Difficulty rating: Easy due to wide, grassy trails

Trail surface: Grass and dirt

Lay of the land: Wooded with gently rolling hills

Other trail users: Equestrians

Canine compatibility: Leashed dogs permitted

Land status: State park

Nearest town: Monticello, MN

Fees/permits: State park vehicle permit required. Annual or day permits are available at the park office. Camping fees are separate.

Schedule: Open for day-use and year-round camping. Cabins are also available. Skiing in winter months.

Maps: USGS maps: Silver Creek, MN; state park map

Trail contacts: Lake Maria State Park, Monticello, MN; (763) 878-2325; Department of Natural Resources, St. Paul, MN; (651) 296-6157 or (888) 646-6367 (only in MN); www .dnr.state.mn.us/parks

Lake Maria

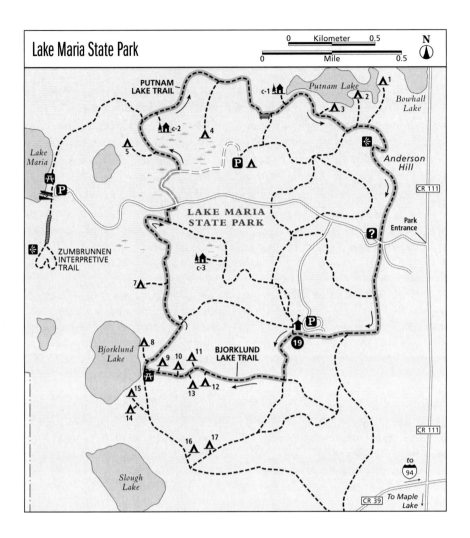

Lake Maria State Park

PUTNAM LAKE TRAIL

Putnam Lake

Bowhall Lake

Lake Maria

LAKE MARIA STATE PARK

Anderson Hill

CR 111

Park Entrance

ZUMBRUNNEN INTERPRETIVE TRAIL

Bjorklund Lake

BJORKLUND LAKE TRAIL

CR 111

Slough Lake

to 94

CR 39

To Maple Lake

Finding the trailhead: From Minneapolis, take Interstate 94 to Monticello, approximately 30 miles. Exit I-94 at the second Monticello exit (exit 193). Turn right off the exit ramp and go two blocks. Turn left on 6th Street, follow brown state park signs to CR 39. Turn left on CR 39 and go 8 miles to CR 111. Turn right and go 1 mile. The park entrance will be on the left. *DeLorme: Minnesota Atlas & Gazetteer.* Page 40 A2.

The Hike

Lake Maria State Park is a precious oasis of forest surrounded by urban activity and miles of farmland. Located a few miles north of the rapidly growing city of Monticello, the park is one of only a few places where you can find wooded seclusion so close to a major metropolitan area (Minneapolis and St. Paul). The park's 1,580 acres were once part of a huge forest extending more than 3,000 square miles, which included part of southern Minnesota. This deciduous forest, dominated by maple and basswood trees, was called Bois Grand or Bois Fort by early French explorers. European settlers later called the area the Big Woods. European settlement eventually reduced the Big Woods to what little remains today.

Three glaciers, the first of which covered the area a million years ago, were responsible for shaping the park's landscape. Red and sandy till from around Lake Superior and clay and loam from the Red River Valley were carried along by these glaciers and deposited in the area of the park. This area is part of the St. Croix Moraine, a place that marks the "edge" of the glacier where it left a pile of debris as it retreated,

Dotted with ponds and marshes and stocked with mature stands of oak, maple, and basswood, Lake Maria State Park makes an ideal home for all sorts of wildlife, including trumpeter swans and the threatened Blanding's turtles. Geese, turkey vultures, white-tailed deer, beaver, fox, and more than 200 bird species make the park their home. More than one hundred bluebird houses in the park encourage the small, colorful bird to nest here.

Blanding's turtles have found habitat to their liking in the park's ponds and marshes. This 5- to 7.5-inch turtle is recognized by its dark-brown or black dome-shaped shell, which is hinged across the front third, and its bright yellow chin and throat. It can be found in shallow water at the edges of ponds and marshes or sunning itself on logs and muskrat houses. Eggs, laid in late spring in sandy, well-drained soil exposed to the sun, usually hatch in September. The turtles, which are observed and studied by park personnel, winter in the muddy bottoms of marshes and ponds. Their survival depends on the plant-filled coves and bogs and the abundance of carrion, insects, and snails. Like so many animal species, this rare turtle has suffered nationwide from habitat loss due to urbanization, agriculture, river channelization, and water impoundment.

Beaver lodge at Lake Maria

Rustic camper cabins and backpack campsites, tucked well off the park's hiking trails, make ideal nature observatories for naturalists, photographers, and bird-watchers.

Lake Maria's 14 miles of hiking trails meander throughout the park, allowing the hiker a variety of choices. This particular hike begins in the main parking area (follow signs) on the south side of the visitor center. Look for a sign that points south to Bjorklund Lake, a small but beautiful little lake where you can launch a canoe (the park has canoes available for rental) and drop a fishing line. Crappie, bluegill, Northern pike, bullhead, perch, and carp can be found in this and the larger Maria Lake to the northwest of Bjorklund. A boat and canoe launch is available on Maria Lake; however, only motors with less than 20 horsepower are allowed on the park's lakes.

Once at Bjorklund, you'll follow the trail north, where you'll eventually cross the main park road that leads west to Maria Lake. This trail heads east, eventually reaching Putnam Lake and then Anderson Hill—a popular lookout—then south and west again to the parking area. There are numerous trails within this large outer loop if you wish to see more of the park or to head to a specific camp spot. Lake Maria is most beautiful in the spring when the trees are adorned with new leaves and violets and other wildflowers are in full bloom, or in mid- to late October when the trees change their colors.

Miles and Directions

0.0 Start at the south side of the visitor center where the sign points the way to Bjorklund Lake. You'll be heading south.

0.4 Turn right (west) where the trail splits, following the Bjorklund Lake sign. Before you get to the lake, you'll see signs marking campsites 12–9.

0.9 An open meadow takes you to the lake where there is a picnic table (in case you want to carry your lunch!) and canoes are available for a cruise on the lake (rent one at the park office). After you've listened to the frogs harmonizing with the redwing blackbirds, had a picnic lunch, or just sat admiring the lake, pick up the trail heading north.

1.6 When you come to the blacktopped main park road, turn right and walk on the road a short distance to where a dirt road is on your left. Turn left onto this road. After rounding a curve to the right, you'll see a sign ahead on your left marking the trail.

1.8 The trail resumes again on your left where it takes you between two marshes that are home to geese, ducks, trumpeter swans, and muskrats, and winter studies are conducted on the rare Blanding's turtles. Continue through the woods past camper cabin 2 and campsite 4.

2.7 When you come to an intersection with a park bench, turn left (east). This will take you past cabin 1 and Putnam Lake.

3.1 Come to a trail intersection, turn left (east) and pass two hike-in campsites; the trail will turn to the south. Eventually, you'll come to a clearing and a sign marking Anderson Hill. Hike to the top to see the view or continue south past the hill.

3.2 Cross the blacktopped main forest road at the park entrance and follow the trail south and then west to the parking lot. Skirt the horse parking area.

4.1 Arrive back at the parking lot and visitor center.

More Information

Local Information
Monticello City Hall: Monticello, MN; (763) 295-2711
Monticello Chamber of Commerce: Monticello, MN; (763) 295-2700; www.monticellochamber
.com

Local Events/Attractions
River Fest Parade and Celebration: July, Monticello, MN
Art in the Park and Taste of Monticello: July, Monticello, MN
Walk and Roll (pathway celebration): June

Accommodations
Lake Maria State Park: Campsites or Cabins, Monticello, MN; (763) 878-2325

Restaurants
Cornerstone Café: Monticello, MN; (763) 295-3888
Pizza Factory: Monticello, MN; (763) 295-5656
Hawks Sports Bar & Grill: Monticello, MN; (763) 295-9990

Local Outdoor Retailers
Gander Mountain: St. Cloud, MN; (320) 654-6600
Cabela's: Rogers, MN; (763) 493-8600

20 Minnesota Valley National Wildlife Refuge

A popular bird haven, Minnesota Valley National Wildlife Refuge lies along the Minnesota River Valley, where the prairies and floodplains provide habitat for approximately 226 species of migrating or nesting birds—including songbirds, waterfowl, and birds of prey. The refuge has much to offer its visitors. It consists of eight units totaling more than 11,000 acres, miles of hiking trails, and a modern visitor center with 8,000 square feet of exhibit space, several classrooms, an observation deck, and a bookstore. The Louisville Swamp Unit has 13 miles of interconnecting trails that take you up onto high bluffs overlooking wetlands, across Sand Creek, and through open prairie, upland forest, and oak savanna.

Start: From the Louisville Swamp parking lot on 145th Street
Distance: 6.7-mile loop
Approximate hiking time: 3.5 hours
Difficulty rating: Moderate due to wide, flat trails, some muddy spots, and a few elevation changes

Trail surface: Wide, grass and dirt trails, muddy in places
Lay of the land: Minnesota River floodplain forest and swamp
Other trail users: Anglers, trappers, and hunters (in season); biking and equestrian use allowed on state trail only!

Canine compatibility: Leashed dogs permitted

Land status: National wildlife refuge, Minnesota Valley State Trail

Nearest town: Shakopee, MN

Fees/permits: None

Schedule: Open year-round. Visitor center hours vary, so call ahead.

Maps: USGS maps: Jordan East and Jordan West, MN; refuge map and brochure

Trail contacts: Minnesota Valley National Wildlife Refuge, Bloomington, MN; (952) 854-5900; http://midwest.fws.gov/Minnesota Valley; Park Manager, Minnesota Valley State Park, Jordan, MN; (952) 492-6400

Finding the trailhead: From Shakopee, take U.S. Highway 169 south to 145th Street where you'll see the brown sign for Louisville Swamp. It's the same exit as the one taken for the Renaissance Festival. Cross the tracks and you'll see the parking lot at the end of the road on the left. *DeLorme: Minnesota Atlas & Gazetteer.* Page 32 A5

The Hike

The Minnesota River, which occupies only a small portion of the huge valley through which it flows, lies as much as 250 feet below the surrounding plains. A miniature version of the Glacial River Warren from which it originated 9,000 to 12,000 years ago, the Minnesota River flows quietly from Brown's Valley near the South Dakota border 355 miles to Fort Snelling, where it discharges into the much longer, mightier Mississippi. The Minnesota's average gradient is 0.8 feet per mile, and its total watershed is 17,000 square miles—14,751 square miles of which are in Minnesota (one-fifth of the state's area). Approximately 2,000 square miles of its watershed lie in South

Standing deadwood on the edge of Louisville Swamp

Dakota and Iowa. The wide, lush valley through which this great river flows—5 miles wide in some areas—has for centuries been a corridor for numerous plant and wildlife species as well as humans.

Minnesota Valley National Wildlife Refuge is part of the national wildlife refuge system created by President Theodore Roosevelt in 1903 to protect native birds from poachers and plume hunters. In later years, Minnesota governor Floyd Olson recognized the need to protect the Lower Minnesota River Valley by creating a plan for a 42,000-acre forest park and recreation area between Fort Snelling and Shakopee. World War II prevented implementation of Olson's plan, but finally, in 1976, the Minnesota Valley National Wildlife Refuge Act was approved. At that time, the Lower Minnesota River Valley Citizen's Committee committed its efforts to protect the river. Today, the refuge encompasses 14,000 acres extending along 34 miles of the river.

Scattered along the river from Fort Snelling to Jordan, the Minnesota Valley National Wildlife Refuge, with its floodplain marshes, wet meadows, fens, and lakes, is a place of restoration, preservation, and observation contained within eight divisions called units. All but one of them are now open to visitors. The 2,600-acre Louisville Swamp Unit, with its 13 miles of trails, mixes old fields, prairie remnants, oak savanna, floodplain forest, and stone farmsteads. Since people began settling Minnesota, they have been altering wetlands to suit their purposes. They have filled, dammed, and channeled, all without thought or concern for the effect their efforts would have on wetlands farther downstream. Louisville Swamp, for instance, now floods three out of five years because more than 90 percent of upriver wetlands, which once acted as a sponge to limit flooding downstream, have been drained. Flooding disrupts human use of the refuge but is beneficial for wildlife. Organizations such as Ducks Unlimited have contributed to refuge management efforts to promote habitat for waterfowl. People aren't the

Ruins of an old homestead

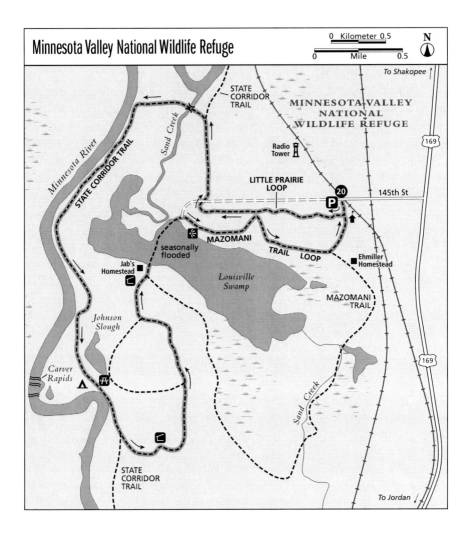

0   Kilometer 0.5

0   Mile   0.5

N

To Shakopee

STATE
CORRIDOR
TRAIL

MINNESOTA VALLEY
NATIONAL
WILDLIFE REFUGE

169

Sand Creek

STATE CORRIDOR TRAIL

Minnesota River

Radio
Tower

LITTLE PRAIRIE
LOOP

20

P

145th St

MAZOMANI

seasonally
flooded

TRAIL   LOOP

Jab's
Homestead

Ehmiller
Homestead

Louisville
Swamp

MAZOMANI
TRAIL

Johnson
Slough

169

Carver
Rapids

Sand Creek

STATE
CORRIDOR
TRAIL

To Jordan

only ones responsible for impacting wetlands. As is obvious in the Louisville Swamp area, beavers have been hard at work constructing dams that cause flooding of private property, as well as roads and trails in the refuge. In addition, their dams have held back water long enough to kill hundreds of acres of trees. Refuge managers have an active trapping program that allows removal of many beavers each year to maintain control of this problem. Although their impact can be viewed as detrimental, beavers also play an important role in the maintenance of wetland areas, which benefits wildlife.

Several tools are used in refuge management to encourage and provide for the nesting of migrating waterfowl. Management includes wetland and grassland restoration and prescribed burning (to maintain prairie areas by preventing the encroachment of trees and shrubs into the prairie). Biologists from the refuge work with private landowners in a thirteen-county area surrounding the Lower Minnesota River Valley to revitalize drained wetlands through a program called Partners for Wildlife. Breaking drainage tiles, building dikes to plug ditches, and installing structures to maintain water levels in the basins are all methods used to accomplish restoration. Other projects include restoration of nearly 300 acres of oak savanna and 2,300 acres of existing or potential floodplain forest. The emphasis here is on regeneration of bottomland hardwood forests to provide nesting areas for neotropical migrants and others in the future.

This hike follows the Little Prairie Loop Trail across a sixty-acre prairie remnant, crosses Sand Creek, heads south along the Minnesota River, and eventually crosses Louisville Swamp before returning on the Mazomani Trail. Insects are rather thick in the summer months, making this area a birders' paradise. More than 220 species of birds have been spotted on the refuge, many of which nest there.

Miles and Directions

0.0   Start from the north side of the parking area and follow signs for the State Corridor Trail. Go west (left). This is actually a connector to the main State Corridor Trail along the Minnesota River.

0.75 The State Corridor trail connector turns right at this junction, continuing 0.25 to its junction with the main State Corridor Trail, a multi-use trail.

1.0   This is the junction with the main State Corridor Trail. Take a left at this three-way intersection. A right follows the main State Corridor Trail downriver toward Chaska and Skakopee. At the bottom of the hill, a bridge crosses Sand Creek and the trail continues west to the Minnesota River. The trail is often wet and muddy here.

1.3   Come into view of the river and follow its bank south. (FYI: Large cottonwoods, ash, and willows line the trail, obscuring the river from view most of the way.)

2.0   Glimpse the river here. (FYI: Start seeing more maple trees mixed with green ash as the trail moves away from the riverbank.)

2.4   Cross from the Louisville Swamp Unit boundary (federal land) onto DNR land, the Carver Rapids Unit.

Anglers looking for roughfish

3.2 Pass a river campsite on the right. There are two picnic tables and fire pits.

3.4 At this junction, the State Corridor Trail continues south along the river. Go left on Flood's Road, toward the group campsite and drinking water. The trail is sandy here, and you'll pass through remnant oak savanna.

3.7 Come to an open area with a shelter, picnic table, fire pit, and garbage can. The drinking water comes from a pump on the other side of this clearing.

3.8 At this junction, turn left on Flood's Road.

4.1 At this trail intersection, go straight (right) to continue north toward Louisville Swamp. Pass a native prairie restoration area.

4.6 Take a right at this intersection. (**Option:** A left loops toward Johnson Slough and back toward the group camp and picnic area.)

4.9 Read about Jab's Homestead and view the three native sandstone buildings of this dairy farmer and his family who settled in the area in 1905. (Note: the smallest of the three buildings is a trail shelter.) Walk downhill and cross a seasonally flooded dam, which anglers frequent. You might see egrets, bald eagles, herons, and other birds. The tall, dead trees of the floodplain forest provide shelter and food for many bird species.

5.3 The trail intersects with the north side of the Mazomani Trail Loop. Take a right onto this trail. In July, it is thick with black raspberries. A left takes you back up to the State Corridor connector trail. The Mazomani Trail continues right, climbing to the top of the bluff and passing through areas of oak savannah restoration. Later, the trail offers good panorama views and an overlook of Louisville Swamp.

6.3 Take the left turn at this junction to head north to the trailhead and parking lot.

6.7 Arrive back at the parking area.

More Information

Local Information
Shakopee Convention & Visitor Center: Shakopee, MN; (952) 445-1660 or (800) 574-2150; www.shakopee.org

Local Events/Attractions
Minnesota Renaissance Festival: September, Shakopee, MN; (952) 445-7361 or (800) 966-8215
Chanhassen Dinner Theatres: Chanhassen, MN; (952) 934-1525 or (800) 362-3515
Canterbury Park: Shakopee, MN; (952) 445-3644
Minnesota Landscape Arboretum: Chanhassen, MN; (952) 443-1400

Accommodations
Canterbury Inn & Suites International: Shakopee, MN; (952) 445-3644 or (877) 291-0622; www.parkinnshakopee.com
Dakotah Meadows Campground: Prior Lake, MN; (952) 445-8800 or (800) 653-CAMP; www.dakotahmeadows.com
Town & Country Campground: Savage, MN; (952) 445-1756
Shakopee Valley RV Park & Campground: Shakopee, MN; (952) 445-7313

Restaurants
Dangerfield's: Shakopee, MN; (952) 445-2245
Emma Krumbee's Restaurant & Bakery: Belle Plaine, MN; (952) 873-3006; www.emma
krumbees.com
OK Corral Restaurant & Saloon: Jordan, MN; (952) 492-6700; www.okcorral.com

Local Outdoor Retailers
Wal-Mart Supercenter: Shakopee, MN; (952) 445-8013

21 Glacial Lakes State Park

Advancing and retreating glaciers carved and molded the landscape into an artistic blend of contrasting highs and lows, lakes, marshes, forests and prairies in the area of Glacial Lakes State Park. You'll see all of this as you hike in the park and learn about kames, eskers, drumlins, kettles, and moraines—especially if you choose the park's half-mile interpretive trail.

Start: From the picnic area 0.6 mile from the park office, near the south end of Mountain Lake
Distance: 4.8 miles out and back
Approximate hiking time: 2 hours
Difficulty rating: Easy due to wide trails over gentle terrain
Trail surface: Dirt, mowed grass, and board-walk trails
Lay of the land: Kettles, kames, drumlins, and eskers
Other trail users: Hikers only
Canine compatibility: Leashed dogs permitted

Land status: State park
Nearest town: Starbuck, MN
Fees/permits: State park vehicle permit required. Annual or day permits are available at the park office. Camping fees are separate.
Schedule: Open year-round for day use and camping
Maps: USGS maps: Starbuck, MN; state park map
Trail contacts: Glacial Lakes State Park, Star-buck, MN; (320) 239-2860; www.dnr.state .mn.us/parks

Finding the trailhead: From Starbuck, drive 5 miles south on Highway 29 and take a left on CR 41. The park entrance is on your left. *DeLorme: Minnesota Atlas & Gazetteer*: Page 44 D3

The Hike

Geologists call it a morainic belt—the 10- to 19-mile band of hundreds of various-sized glacial lakes and prominent knolls and ridges—that stretches 150 miles from Detroit Lakes to Willmar. This unique geological area, which includes Glacial Lakes State Park, is referred to as Leaf Hills, an area where the landscape is anything but flat.

The topographic features in these counties (Otter Tail, Becker, Douglas, and Pope) mark the glacial boundaries, where the debris of terminal moraines was deposited. The area is known as the Bemis-Altamont-Gary moraine system, and some of the highest hills in these counties are from 1,700 to 1,800 feet above sea level. More than 10,000 years ago, glaciers inched their way into Minnesota and, like giant bulldozers, scraped hills and bluffs down to the bedrock. As the glacial ice melted and retreated, it dropped its collection of gravel, rock, and sediment (or drift)—up to 400 feet high in some areas. The result was a spattering of prominent glacial formations: moraines, kames, kettles, drumlins, and eskers—all of which are obvious landmarks in Glacial Lakes State Park.

Kames are conical-shaped hills formed when meltwater dripped into holes in the ice, depositing debris in the holes. Kettles are depressions in the ground scooped out by glacial ice. Some of these are filled with enough glacial debris to create swamps. Drumlins are another type of glacial deposit forming elongated or oval hills. Eskers result from rivers that tunnel under the giant ice sheet. As the river gradually retreats, it drops loads of debris at its mouth, forming a long, high ridge. (The park map—available at the park office—indicates where these glacial features are located.)

In southwestern Minnesota, the landscape makes a gradual transition from the hardwood forest of the east to the western prairie. Glacial Lakes State Park preserves a small portion of the one-tenth of 1 percent of original Minnesota prairie remaining from pre-European settlement days. Big and little bluestem, Indian grass, prairie clover, pasque flowers, coneflowers, and goldenrods, plus shrubs such as wolfberry and rose, are among original prairie remnants found in the park.

Ants are essential to the health of the prairies. These industrious workaholics keep the prairies alive by mound building and tunneling, thus providing the essential service of soil aeration. Prairies wouldn't survive without aeration, which allows water drainage, exchange of gases by root hairs, and the decomposition of dead plants and animals by gasses infiltrated into the soil. Ants also build mounds under which their nests are constructed. Discarded plant and animal material in the mounds provides a rich source of nutrients for plants growing on the surface of abandoned nests. Sometimes ants share their nests with other prairie helpers like scarab beetles. One of the results of this relationship is a healthy, enduring ecosystem.

Adding variety to the prairie are scattered stands of bur oak. Because of their location along wetland firebreaks and their tolerance to fire and drought, they have been able to survive natural and prescribed burns. The bur oak's thick, corky bark and extensive root system make it more fire resistant than any other tree species. Even this hardy tree has enemies that thwart its growth. One of these is the European buckthorn, which, as its name implies, is not native to the United States. It moves into bur oak territory and, growing higher and thicker than the bur oak seedlings, robs them of the nutrients and sunlight they require for growth into mature trees.

Along the hike you'll see something called woodland litter, or duff. It consists of dead plant material that forms a spongy blanket covering the forest floor, and it's necessary for maintaining healthy soils and preventing erosion. Without rich topsoil, insects, earthworms, fungi, and bacteria couldn't do their important work of recycling dead plant and animal material into simple chemicals, which, in turn, are converted into living tissue. This process helps preserve the ecosystem. It is important that people do not release worms from fishing in the park, as an infestation can destroy the duff levels.

Several wet areas in the park serve as drainages, channeling runoff into Mountain Lake and providing watering sites for white-tailed deer. Spring-fed Mountain Lake was created by an esker, which blocked drainage, and by ice blocks from glaciers that were trapped under debris. Known to be exceptionally clean, the lake is landlocked with no surface outlets and is home to northern pike, large-mouth bass, sunfish, crappies, and perch. Canoes and rowboats can be rented in the park. Only electric motors are allowed on the lake. Most of the park's notable features are visible from the park's highest point, a hill rising 1,352 feet above Mountain Lake.

Miles and Directions

0.0 Start from the picnic area 0.6 mile from the park office at the south end of Mountain Lake (there are two picnic areas). At the east end of the parking lot, look for the Hiking Club Trail sign and begin here. Walk east up a glacier-formed kame (hill) into a basswood and oak forest. The trail is wide and well maintained. At the top, you will be treated to a northern view of Mountain Lake (on your left).

0.2 Turn left at this intersection to circle the lake.

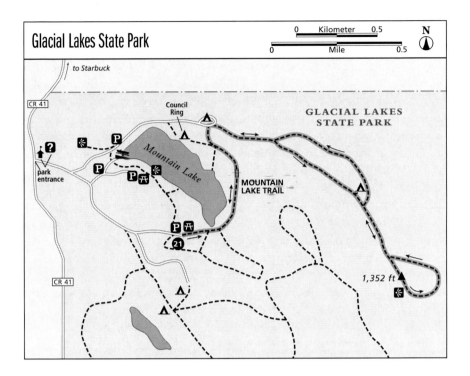

0   Kilometer   0.5   N

0   Mile   0.5

to Starbuck

CR 41

Council
Ring

GLACIAL LAKES
STATE PARK

Mountain Lake

park
entrance

MOUNTAIN
LAKE TRAIL

21

CR 41

1,352 ft

0.3   This may appear to be a four-way intersection, as there is a path on the left that leads down to the lake. A right follows a loop trail; proceed straight ahead to continue around the southwest side of Mountain Lake.

0.4   Cross a small stream that empties into Mountain Lake where beaver have taken up residence.

0.6   Cross a boardwalk over a marsh.

0.7   Take a right at this four-way intersection and walk to the campground road. (FYI: Going straight at this intersection leads to the council ring.) Turn right onto the park road and walk 100 feet to the parking area for the hike-in campsites.

0.8   Turn right at the Hiking Club Trail signs and follow a single footpath that winds through prairie grasses, large patches of sumac, wild plum trees, and quaking aspen.

1.0   Turn right. Here the trail climbs up onto a kame and straddles it, providing good views of the area landscape of hills and depressions.

1.5   Pass a spur trail on the left that leads to a hike-in campsite. Stay right on the main trail. (FYI: Look for purple prairie clover growing along the slopes.)

1.6   Take a right at this intersection to head south toward the highest elevation in the park, at 1,352 feet above sea level. The trail then loops back to the west. Hike through oak forest on a series of short, steep hills.

2.7 Take a right at the beginning of the loop you just finished and retrace your steps along this section of trail before it forks again.

3.0 Turn right and descend a small hill through oak forest. (FYI: Look for examples of woodland litter, the spongy blanket of dead plant material that aids in maintaining healthy soils.)

3.2 Pass the same hike-in campsite on your left. (FYI: View a new beaver pond on the right. Walk through open prairie where you'll see many piles of rich black dirt created by pocket gophers, woodchucks, and badgers making homes in the cool, protective underground.)

3.8 Take a right to head back toward the campground.

4.0 Back at the campground, retrace your steps to the park road.

4.1 Turn left at this four-way intersection. A right leads to the council ring and straight ahead to a fishing dock on the east side of Mountain Lake.

4.2 Cross back over the marsh on a boardwalk.

4.4 Cross a small stream and watch for painted snapping turtles.

4.5 Proceed straight ahead to walk back to the picnic area.

4.6 Stay right and walk down the hill.

4.8 Arrive back at the parking lot.

More Information

Local Information
Morris Chamber of Commerce: Morris, MN; (320) 589-1242; www.morrismnchamber.org

Local Events/Attractions
Prairie Pioneer Days: Second weekend in July, Morris, MN; Morris's largest community festival
Morris Wetland Management District Birding Event: May, Morris, MN; (320) 589-1970
Donnelly Threshing Bee: Last weekend in August, Morris, MN
Morris Harvest Craft Show: Third Saturday in September, Morris, MN; (320) 589-1212
Stevens County Fair: August, Morris, MN; (320) 795-2948

Accommodations
Smith's Lodging House: Morris, MN; (763) 767-3959
Best Northland Prairie Inn: Morris, MN; (320) 389-3030 or (800) 535-3035

Restaurants
Best Northland Prairie Inn (Ranch House): Morris, MN; (320) 589-3030
Old #1 Bar & Grill: (320) 589-2270
Common Cup Coffeehouse: (320) 589-1200

Local Outdoor Retailers
Pamida: Morris, MN; (320) 589-2264

22 Maplewood State Park

If brilliant color and variety in landscape are what you're looking for, Maplewood State Park is not to be missed. Late summer or fall, when the park's leaves are at their peak, are the best times to visit this area. It is a region of dramatic relief and the home of the state's largest ironwood tree. Although the woods consist primarily of hardwoods, tamarack and a few red cedar also grow in the park. Maplewood lies on the eastern edge of the Red River Valley, within the kame- and kettle-marked Alexandria Moraine. Several trails, including an interpretive trail, encircle the park's small lakes. Although some of them are marked equestrian, hikers are welcome on all.

Start: From Knoll Campground off Highway 108
Distance: 4.6-mile loop
Approximate hiking time: 2 hours
Difficulty rating: Moderate due to many hills
Trail surface: Mowed grass and wide dirt trails
Lay of the land: A series of hills and lakes— part of the Alexandria Moraine
Other trail users: Equestrians
Canine compatibility: Leashed dogs permitted
Land status: State park
Nearest town: Pelican Rapids, MN
Fees/permits: State park vehicle permit

required. Annual or day permits are available at the park office. Camping fees are separate.
Schedule: Open year-round; day use and camping
Maps: USGS maps: Lake Lida, MN; state park map
Trail contacts: Maplewood State Park, Pelican Rapids, MN; (218) 863-8383; Department of Natural Resources, St. Paul, MN; (651) 296-6157 or (888) 646-6367 (only in MN); www .dnr.state.mn.us/parks

Finding the trailhead: From Fergus Falls, go northwest on Interstate 94 to U.S. Highway 59. Drive north on US 59 to Pelican Rapids, then east on Highway 108 approximately 7 miles to the park entrance. *DeLorme: Minnesota Atlas & Gazetteer.* Page 51 A9

The Hike

The west central part of Minnesota is known for its concentration of lakes, ponds, streams, and rivers, which are embedded in a terrain of hills and depressions. Encompassing a prairie/hardwood forest boundary, Maplewood State Park lies along the Alexandria Moraine, which is responsible for the numerous lakes and the rolling terrain. Throughout the park are conical hills of various sizes and heights (called *kames*), made up of gravel and sand, and now blanketed by trees and prairie grass. These kames are the handiwork of melting, debris-carrying glaciers and are typical of the area along the Alexandria Moraine. Maplewood State Park contains several kames, some of them as high as 1,600 feet with abrupt elevation changes of 300 feet in less than a mile. Glaciers also formed the park's lakes when huge blocks of ice broke off, leaving scattered depressions (or kettles) in the earth. These later filled with water, creating lakes of varying shapes and depths.

The Otter Tail River drains this section of Minnesota. Its main tributary, the Pelican River, flows through the city of Pelican Rapids. A relatively short river, the Pelican flows 60 miles, drains 518 square miles, and has a gradient of 3.5 feet per mile. The Otter Tail travels roughly 200 miles to drain into the Red River to the west.

The Pelican River, the falls, and the city all owe their names to the American white pelican, which uses the area as a stopping place on its migration route. Once common in Minnesota before human pressure disturbed its habitat, the white pelican has only recently begun nesting once again in the state. Listed as a threatened species, the bird's nesting habits are being studied under the state's wildlife management program through the banding of birds. At 60 inches long and with a wingspan of 8 to 9.5 feet, the American white pelican is one of the largest of eight species of pelicans. People like to watch their well-developed fish-catching techniques at feeding time. The birds line up and together herd the fish into shallow water, where they surround them and scoop them up in their huge, pouched bills. A pelican's pouch can hold three gallons of water, and once the fish are caught, the bird points its bill downward, allowing the water to drain. Fish are a small part of their diet, which also includes a good number of salamanders and crayfish. Small numbers of these large birds use the lakes and marshes of the Pelican Rapids area as a rest stop for a few weeks each spring and fall, filling their stomachs before continuing their journey.

One of the park's most spectacular features, especially in the fall when colors peak, is its mixed forest of sugar maples, ironwoods, basswoods, American elms, and aspen. Minnesota's hardwood forests covered much of the state at the time of European settlement. However, a great deal of it was cleared for farming and timber harvest. Today, only a small fraction of those woods remains. Called Mesic forests, these woods

View from the top of Hallaway Hill

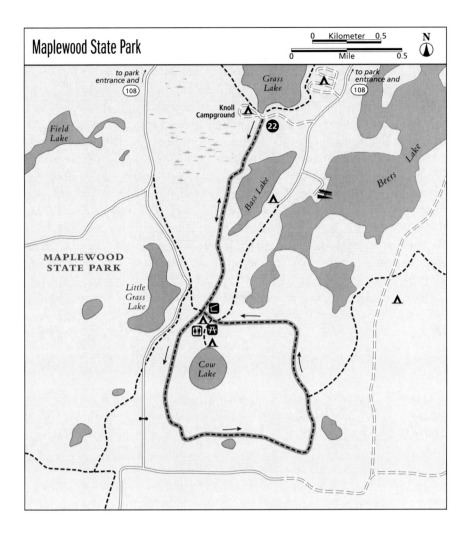

0   Kilometer   0.5

0   Mile   0.5

N

to park
entrance and
108

Grass
Lake

to park
entrance and
108

Knoll
Campground

22

Field
Lake

Bass Lake

Beers Lake

MAPLEWOOD
STATE PARK

Little
Grass
Lake

Cow
Lake

are typified by maple-basswood growth whose development is protected from fire by wetlands, rivers, and topography, fertile leaf litter, and rich soils left by glacial deposits. These woods, mixed with prairie, encourage diverse plant and animal populations. Common in the park are trillium, bloodroot, and liverwort, and on the prairie, wild onion, showy milkweed, beardtongue, and prairie rose.

Like other Minnesota state parks, Maplewood is rich in history. Archaeological evidence reveals a human presence at least 6,000 years ago. In 1931, the skeleton of what was thought to be a prehistoric man (once named Minnesota Man) was discovered 9 feet under laminated glacial lake clay near Pelican Rapids. It was only in later years that further study revealed the man to be a prehistoric teenage girl, now named Minnesota Woman, or Minnie. The location of the find, plus other archaeological evidence, supports the idea that the girl drowned in a glacial lake. A state archaeologist determined in 1969 that the bones date back to between 5,000 and 1,000 B.C., making it the oldest skeleton found in Minnesota.

Trails in the 9,000-acre park are designated for hikers only, horseback/hiking, and interpretive (hiking only). The selected hiking trail is a hiking-only trail and includes a small portion of hiking/horseback trail that skirts Cow Lake. This hike will give you a good sampling of the kettle and kame topography. Surrounded by hardwood forest, it is a cool, shaded hike in the heat of summer and a brilliant, colorful hike in autumn.

Miles and Directions

0.0 Start from Knoll campground on the south side of Grass Lake. At the turnaround, park at the side of the road and walk east (uphill) on the road approximately 100 feet to the trailhead. Turn right onto the trail and continue uphill into open prairie and oak savanna with lots of sumac growing along the mowed grass trail.

0.2 The trail enters the woods here.

0.3 Come out of the woods, skirt the edge of Bass Lake, walk across a beaver dam, and reenter the forest. Notice the large boulders left by glaciers on the floor of the maple, basswood, elm, and oak forest. The trail has joined an old road. Continue climbing a series of moderate hills.

1.1 As you climb, come to a four-way intersection that has a hike-in campsite, picnic table, open shelter, fire ring, and latrine. Proceed straight ahead, crossing the equestrian trail.

1.4 Glimpse Cow Lake through the trees. The hills are steeper, and the forest consists of maples mixed with a few paper birches.

1.7 Come out into an open field of grasses and purple thistle.

1.8 Back in the heavy canopy of the woods, watch for a tiny kettle lake through the trees on the right. Proceed down a steep hill through some large quaking aspen and elm trees.

2.1 Look for beaver sign here.

2.4 There's a small kettle lake on the right.

2.5 The hiking trail meets the equestrian trail. Turn left on the equestrian trail to complete the loop around Cow Lake.

2.8 Come into an open meadow and view Cow Lake on the left as you complete the loop around it. Beers Lake is on the right, or north.

2.9 Hike along the south shore of a bay on Beers Lake.

3.3 The trail turns away from the lake and back into the woods.

3.4 An equestrian trail joins here, and the trails parallel for a short distance. A right leads north to the group camp. Turn left. (**Option:** Take a moment to walk down to the excellent hike-in campsite on Cow Lake on the left.)

3.5 Back at the four-way intersection, take a right to retrace your steps north back to Grass Lake.

4.3 Walk back across the beaver dam and skirt the edge of Bass Lake.

4.4 Leave the woods and enter open prairie, back onto the mowed grass trail.

4.6 Arrive back at the road and vehicle.

More Information

Local Information

Pelican Rapids Chamber of Commerce: Pelican Rapids, MN; (218) 863-6571; www.pelican rapids.com

Fergus Falls Convention and Visitor Center: Fergus Falls, MN; (218) 332-5425 or (800) 726-8959; www.fergusfalls.com

Oktoberfest & Maplewood State Park Days: Mid-October, Pelican Rapids, MN
Turkey Festival: Mid-July, Pelican Rapids, MN
West Otter Tail County Fair: Mid-July, Fergus Falls, MN

Accommodations

Pelican Motel: Pelican Rapids, MN (218) 863-3281 or (800) 423-1172
Leisure Lane Resort: Pelican Rapids, MN; (218) 863-4490 or (800) 358-1883

Restaurants

The Muddy Moose: Pelican Rapids, MN; (218) 863-2900
Cornfield Café: Pelican Rapids, MN; (218) 863-5777
The Viking Café: Fergus Falls, MN; (218) 736-6660
Mabel Murphy's: Fergus Falls, MN; (218) 739-4406

Local Outdoor Retailers

Dalton Outdoors: Fergus Falls, MN; (218) 589-8679

23 Itasca State Park

This is the place where the continental glaciers of the last great ice age decided to leave a significant footprint. It is the place where the Mississippi River begins as a tiny stream, later to grow into one of the world's mightiest rivers. Thirty-three miles of hiking trails loop through Itasca State Park's wilderness, and when you've finished exploring the park on foot, there's a lot more to do within the park's boundaries including boating, biking, rollerblading, fishing, and listening to live music.

Start: From the parking lot at Douglas Lodge
Distance: 5.2-mile loop
Approximate hiking time: 2.5 hours
Difficulty rating: Easy due to wide trails over gently rolling terrain
Trail surface: Grass and dirt
Lay of the land: One of the last large tracts of old-growth pine in Minnesota
Other trail users: Mountain bikers (on paved designated trails only, not hiking trails)
Canine compatibility: Leashed dogs permitted (leash must not exceed 6 feet)
Land status: State park
Nearest town: Lake George, MN (to the east); Park Rapids, MN (to the south)

Fees/permits: State park vehicle permit required. Daily or yearly permits available at the park office. Camping fees are separate.
Schedule: Open year-round, including the Jacob V. Brower Visitor Center. Winter lodging is available at the Itasca Suites or at the Mississippi Headwaters Hostel.
Maps: USGS maps: Lake Itasca, MN; state park map
Trail contacts: Itasca State Park, Park Rapids, MN; (218) 266-2100; Department of Natural Resources, St. Paul, MN; (651) 296-6157 or (888) 646-6367 (only in MN); www.mnstateparks.info

Finding the trailhead: From Park Rapids, drive 21 miles north on U.S. Highway 71 to the park's entrance. *DeLorme: Minnesota Atlas & Gazetteer.* Page 61 A6

The Hike

Of all the hiking destinations in Minnesota, you won't want to miss Itasca State Park, the popular birthplace of the Mississippi River, with its 33 miles of hiking trails, Northern Minnesota woods and wildlife, more than one hundred of the state's 10,000 lakes, and fascinating history. Itasca State Park has been designated one of the state's seven National Natural Landmarks.

Itasca is Minnesota's oldest state park, receiving its designation in 1891, at a time when public awareness was drawn to the need for preserving nature's resources. Two other park proposals in the late nineteenth century—Minnehaha being one of them—were dropped temporarily due to continuing debate and lack of funds. As legislative debate continued, the decision was made to preserve what remained of Itasca's virgin pine and to protect the basin surrounding the Mississippi River's source. Red, white, and Jack pine, as well as birch, spruce, fir, aspen, oak, maple, and basswood thrive in the park along with lakes and wetlands, supporting a diversity of plant and animal life. Twenty-five species of orchids grow in the park. Wildlife residents include fisher, raccoon, gulls, bald eagles, pelicans, cormorants, otter, black bear, wolves, bobcat, and white-tailed deer. Itasca's diverse habitats also support many species of birds, includ-

Headwaters of the Mississippi River

ing trumpeter swans, loons, warblers, hawks, shorebirds, and owls. This is an excellent place for avid birders to visit.

Glaciers shaped Itasca State Park's water-dotted landscape thousands of years ago. The massive ice sheets deposited debris, such as boulders and course gravel, along their edges. The action of the glacial ice, combined with meltwater streams, created the more than one hundred lakes in the park. That the state's largest white pine still stands here adds to the park's uniqueness and significance. It's recommended that you begin your Itasca State Park experience by visiting the Jacob V. Brower Visitor Center located near the junction of the east and south entrance roads. This 13,000-square-foot facility is an excellent orientation point for learning about what the park offers. A good place to go from here is the famous Mississippi Headwaters, where you can walk across the small stream that gradually gathers speed, width, and strength as it winds its way 2,552 miles to the Gulf of Mexico. From its beginning 1,475 feet above sea level, the river flows north before turning east and south to continue its long journey to the sea.

It took 348 years from the time Hernando DeSoto found the mouth of the Mississippi River in 1541 until Jacob V. Brower settled the dispute as to the source in 1889. In 1832, Henry Rowe Schoolcraft asked a local Ojibwe leader named Ozawindib to take him to the source of the river, which Schoolcraft named Lake Itasca. Soon after this trip, another explorer challenged his discovery, claiming to have uncovered the real source. A controversy ensued, but in the end, the Minnesota Historical Society confirmed Schoolcraft's claim of Lake Itasca as the true source, and the matter was laid to rest. The fascinating history of the search for this great river's birthplace plus numerous other publications about the park, its wildlife and plants are available at the park's interpretive centers. Tour guide booklets will keep you informed as you drive through the park or hike its nature trails.

From the Headwaters, you can drive down to the historic Douglas Lodge where the 2-mile Dr. Roberts Trail begins. This trail, which features an abundant variety of plant life (described in a trail guide available at the park gift shops or at the trailhead), follows Lake Itasca for approximately half its distance, then loops back to a point near its beginning. From there, a right turn (south) will take you down Deer Park Trail, which passes several lakes where you're likely to see signs of otter and deer. It eventually merges with Red Pine Trail. As the name implies, this trail takes you through impressive stands of large red pine. It also offers great views of several lakes. Red Pine Trail intersects with Ozawindib Trail, which takes you north to the historic Douglas Lodge, built in 1905. This Hiking Club Trail wanders through a mix of pine, birch, maple, and aspen, as well as a variety of wildflowers. If you're looking for longer hikes, Ozawindib or Deer Park Trails will lead you to several longer loop options that meander through the park.

You'll probably want to spend more than a day at Itasca State Park to investigate all it has to offer, including the 10-mile Wilderness Drive, the scenic road that winds through the park. Many visitors also bicycle along Wilderness Drive. In this 32,000-

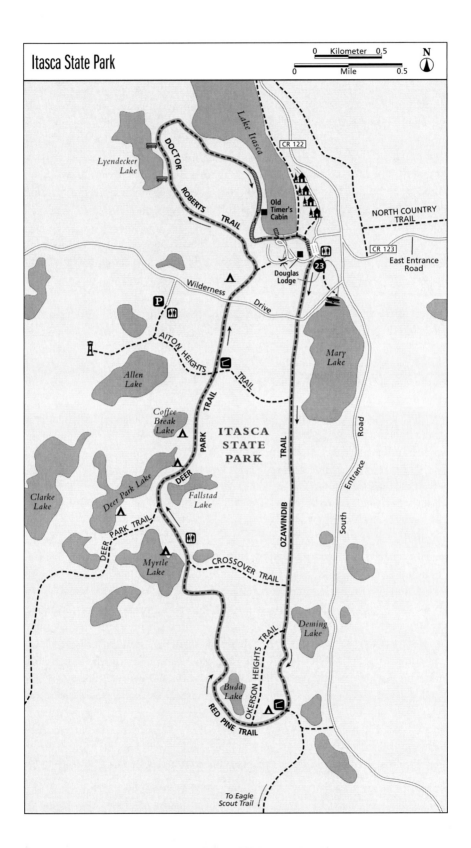

acre park, you'll find not only parking, restrooms, information centers, a lodge, cabins, food service, gift shops, a tour boat, sports rentals, and boat ramps, but also hiking, interpretive, and bike trails.

Miles and Directions

0.0 Start from the parking lot by Douglas Lodge and Forest Inn Gift Shop. Go to the northwest corner of the parking lot, find an information sign near a drinking fountain, and walk south, following signs marking Ozawindib and Hiking Club trails.

0.1 Cross Wilderness Drive, a scenic, paved road through the park. Mary Lake is on the left. Continue south. This trail parallels the park's South Entrance Road, although the road isn't within sight.

0.4 Aiton Heights Trail comes in from the right. Continue left (south) on Ozawindib Trail. (FYI: Trilliums are in bloom along this stretch in early June.)

0.8 Pass a beautiful ash swamp on the right.

1.0 Crossover Trail turns right (west) to join Deer Park Trail. Continue straight ahead (south) on Ozawindib Trail.

1.2 Catch a glimpse of Deming Lake on the left (east) and pass a stand of large, old red pines.

1.3 Come to Okerson Heights Trail intersection. This trail receives minimal maintenance and may be overgrown. Stay left (south) on Ozawindib Trail.

1.5 Turn right (west) onto Red Pine Trail. There is a shelter and fire pit at this intersection. A left continues south on Ozawindib Trail to eventually meet up with Eagle Scout Trail.

1.7 Pass the other end of Okerson Heights Trail on the right (north). Stay on Red Pine Trail.

1.8 Pass Budd Lake on the right. The trail then turns north.

2.3 Myrtle Lake comes into view on the left. Look for beaver activity and sign, including slides and dams.

2.4 An unmarked trail intersection comes in from the right. Continue left and follow the Myrtle Lake shoreline. Then come to Crossover Trail. Take a left onto this wide mowed path. This is where Red Pine Trail joins Crossover Trail for a short distance. (**Option:** A right [east] follows Crossover Trail back to Ozawindib Trail.)

2.6 Pass Myrtle Lake campsites on the left and a latrine on the right.

2.7 At this three-way intersection Red Pine/Crossover Trail ends. Take a right (north) onto Deer Park Trail to head back toward Douglas Lodge. Continuing left (south) is Deer Park Trail with a crossover trail to DeSoto Lake.

2.8 Pass Deer Park Lake on the left (west) and Fallstad Lake on the right (east). Notice the large beaver lodge.

3.1 Pass Coffee Break Lake and hike-in campsites on the left.

3.5 Aiton Heights Trail crosses Deer Park Trail. There is a trail shelter at this four-way intersection. Continue straight ahead (north) on Deer Park Trail.

3.7 Cross back over Wilderness Drive.

3.8 Take a left onto Doctor Roberts Trail. (FYI: A right leads directly back to the lodge. Dr. Roberts trail has many interpretive signs. A guide to the trail can be purchased at the gift shop or borrowed at the trailhead near Douglas Lodge. Be sure to pick up your guide before starting this hike.)

4.3 A bench overlooks Lyendecker Lake, a glacier-formed lake of the knob and kettle topography of the park. The common loon nests here in the summer.

4.5 Another bench overlooking Lyendecker Lake and a spur trail that leads out to an overlook are on the left.

4.6 A long boardwalk over a marsh environment begins here.

4.9 The boardwalk ends by the Old Timer's Cabin, a cabin constructed of enormous logs by the Civilian Conservation Corps in the 1930s. Just past the Old Timer's Cabin another boardwalk begins, leading over a conifer bog. Please stay on the trail to protect this fragile ecosystem. Walk by tamarack trees, and listen for the buzzy trill of the Northern Parula warbler, which breeds in northern Minnesota.

5.0 Pass the discarded wheels of the track that was used to bring the tour boat *Itasca* ashore each fall. (FYI: Look for the showy lady's slipper, an orchid growing in conifer swamps that's Minnesota's state flower. This orchid requires up to fifteen years of growth before flowering.)

5.1 Exit the woods and enter an open area next to Lake Itasca. Pass by the tour boat *Chester Charles II* and cross the parking lot, keeping the lake on your left. Cross Mary Creek, which flows into Lake Itasca from Mary Lake. Pass a fishing pier and Brower Trail on the left at the base of fifty-one wide, stone steps. Climb the steps to reach Douglas Lodge and follow the sidewalk past the lodge.

5.2 Arrive back at the parking lot.

More Information

Local Information

Park Rapids Area Chamber of Commerce: Park Rapids, MN; (218) 732-4111 or (800) 247-0054; www.parkrapids.com

Local Events/Attractions

Annual Headwaters Rodeo: July, Park Rapids, MN
Founder's Day Social: July, Park Rapids, MN
Northland Bison Ranch: Nevis, MN; (218) 652-3582
Paul Bunyan Days: June, Akeley, MN
Pine Point Pow Wow: Second weekend in August, Park Rapids, MN
Blueberry Festival at Lake George: Lake George is located 19 miles north on CR 4 from Park Rapids. The festival is in late July each year. See www.exporeminnesota.com for more info.
Lakes, Loons, and Legends: August, Park Rapids, MN
Lake and Pine Craft Fair: June, Park Rapids, MN

Accommodations

Bert's Cabins: Lake Itasca, MN; (218) 266-3312
Mississippi Headwaters Hostel: Hostelling International, Lake Itasca, MN; (218) 266-3415; www.himinnesota.org
Historic Douglas Lodge: Park Rapids, MN; (218) 266-2100
Carolyn's Bed & Breakfast: Park Rapids, MN; (218) 732-1101 or (800) 484-1058 King's Cottages Resort & Motel: Park Rapids, MN; (218) 732-4526; www.kingscottages.com

Restaurants

Y Steak House: Park Rapids, MN; (218) 732-4565
Blueberry Pines Restaurant: Menahga, MN; (218) 564-4653
Historic Douglas Lodge: Park Rapids, MN; (218) 266-2100
Mary Gibbs Headwaters Restaurant: in the park

Hike Tours

Itasca State Park offers scheduled programs throughout the summer. Check the park bulletin boards for current programs.

Local Outdoor Retailers

L & M Fleet Supply: Park Rapids, MN; (218) 732-4465
Itasca Sports Rental: Lake Itasca Public Access (within Itasca State Park); open May through October; (218) 266-2150 or (218) 657-2420 (off-season)

MISSISSIPPI RIVER: MINNESOTA'S GREAT RIVER

The term headwaters may be a little misleading when used in reference to the Mississippi River at Itasca State Park. While this is where the powerful river begins, it's believed that the actual source is in the many small tributaries draining into Lake Itasca from higher elevations. Also, there are those who believe the Minnesota rather than the Mississippi is the main river and that the Mississippi is merely a tributary. Downstream, the Missouri and Ohio fuel the debate (claims have also been laid on their behalf for being the main rivers). Thus, the controversy regarding the river goes on, but it isn't likely that the Mississippi's status will ever change. The river begins its journey as water discharges from the north end of Lake Itasca at 1,475 feet above sea level. It starts out as a narrow stream (only a few steps across) that stretches out from the lake something like a long umbilical cord winding north, east, and then south 2,492 miles to rendezvous with the Gulf of Mexico.

Long before the Mississippi existed, the earth was shaped and molded like a huge ball of soft clay by nature's tools: volcanic eruptions, glaciers, advancing and retreating oceans, wind, rain, and water. These energies formed the rocks, hills, and valleys. Each of these forces left its distinct mark on the North American continent, and Minnesota's varied and contrasting landscape is no exception. Retreating glaciers left huge bodies of water that later drained. Large ice blocks buried under glaciers caused deep depressions in the earth that resulted in what are called ice-block lakes. These include Lakes Allen, Mary, and Itasca in Itasca State Park as well as many lakes in other areas of the state.

Glacial Lake Agassiz, an enormous body of water, once covered much of Canada, northwest Minnesota, and North Dakota. As conditions changed, water began to trickle out of the lake, forming Glacial River Warren. With the force of its great volumes of water—one hundred times the volume of the present Minnesota River—the River Warren scooped out the Minnesota Valley and eroded the Mississippi Valley south of the confluence of the Mississippi and Minnesota Rivers. Nature's forces were at work preparing a place for North America's greatest river.

As it travels from its meek beginnings on its way to meet the ocean, the Mississippi meanders, widens, deepens, and changes mood and character. For several miles after its beginning the river flows, sometimes quietly, sometimes with turbulence, through lands clothed in spruce, fir, pine, and dotted with wild rice marshes. Along its way, it loses itself in many lakes, eventually emerging on the opposite side to continue its journey. It passes through small towns, farm country, and big cities, spreading out into ever-wider valleys as it goes.

The river's volume increases significantly from its source at Lake Itasca due to numerous tributaries, both large and small, that drain the land and carry accumulating water many miles to deposit into the Mississippi. Thus the river drains 45,000 square miles in Minnesota alone. As water volume steadily increases, flow becomes 100 cubic feet per second at Bemidji, 1,000 cubic feet at Grand Rapids, 3,500 at Aitkin, 7,000 at the Twin Cities, 10,000 at St. Paul after the junction of the Minnesota River, and 15,000 cubic feet per second below the St. Croix River. The river also drops quite a bit in elevation (an average of 4 feet per mile) between Lake Itasca and Lake Bemidji, increasing the river's speed. In Minnesota, the Mississippi drops 833 feet, which is 57 percent of the river's total drop in elevation.

In Minnesota, the Mississippi travels through seven state forests and the Chippewa National Forest. A favorite recreation area is the greatly swollen portion of river at Red Wing. Lake Pepin, often referred to as a river-lake, buzzes with activity during summer when sailboats, water-skiers, and anglers occupy the lake during fair weather. Bald eagles join the fun by soaring through the air currents above them.

Much of the upper Mississippi is within the jurisdiction of the Upper Mississippi River Wildlife and Fish Refuge. Fishing, hunting, camping, and other recreation are allowed within most of the 200,000-acre refuge except for designated areas during certain times of the year when wildlife is protected. Thirty-three thousand acres of this refuge are in Minnesota, 88,000 are in Wisconsin, 51,000 in Iowa, and 23,000 in Illinois. Refuge headquarters are in Winona with several district offices scattered through Minnesota, Wisconsin, Iowa and Illinois.

People in Minnesota are very interested in preserving this mighty and famous river—snatching it from the lethal grip of pollution. Citizen groups have formed in several areas of the state to study water quality, protect the plant and animal life, and keep watch on the industry along its course. Although great strides have been made in cleaning up the Mississippi, the Minnesota River—a tributary of the Mississippi—is the most polluted river in the state. The Mississippi's future as a thriving river lies in the hands of citizens living near it. There are several contacts for finding out how you can help. Here are a few:

Department of Natural Resources, St. Paul, MN;
    (651) 296-6157 or 888-MINNDNR (only in MN), www.dnr.state.mn.us
Steve Johnson, River Project Coordinator, Community Stewardship Supervisor,
    (651) 296-4802
Amy Denz, Community Stewardship Planner, (651) 296-0528

24 Scenic State Park

This is a relaxing hike through a marsh and out onto a needle-cushioned path among aromatic pines. Here blue water and picturesque panoramic views merge. This area is the former home of a huge glacier that left the long, shapely esker that now divides Coon and Sandwick Lakes. It's also home of the osprey, a large raptor whose nest of twigs looms in the upper branches of the tallest trees.

Start: From the information center
Distance: 2.9-mile loop
Approximate hiking time: 1.5 hours
Difficulty rating: Moderate due to a mix of hilly terrain with wide, flat trails
Trail surface: Dirt, grass, and pine needle-covered trails
Lay of the land: Marsh and pine-forested esker jutting out between two lakes
Other trail users: Hikers only
Canine compatibility: Leashed dogs permitted
Land status: State park

Nearest town: Bigfork, MN
Fees/permits: State park vehicle permit required. Daily or yearly permits available at the park office. Camping fees are separate.
Schedule: Open year-round
Maps: USGS maps: Coon Lake, MN
Trail contacts: Scenic State Park, Bigfork, MN; (218) 743-3362; Department of Natural Resources, St. Paul, MN; (651) 296-6157 or (888) 646-6367 (only in MN); www.dnr.state .mn.us/parks

Finding the trailhead: Follow Highway 38 north to Bigfork and then turn east on CR 7. The park entrance is 7 miles on the left. *DeLorme: Minnesota Atlas & Gazetteer:* Page 73 B9

The Hike

From an aerial view or on the map, the high, narrow piece of land that divides Sandwick and Coon Lakes looks much like a long snake slithering across the water. At nearly a mile long, this twisted, wooded landform, believed to be an esker, rises 25 to 30 feet above the lakes and culminates in Chase Point, where you're given panoramic views of the blue water and mature pine forests with its undeveloped, natural shoreline.

The word *esker* is derived from the Irish word *eiscir*, which means narrow, winding ridges. Resulting from the most recent glacier, this landform sometimes appears as a large serpentine ridge. As temperatures slowly warmed, the glacier began to melt, dripping water into a crack in the ice, accumulating until it became a rushing tunnel river carrying sand, gravel, and debris. The sediment settled out in the tunnel of the glacial ice and, as the ice melted, the sediment remained as a continuous ridge. When a single deposit was left, it was called a *kame*, seen as a large, rounded hill. Eskers are one of several landforms left behind by glaciers. The many lakes within the park's boundaries are water-filled depressions scooped out by glaciers and filled with water left over from Glacial Lake meltwater, and the surrounding gently rolling hills are huge piles of debris left by receding glaciers.

Once covered with stately pines, this region of northern Minnesota was heavily logged in the late nineteenth century. Settlers moved in and tried to farm the open land, but the soil didn't lend itself to farming. Other ways of making a living had to be found. Residents of Bigfork saw the area's wilderness slowly slipping away under the pressure of logging and decided to take action to preserve the remaining virgin pine surrounding Coon and Sandwick Lakes. The result of their efforts was the establishment of Scenic State Park in 1921.

Dense white cedar, spruce, and red pine stands provide ideal nesting places for a variety of bird species including the osprey, a bird of prey listed by the Raptor Center in St. Paul as a species "of special concern" in Minnesota. Nesting high in the tallest trees along the water, ospreys build their homes of twigs and feed on fish. At a length of 22 to 25 inches, these brown and white birds measure 4.5 to 6 feet from wingtip to wingtip in adulthood and possess a distinctive cry. Ospreys have unusual body, wing, toe, and feet adaptations that help with fishing. Their feet have rough bumps on the bottom that enable the bird to grasp its slippery prey, and reversible end toes that allow a firm grasp from which prey cannot escape. Special joints in their wings allow ospreys to bend them backward for a quick retreat from the water.

Ospreys have a worldwide population distribution. In Minnesota, they're likely to be seen on northern lakes and along the St. Croix River during the summer. A few pairs nest in the Twin Cities area due to the Raptor Center's efforts at reintroduction, which began in 1984. Besides tall trees, the osprey will nest on power poles, channel markers, or specially made osprey platforms. A team of biologists began a banding program in August of 1995 to track their migration and wintering habits. Apparently Minnesota ospreys spend their winters in a wide range of places, making tracking

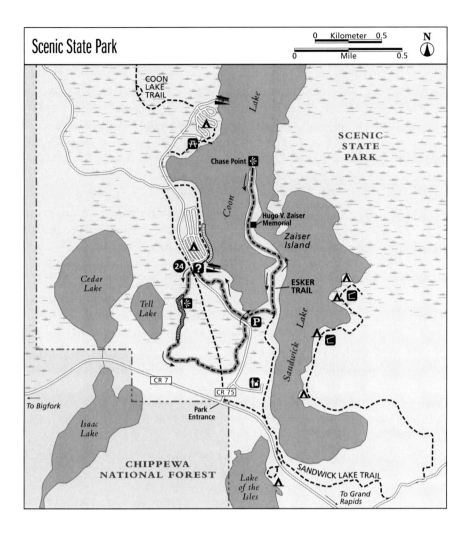

0   Kilometer   0.5

0   Mile   0.5

N

COON
LAKE
TRAIL

SCENIC
STATE
PARK

Lake

Chase Point

Coon

Hugo V. Zaiser
Memorial

*Zaiser
Island*

24

*Cedar
Lake*

ESKER
TRAIL

*Tell
Lake*

Sandwick Lake

P

CR 7

CR 75

To Bigfork

Park
Entrance

*Isaac
Lake*

CHIPPEWA
NATIONAL FOREST

*Lake
of the
Isles*

SANDWICK LAKE TRAIL

To Grand
Rapids

difficult and leaving many questions regarding the bird's migration habits. Since ospreys eat fish almost exclusively, the continuation of the species is of concern due to contamination of rivers and lakes from which they obtain their food. Once their numbers are diminished, they'll be hard to re-establish, since their nervousness and unwillingness to eat in captivity makes it difficult for humans to raise them.

As you hike the interpretive trail through marsh and mature white cedar, maple, ash, black spruce, white pine, and red pine, search the treetops for an osprey nest. Watch for interpretive signs that describe the area's various habitats. There are benches along the trail and an overlook deck at the esker's end for those who want to sit and soak in the magic of water, woods and the aroma of fresh pine.

Miles and Directions

0.0 Start from the information center. Proceed west across the park road and look for the interpretive trail sign by the RV dump station.

0.1 Cross a long boardwalk through a marsh environment.

0.3 Continue out of the marsh and up on a forested trail. Here, there is a bench overlook to the left. Look toward the distant treetops for a nesting osprey. The trail here is wide and grassy.

0.6 A snowmobile trail crosses the hiking trail here. Continue straight ahead.

0.8 An interpretive sign tells you how to identify quaking aspen, large-toothed aspen and balsam poplar as you pass by these trees.

1.0 The hiking trail crosses the park road to the parking area before the Chase Point Trail and forks. A left takes you back toward the information center. Go right to reach Esker Trail.

1.1 You'll see a black spruce bog bordered by large red and white pine atop the well-drained esker. Take a left onto Esker Trail to go out to Chase Point. A right leads south around Sandwick Lake to hike-in camping.

1.5 A memorial to Hugo V. Zaiser, the first park superintendent in 1956, stands here, where you can see Zaiser Island to the right. This memorial commemorates his contributions to Scenic State Park.

1.7 Rest on the bench here and take in the sunlight filtering through the pines.

1.8 Reach the end of Chase Point, which overlooks Coon Lake. A set of wooden stairs leads to a deck at the water's edge. Retrace your steps from here back to the parking lot.

2.6 Back at the parking area, take a right at the fork to parallel the park road toward the information center. This trail leads through a splendid old-growth maple forest and hills overlooking the lake.

2.9 Arrive back at the information center and parking.

More Information

Local Information

Grand Rapids Area Chamber of Commerce: Grand Rapids, MN; (218) 326-6619 or (800) 472-6366; www.grandmn.com

Local Events/Attractions
Effie Rodeo: Last weekend in July, Effie Rodeo Grounds
Itasca County Fair: In mid-August, Itasca County Fairgrounds
Hill Annex Mine State Park: Calumet, MN (218) 247-7215; www.dnr.state.mn.us/parks
Judy Garland Museum: Grand Rapids, MN; (218) 327-9276; www.judygarlandmuseum.com
Itasca Vintage Car Club: Grand Rapids, MN; (218) 326-8558

Accommodations
Hillcrest Resort: Big Fork, MN; (218) 832-3831
Scenic Pines Lodge: Big Fork, MN; (218) 245-1818
Judge Thwing House Bed & Breakfast: Grand Rapids, MN; (218) 326-5618; www.paulbunyan
.net/bedandbreakfast
Antler Lake Motel: Bigfork, MN; (218) 245-2369 or (888) 326-8537
Country Inn: Grand Rapids, MN; (218) 327-4960 or (800) 456-4000
Jessie View Resort & RV Campground: Deer River, MN; (218) 832-3678 or (877) 537-7438

Restaurants
Cedars Dining Room: Saw Mill Inn, Grand Rapids, MN; (218) 326-8501
Antler Lodge: Bigfork, MN; (218) 245-1136 or (800) 326-8537; www.antlerlodge.com
Arcadia Resort & Restaurant: Bigfork, MN; (218) 832-3852
Huskie Café: Bigfork, MN; (218) 743-6688
Loggers Supper Club: Bigfork, MN; (218) 743-3847
Eagles Nest Dining Room: Arcadia Lodge, Bigfork, MN; (218) 832-3852 or (888) 832-3852;
www.arcadialodge.com
Scenic Pines Lodge & Store: Bigfork, MN; (218) 245-1277

Local Outdoor Retailers
Glen's Army Navy: Grand Rapids, MN; (218) 326-1201

Honorable Mentions

Compiled here is an index of great hikes in the Glacial Lakes and Landforms region that didn't make the A-list this time around but deserve recognition. Check them out and let us know what you think. You may decide that one or more of these hikes deserves higher status in future editions or, perhaps you may have a hike of your own that merits some attention.

Lost Forty Trail

What makes this 1-mile hike unique is twenty-eight acres of old-growth red and white pine, left standing due to a surveying error. The scenic trail winds through part of this stand, where you can see impressive trees that are more than 350 years old. Near Scenic State Park, Lost Forty Trail is a little-used gem that is off the beaten path but well worth the visit.

To get there from Blackduck, proceed west on CR 30 for 13 miles to Alvwood (CR 30 turns into CR 13 when it crosses the Itasca County line). Turn north on Highway 46 for a half mile and turn right onto CR 29. Proceed 10 miles on CR 29 to Dora Lake, and then turn left onto CR 26. Drive north for 2 miles and turn left on Forest Road 2240. Continue 1.5 miles to the parking area and trailhead. *DeLorme: Minnesota Atlas and Gazetteer*: Page 73 A6

Lake Carlos State Park

Lake Carlos State Park is known for its maple basswood forest and gently rolling glacial landscape. Although many people are drawn to the deep, clean waters of Lake Carlos for fishing and boating, the hiking trails are wooded and beautiful. This 3-mile loop combines Red Oak and Hidden Lake trails, circumnavigating Hidden Lake and following the west shore of Lake Carlos. Begin at the parking area near the swimming beach.

From Alexandria, drive north on Highway 29 for 8 miles. The park entrance is on the left. *DeLorme: Minnesota Atlas and Gazetteer*: Page 45 A5

Myre Big Island State Park

This hike is unusual in that the area's hardwood forest has survived the harsh prairie wildfires because of Albert Lea Lake and its associated marshland. A haven for waterfowl and birds in general, the park also has trails on top of an esker left by the last glacier. From Albert Lea, exit off I-35 on CR 46 (exit 11) and proceed east a half mile to CR 38. Turn right (south) and proceed for 1 mile to the park entrance. *DeLorme: Minnesota Atlas and Gazetteer*: Page 24 E2

G eologists are still discovering pieces of history within Lake Agassiz's ancient lakebed. That this giant lake once existed is obvious in northwestern Minnesota where the landscape is flat and streams meander aimlessly toward their destinations. Lake Agassiz's beach ridges are prominent here, visible signs of the lake's indecisive advances and retreats until the lake left Minnesota for good approximately 8,000 years ago. It is only these ridges and the streams cut into glacial deposits that offer relief from the flat region's landscape. Two of these ridges, Campbell and Herman, named for towns along their path, are especially significant. These two beaches, as they are called, are the most continuous of all of Lake Agassiz's remnant beaches and represent periods when the lake level was stable for a long enough period to build prominent ridges.

No bedrock is exposed in this region, which stretches a short distance east of International Falls, follows the international border west to North Dakota, then south to Brown's Valley. The bedrock here lies well hidden beneath hundreds of feet of glacial deposits and lake sediment. Sand and gravel deposits make up lakebed ridges, and clay is found in the bed itself. Wetlands containing bogs and fens make up the eastern edge where peat is the most common soil type. Drainage ditches are frequent here, where the water table is high and has nowhere to go. All that's left of Glacial Lake Agassiz now are Upper Red and Lower Red Lakes, Lake of the Woods, and Lake Winnipeg. Other than that, this region of Minnesota is mostly devoid of lakes.

Once covered by a vast prairie, the western portion of the region is now relatively treeless farmland, its sandy, gravely soil ideal for growing sugar beets, potatoes, and grain crops. Small stands of bur oak, aspen, and cottonwood grow in the savannas and along river bottoms. To the east, where the ground is moist, grow forests of spruce, cedar, sedge, heath, and sphagnum moss. From prairies in the west to wetlands and forests in the east, wildlife is varied and abundant, and endangered and protected species find refuge here.

Glacial Lake Agassiz Plain Overview

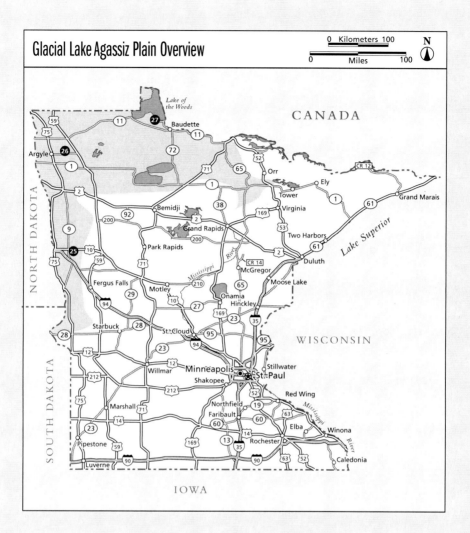

25 Buffalo River State Park

Buffalo River State Park is one of many western Minnesota areas where prairie preservation is going on. With 900 acres of grassland as a part of its 1,322 acres, it joins The Nature Conservancy Lands and Moorhead State University Regional Science Center in preserving 5,000 acres—one of the largest of Minnesota's remaining grasslands. The trail takes you through a portion of prairie but also along the beautiful Buffalo River where northern pike, walleye, and channel catfish are common catches. The Buffalo winds its way from tiny Lake Tamarack for 88 miles to the North Dakota border, dropping 635 feet, where it drains its gathered waters into the Red River. Along the way, you're likely to see deer, evidence of beaver activity, and other wildlife. The park has 12 miles of hiking trails through prairie and along the river.

Start: From the picnic and swim area parking lot
Distance: 2.5 miles
Approximate hiking time: 1 hour
Difficulty rating: Easy due to wide flat trails
Trail surface: Mowed grass and dirt trails
Lay of the land: Lake Agassiz beach ridge and Buffalo River valley
Canine compatibility: Leashed dogs permitted (leash must not exceed 6 feet)
Land status: State park
Nearest town: Glyndon and Hawley, MN

Fees/permits: State park vehicle permit required. Annual or day permits are available at the park office. Camping fees are separate.
Schedule: Open year-round for camping, swimming, hiking, skiing, and picnicking
Maps: USGS maps: Downer, MN; state park map
Trail contacts: Buffalo River State Park, Glyndon, MN; (218) 498-2124; Department of Natural Resources, St. Paul, MN; (651) 296-6157 or (888) 646-6367 (in MN only); www .dnr.state.mn.us/parks

Finding the trailhead: From the Twin Cities, drive north on U.S. Highway 10 to Detroit Lakes. The park entrance is on the left side of US 10 approximately 30 miles past Detroit Lakes. (Note: It's also 4.5 miles east of Glyndon and 14 miles east of Moorhead. Coming north on State Highway 94 take the Barnesville exit and go north on CR 15. Watch for signs.) *DeLorme: Minnesota Atlas & Gazetteer.* Page 59 C6

The Hike

As glaciers retreated into Canada, meltwater spilled into Minnesota, filling the Red River Valley and beyond. Called Glacial Lake Agassiz, this huge body of water was a key player in the development of Minnesota's varied landscape, especially in the northwest where retreating lake water left behind the debris, silt, sand, and gray clay collected and dumped by glaciers. The Red River Valley was shaped by these deposits, not by the Red River, as one might imagine. The Red River is merely a remnant of that ancient Glacial Lake Agassiz, collecting drainage off its dry lakebed from numerous tributaries including the Buffalo River. Prominent beach ridges left over from Lake Agassiz are characteristic of the Red River Valley. The rivers that flow over them, such as the Buffalo River, have slowly worn these high points in the prairie, leaving deep gorges and rocky rapids.

It was here in the Red River Valley that early settlers found the rich farmland they had traveled so far to find. Named after Louis Agassiz, a well-known geologist referred to as the father of glacial geology, Lake Agassiz once covered 17,000 square miles in northwest Minnesota. With the rise and fall of the lake water levels and centuries of glacial activity, the terrain was shaped such that the Red River flows north into Canada. As Lake Agassiz dried up, it left a fertile lake bottom along with prominent gravel ridges, one of which can be seen along the eastern edge of Buffalo River State Park.

Grasses of all types gradually migrated into the dry lake bottom, creating the rich, fertile, colorful prairie not seen since pioneer days. Only along the banks beneath the hardwood trees lining the Buffalo River can a person find shade from the intense afternoon sun. The river gets its name from the herds of bison that once roamed through here in massive herds. Bison bones occasionally peek out from beneath the soil, making this an area of great archaeological potential.

As with much of the surrounding area, the recent history of Buffalo River State Park is punctuated by land possession conflicts between the Native Americans, white settlers, and the U.S. government. By 1855, the land had been ceded to the U.S. government, and the Pembina Trail became an important and popular oxcart route in the fur trade business between St. Paul and Pembina, North Dakota. It wasn't until 1937, however, that Buffalo River State Park was established, thanks in part to the Moorhead Rod and Gun Club. The park began with just 242 acres, expanding throughout the years to 1,367 acres. Its prairies and river woods of elm, ash, cottonwood, oak,

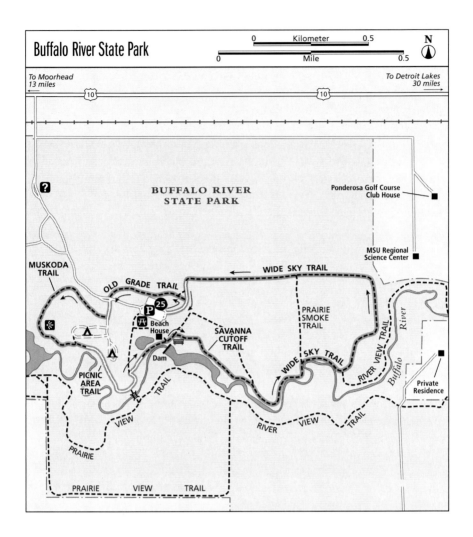

and basswood are alive with more than forty species of mammals including red fox, coyotes, and badgers. As the trail takes you through the open prairie and skirts the river, there's a good chance you'll see deer, which are plentiful in the park. Beaver are also abundant, as their many dams along the river will attest. Moose have occasionally been known to pass through the park, and more than 200 species of birds can be seen and heard including woodpeckers, great crested flycatchers, bobolink, phoebes, warblers, vireos, and colorful orioles.

Visitors can pick up interpretive brochures at the park office and explore self-guided trails to learn more about the park's natural history. Adjacent to the park is the Regional Science Center, an extension of the University of Minnesota, which hosts more than 24,000 visitors each year.

Prairie restoration is going on in many sections of Minnesota; however, the prairie in Buffalo River State Park and the adjoining scientific and natural area are known to be one of the finest and largest remaining prairie tracts in the state with more than 250 species of wildflowers and grasses. Researchers are finding that prairie grasses, with their dense root networks, greatly improve the productivity of soils. Most of this beneficial activity takes place underground as millions of microbes break down dead roots, turning them into soil nutrients. In addition, these microbes produce substances that glue the soil into small chunks through which ants, beetles, larvae and nematodes bore passageways. These passageways allow air and water to penetrate every inch of soil, allowing the prairie to regulate moisture. The porous nature of this soil allows new roots to find the nutrients and moisture they need to become vigorous plants.

Miles and Directions

0.0 Start from the east end of the picnic area and swimming beach parking lot. Follow the service road 0.1 mile, then turn left onto Old Grade Trail. Walk along the mowed trail over the flat, open lakebed of Glacial Lake Agassiz, now covered with prairie grasses and flowers.

0.2 Cross the paved park road and walk the dirt campground road past the dump station, and turn right onto Muskoda Trail. Hike west toward the Buffalo River. (FYI: Along the river, you will see white bur oak and basswood trees.)

0.6 A left at this intersection leads to the campground. Stay right to continue along the winding riverbanks. Here the trail drops into the wide, wooded floodplain of the Buffalo River and follows an old gravel/sand two-track road.

0.8 A right turn here crosses the river. Turn left toward the swimming beach, walk past the beach house, and follow the riverbank toward the beach house (leaving the two-track and walking across the grass between the river and swimming hole).

1.0 Walk past the beach house (to your left) and turn right onto Savanna Cutoff Trail, following Hiking Club Trail signs. The trail drops into an abandoned oxbow of the river here. Rest on the bench and watch for beavers and great blue herons.

1.3 A left completes the Savanna Cutoff loop. Stay right to follow Wide Sky Trail and continue along the river.

1.5 Prairie Smoke Trail intersects with Wide Sky Trail here. Continue east (right) on Wide Sky Trail.

BETTER BISON

Bison are becoming preferred grazers over cattle, and there's been a growing demand for bison products. Bison are easy keepers, better able to withstand the cold with no need for shelter. Because they're less finicky eaters than cattle, consuming more grass, bison also help retain and refurbish the natural prairies by grazing while on the move.

1.6 Wide Sky Trail intersects with River View Trail. Turn left to stay on Wide Sky Trail and head northeast across open prairie and away from the river. Look for wild asparagus, prairie sage, common milkweed, big bluestem, or turkey foot grasses.

1.9 You will see the Moorhead State University (MSU) Regional Science Center on the right.

2.1 Continue straight ahead on Wide Sky Trail, and walk across the prairie west toward the campground. A left turn follows Prairie Smoke Trail south.

2.4 Wide Sky Trail takes a jog left here onto an old asphalt road. Stay left at the intersection with Old Grade Trail, and follow the old road back to the parking area.

2.5 Arrive back at the parking area.

More Information

Local Information
Fargo-Moorhead Convention & Visitors Bureau: Fargo, ND; (800) 235-7654; www.fargomoor head.org

Local Events/Attractions
Barnesville Potato Days: Barnesville, MN; (800) 525-4901
Western Minnesota Steam Threshers Reunion: Labor Day Weekend, Rollag, MN; (701) 212-2034
We Fest: August, Detroit Lakes, MN; (800) 493-3378
Heritage Hjemkomst Interpretive Center: Moorhead, MN; (218) 299-5511
Clay County Museum & Archives: Moorhead, MN; (218) 299-5500
Red River of the North Riverkeepers: (701) 235-2895; www.riverkeepers.org; fishing, wildlife observation, nature trails, festivals, etc.

Accommodations
Buffalo River State Park: Glyndon, MN; (218) 498-2124 (Minnesota state parks)
Courtyard By Marriott: Moorhead, MN; (218) 284-1000
Red River Lodge: Fargo, ND; (701) 282-9100
Grand Inn: Moorhead, MN; (218) 233-7501

Restaurants
Hi-Ho Tavern: Dilworth, MN; (218) 287-2975
The Whistle Stop: Hawley, MN; (218) 483-4648
Castle Rock Supper Club: Hawley, MN; (218) 483-4604
Mr. Steak: Fargo, ND; (701) 232-2400

Local Outdoor Retailers
Scheels: Fargo, ND; (701) 232-8903
Gander Mountain: Fargo, ND; (701) 277-9979

26 Old Mill State Park

A fascinating history surrounding the preserved mills in Old Mill State Park makes this hike a must for history buffs. Nature lovers will enjoy it as well, for a variety of wildlife including moose frequent the area. In addition, the flat terrain allows spectacular views of northern lights. The trail takes you into the open prairie, through the riverine forest along the Middle River, across the river on a footbridge where the trail leads to a small swimming lake, and, at the north end of the park, to the old mills. The park is a combination of prairie, oak savanna, riverine forest, and Agassiz beach ridges created by the glacial lake that once covered much of northwestern Minnesota. Several scenic overlooks along the way will give you a good view of the river and the landscape's vast open area.

Start: From the south end of the parking area, at the start of the Agassiz Self-Guided Trail
Distance: 3.6 miles
Approximate hiking time: 2 hours, taking time to explore the old mill
Difficulty rating: Easy due to wide, flat trails
Trail surface: Mowed grass and dirt trails
Lay of the land: Riverine forest along the Middle River, oak savanna and prairie on old Lake Agassiz beach ridges
Other trail users: None
Canine compatibility: Leashed dogs permitted
Land status: State park

Nearest town: Warren and Thief River Falls, MN
Fees/permits: State park vehicle permit required. Annual or day permits are available at the park office. Camping fees are separate.
Schedule: Open year-round
Maps: USGS maps: Florian SE, MN; state park map
Trail contacts: Old Mill State Park, Argyle, MN; (218) 437-8174; Department of Natural Resources, St. Paul, MN; (651) 296-6157 or (888) 646-6367 (in MN only); www.dnr.state .mn.us/parks

Finding the trailhead: From Argyle, take CR 4 east 13 miles. The park entrance is a half mile north of CR 4 on CR 39. Watch for signs. *DeLorme: Minnesota Atlas & Gazetteer:* Page 80 B5

The Hike

Surrounded by flat, sparsely populated farmland in the northwestern corner of Minnesota lies an historic treasure. Old Mill State Park—where lovely prairie flowers bloom (bottle gentians, purple coneflowers), and morel mushrooms make the mouths of mushroom-lovers water—is a place where history is relived each year. This flat, rich farmland is located at what was once the lake bottom of the ancient Glacial Lake Agassiz. This was the place Lars Larson chose to settle in 1881 when he arrived in America from Sweden, bringing with him his family and his trade. The Middle River most likely figured highly in his decision to locate there, as water was necessary for powering the flour mill he planned to build. Completed in 1886, the mill was destroyed by a flash flood just two years later. Undaunted, Lars built another mill, this time powered by wind. To his dismay, this mill also fell, this time to a powerful windstorm that brought it down in 1889, just one year after being built. For his third mill, Larson decided to return to waterpower.

Larson's son, John, also built a mill in 1889; however, he decided to use an 8-horsepower Case steam engine purchased in Wisconsin. It's this mill and the Case 359 steam engine, rebuilt in 1957, that are fired up at the park each year on the last Saturday in August so visitors can experience flour making nineteenth-century style. After the grain is ground into flour by the huge granite grindstones, it's packaged and sold to visitors. This event is sponsored by the Marshall County Historical Society, volunteers from the Friends of Old Mill State Park, and park staff. John's mill and his father's third mill were moved to the park in 1897 and were owned and operated by several people before finally being sold to the state in 1937.

While the old gristmill is the focus of Old Mill State Park, the northern lights, animal life, colorful prairie wildflowers, and tasty morel mushrooms are also attractions for visitors, who number more than 21,000 annually. If it's morels your mouth is watering for, head down to the forest along the river in the spring where you'll find stands of bur oak, aspen, and cottonwood—all providing just the right habitat for this highly sought-after mushroom. The park advises not to over-pick but to leave enough mushrooms to perpetuate and for others to enjoy. Before picking, ask park officials to help you identify this mushroom, and be certain not to eat anything you can't positively identify.

Larson Homestead

It's said that this portion of northwestern Minnesota, with its flat farmland that stretches for miles in a country nearly devoid of interfering lights, is a good place to watch the northern lights. In addition, the park is geographically situated in an area where northern lights make regular appearances. The aurora borealis appears at all times of the year up here, but will light the night skies more frequently in the fall.

As you make this hike, which includes a small section of the Agassiz Self-Guided Trail, you may encounter some of the park's wildlife. Moose frequently move through the area. Bear, timber wolves, otter, beaver, fox, white-tailed jackrabbits, and snowshoe hare are also common. Among the more than 100 bird species are marsh and red-tailed hawk, sharp-tailed grouse, scarlet tanagers, saw-whet owls, pileated woodpeckers, meadowlarks, warblers, finches, and hawks.

Prairie clover

Also watch for the beautiful closed or bottle gentian *(Gentiana andrewsii)*. The flowers of the bottle gentian plant appear closed due to inward-projecting lobes at the tops of united petals, and it takes a large, strong bee to force its way inside to get at the nectar. The plant blooms in late August through much of September. Occasionally flowers have been known to bloom into November. Bottle or closed gentian thrives in rich low prairies, meadows, and woodland openings. The gentian family derives its name from King Gentius of Illyria who discovered the medicinal value of the plant. Bitters made from the plant act as stimulating tonics for the digestive system through a reflex via the taste buds. The plant is also used to tone and strengthen the liver, to stimulate the secretion of saliva from the salivary glands, and as a stimulant to quicken and enliven the physiological function of the body.

Miles and Directions

0.0 Start from the south end of the parking area, The wide, mowed trail is marked as a hiking/skiing trail. Proceed south. View a patch of open prairie to the left.

0.1 Enter oak savanna.

0.3 The trail forks; take a left. Next, take a right onto a well-maintained trail. Pass by some very large oaks, one with a 5-foot circumference.

0.4 Stop and rest on the wooden benches to enjoy an overlook of the Middle River and beaver dam. The trail turns to the east after the overlook.

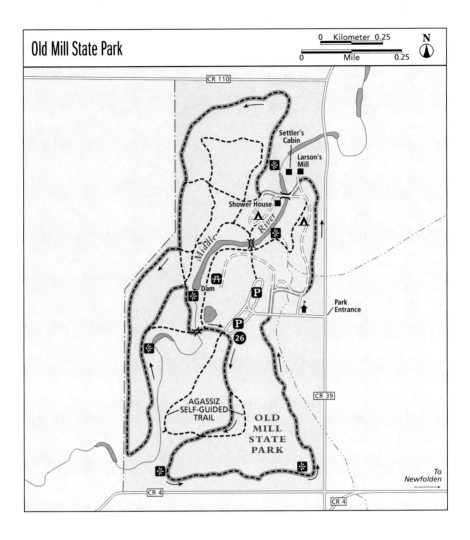

0   Kilometer   0.25   **N**

0   Mile   0.25

CR 110

Settler's Cabin

Larson's Mill

Shower House

River

Middle

Dam

P

Park Entrance

26

CR 39

AGASSIZ SELF-GUIDED TRAIL

OLD MILL STATE PARK

CR 4

CR 4

To Newfolden

0.6   Away from the riverine environment, reenter open prairie. (FYI: Notice new plant growth and evidence of controlled burns used by the park to keep the forest from encroaching.)

0.7   Pass a stand of jack and red pine and another bench from which to admire the prairie, or look for birds and wildflowers.

1.1   Cross the paved park road. The trail joins the gravel service road for 100 feet. Then take a right before entering the service area at Hiking Club Trail signs. Watch for wild asparagus.

1.3   Cross a gravel road that leads to the group campground, and walk through a small red pine plantation. Look for deer sign. Here, you will be back on the trail.

1.5   The mowed trail comes close to a gravel road. Stay on the trail. Round a corner and come out into a large clearing where the Settler's Cabin and Larson's Mill are located. Another trail on the right dead-ends a few feet into the woods. (FYI: This was the original wagon road farmers used to take their grain to the mill. Ruts cut by the wagon wheels are still clearly visible. The Larson Homestead was built in 1883. Interpretive signs provided by the Marshall County Historical Society tell the story. Learn how the Larsons brought Scotch pine seeds from the old country and scattered them around the property.) Continue on past the mill and along the river, to the left of the mill.

1.6 Cross a bridge over the Middle River and enter the north side of the campground, keeping the shower house to your left. Turn right where the trail departs from the campground and head north.

1.7 Come to a river overlook and riverine forest of ash and oaks mixed with some patches of prairie encouraged by prescribed burns. Then, pass through a large stand of quaking aspen.

2.3 The trail follows along the edge between woods and prairie.

2.4 A left heads east, back toward the campground. Take a right and proceed south.

2.5 Take a right at this four-way intersection and enjoy the hundred-year-old scotch pines that live on from the Larson's seeds.

3.3 Enjoy an overlook of the river at a sharp bend, common in the relatively young rivers that cut across the old Glacial Lake Agassiz lakebed.

3.4 A right here leads back toward the parking area. Keep left for another overlook opportunity before reaching the car.

3.5 Take a right at this intersection and view the dam on the Middle River. Follow signs to the swimming pond. Turn left and cross a cable suspension bridge with massive granite archways on either side of the river. Stay to the right of the spring-fed swimming pond.

3.6 Arrive back at the parking area and your vehicle.

More Information

Local Information
Thief River Falls Convention & Visitor Center: Thief River Falls, MN; (218) 681-3720 or (800) 827-1629; www.visitthiefriverfalls.com

Local Events/Attractions
Historic Riverwalk: Thief River Falls, MN
Peder Engelstad Pioneer Village: Turn-of-the century village open 1:00 to 5:00 p.m. daily from Memorial Day to Labor Day, (218) 681-5767
Bountiful Harvest: August, Peder Engelstad Pioneer Village; (218) 681-5767
Pennington County Fair: Thief River Falls, MN; contact visitor center

Accommodations
Hartwood Motel: Thief River Falls, MN; (218) 681-2640
Tourist Park, Parks and Recreation Department: (218) 681-2519. There are a number of parks for camping in Thief River Falls.

Restaurants
Dee's Kitchen: Thief River Falls, MN; (218) 681-9907
Handy Farms Country Cookin': Thief River Falls, MN; (218) 681-7686
Lantern Restaurant and Lounge: Thief River Falls, MN; (218) 681-8211

Stone suspension bridge over the creek

Minnesota State Parks Hiking Club: DNR Information Center, Twin Cities; (218) 437-8174 or (888) 646-6367. Naturalist programs are offered on a seasonal basis from Memorial Day weekend through Labor Day.

Local Outdoor Retailers

Fleet Supply: Thief River Falls, MN; (218) 681-2850

27 Zippel Bay State Park

Lake of the Woods and Rainy River are great fishing grounds if you like walleye. Fishing, swimming, and hiking are only a few of the recreation opportunities at Zippel Bay State Park, where wildlife is prolific and bird-watching is a popular activity. Numerous flowers including four species of lady's slippers, a variety of edible berries including cranberries and Juneberries, and edible mushrooms grow along the hiking trail and in the woods. This is a place where you are likely to see sandhill cranes, white pelicans, and double-crested cormorants, along with several species of shorebirds. It's also home to the endangered piping plover.

Start: From the swimming beach/picnic area parking lot

Distance: 1.3 miles

Approximate hiking time: 1 hour

Difficulty rating: Easy walking along a beach

Trail surface: Sand and grass

Lay of the land: Remnants of Glacial Lake Agassiz, flat lakeshore, and sandy beach of North America's largest lake, excluding the Great Lakes

Other trail users: None

Canine compatibility: Leashed dogs permitted

Land status: State park

Nearest town: Baudette, MN

Fees/permits: State park vehicle permit required. Annual or day permits are available at the park office. Camping fees are separate.

Schedule: Open year-round

Maps: USGS maps: Williams SE, MN; state park map

Trail contacts: Zippel Bay State Park, Williams, MN; (218) 783-6252; Department of Natural Resources, St. Paul, MN; (651) 296-6157 or (888) 646-6367 (in MN only); www.dnr.state .mn.us/parks

Finding the trailhead: From Baudette, drive northwest 10.5 miles on Highway 172 and take a left (west) onto CR 8. Travel 6 miles to the park entrance road, which is CR 34, and take a right (north). *DeLorme: Minnesota Atlas & Gazetteer:* Page 93 C9

The Hike

A narrow channel links a small, quiet bay from giant-sized Lake of the Woods—the focus of Zippel Bay State Park, with its 3,000 acres of jack pine, birch, and sandy beach. The lake itself is more than 55 miles across, encompassing 1,485 square miles.

One-third of it is in Minnesota. Although the lake contains many twists, turns, islands, bays, and peninsulas, Minnesota's portion is a wide expanse of open water known to early voyageurs as Big Traverse. Canada owns a much larger portion including the lake's 14,000 islands and countless peninsulas. Lake of the Woods was named for its pine-covered islands.

Named after one of the area's first white settlers, Wilhelm Zippel, the park harbors a variety of wildlife including the endangered piping plover. This small, stocky shorebird, resembling a sandpiper, feeds on worms, fly larvae, beetles, crustaceans, and other invertebrates it finds in the sand. Nearly extinct in the Great Lakes states, the piping plover has dwindled to 1,348 pairs in the United States. Human disturbance and habitat destruction are major causes of the piping plover's decline. Additionally, increased human habitation near beaches encourages the plover's enemies to move in—skunks, raccoons, and gulls attracted by human refuse. With only fifty breeding individuals, Lake of the Woods is considered the largest piping plover breeding area remaining in Minnesota and the Great Lakes region. Zippel Bay is one of these areas. Visitors can help ensure this species' survival by keeping their distance from nesting and feeding birds. Pine and Curry Islands near the southwest corner of Lake of the Woods also harbor nesting plovers and are protected by The Nature Conservancy and the State Scientific and Natural Areas Program.

Lake of the Woods and Zippel Bay State Park lie on the eastern portion of the Lake Agassiz lowlands. A flat, poorly drained lake plain where topographical relief is generally less than 50 feet characterizes this area. Peatlands are common in the low-

Lake of the Woods shoreline looking west

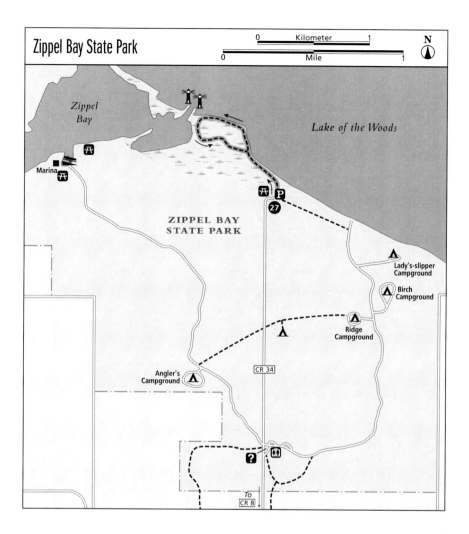

Zippel Bay

Lake of the Woods

Marina

ZIPPEL BAY
STATE PARK

Lady's-slipper
Campground

Birch
Campground

Ridge
Campground

Angler's
Campground

CR 34

To
CR 8

land, dominated by bog forest species of black spruce and tamarack. Aspen, birch, and jack pine clothe the upland regions. Peatlands in this area developed from a process called lake filling, where aquatic vegetation of various types invades the lake, creating floating mats and filling in the lake. Infilling changes water depth, allowing semi-aquatic plants and mosses to move in. Peat bogs began to develop nearly 5,000 years ago when the climate was cooler and wetter, slowly developing into two types of peat lands—bog and fen. Bogs are dominated by sphagnum moss and stands of black spruce and tamarack. Grasses, sedges, and reeds cover fens. If left long enough, these peat deposits will eventually be compressed into coal.

Lake of the Woods is home to the mouth of the Rainy River, which begins its Minnesota journey in Rainy Lake near Baudette. It's a fairly mild river with few rapids and a low gradient, dropping just 10 feet on the way to its destination. The river's gradient reflects the flatness of Lake Agassiz's lakebed, which is included in its watershed at Lake of the Woods (a remnant of that giant glacial lake). The Rainy River was used extensively during logging days for transporting logs from Big Fork, Little Fork, Black and Rapid River pineries to mills in Baudette and Canada. The peak year for logging was 1917, but by 1937 the last of the big sawmills closed when readily available timber was exhausted. Today, large paper mills operate in Baudette and International Falls, where stringent water-quality laws are slowly improving waterways that had long suffered from the industry's effects.

The sandy beach of Lake of the Woods where the hike begins reveals an excellent record of birds and mammals that have walked along the shore. The immense lake is so impressive that, on a clear day, hikers can see the curvature of the earth, and islands seem to float on the distant lake surface. At the hike midpoint, Zippel Bay comes into view through an inlet from Lake of the Woods bordered by two lighted rock jetties. Here, where large ash trees have taken hold in the sandy soil, you may observe a double-crested cormorant drying its wings or hear the repeating call of the sandhill crane, which nests in the park. This is a peaceful spot to watch the waves wash up onto the beach and listen to bird activity.

Miles and Directions

0.0   Start from the parking lot by the picnic area/swimming beach. Walk north toward the swimming beach and take in the expansive view of this gigantic lake. On the west side of the beach area is an information sign that describes how Zippel Bay got its name. This is

Lighthouse at the entrance to Zippel Bay from Lake of the Woods

the beginning of the Hiking Club Trail. The trail begins as a wide, mowed path with willow, vetch, and poison ivy lining the edges.

0.3 The trail forks. Turn right and walk out onto the lakeshore. From this point, the trail leads along the sand beach, where you are likely to get your feet wet.

0.6 Reach the lighted rock jetties built by the Coast Guard that mark the inlet to Zippel Bay. Turn east and head back on a shaded trail, scattered with oaks and ash trees, which offers glimpses of interior marshlands.

0.9 This intersection marks the loop where the beach walk began. Stay right to continue toward the parking area.

1.3 Arrive back at the parking area.

More Information

Local Information

Lake of the Woods Tourism: Baudette, MN; (218) 634-1174 or (800) 382-3474; www.lake ofthewoodsmn.com

Local Events/Attractions

Annual Kenora Harbourfest: Beginning of August, Kenora Recreation Centre & Grounds
Lake of the Woods County Fair: Baudette, MN; (218) 634-1034

Accommodations

Walleye Inn Motel: Baudette, MN; (218) 634-1550
Baudette Motel: Baudette, MN; (218) 634-2600
Lakeroad Lodge Motel: Baudette, MN; (218) 634-2336
Royal Dutchman Motel: Baudette, MN; (218) 634-1024 or (800) 908-1024

Restaurants

Rosalie's Restaurant and Lounge: Baudette, MN; (218) 634-9422
Northlake Café: Baudette, MN; (218) 634-9807

Local Outdoor Retailers

Randle's Ben Franklin: Baudette, MN; (218) 634-2332

Framed by the Boundary Waters Canoe Area Wilderness (BWCAW) along the Minnesota/Ontario border and Lake Superior's rugged North Shore, northeastern Minnesota is one of the most spectacular areas in the United States. Also called the Arrowhead (for its shape), its typical landscape features are glacier-scoured ridges, granite domes, and volcanic cliffs. Located entirely within the coniferous forest biome, the northeastern Minnesota landscape is covered with pine, spruce, fir, cedar, and birch. Near Lake Superior, where the large body of water moderates temperatures, eastern hardwoods, such as maple and oak, flourish. Lakes, rivers, and a tri-continental divide separating Hudson Bay, Lake Superior, and Mississippi watersheds dominated the area. Paralleling the scenic coastline of Lake Superior, the largest freshwater lake in the world, is an ancient volcanic mountain range called the Sawtooth Mountains. These much-eroded hills provide a rugged and scenic setting for one of the premier hiking trails in the United States, the Superior Hiking Trail. Rivers along the North Shore are relatively short, cutting dramatic canyons and gorges through bedrock in their steep descent to Lake Superior. BWCAW and Voyageurs National Park consists of a network of thousands of lakes that stretch westward across Minnesota's northern border from Lake Superior and flow north into Hudson Bay.

Rocks in this region were formed during the earliest geologic time, more than 600 million years ago, according to scientists. They are part of the Canadian Shield, a mass of Precambrian rock that extends northward more than 3,000 miles and is part of the ancient core of North America. Each continent has such a core. Because they have been exposed from glacial scouring, these Precambrian rocks in northeastern Minnesota are among the most well known in the world. They include granites formed from molten lava within the earth's crust, and greenstones formed from underwater lava flows. Shallow inland seas left sedimentary iron deposits at the western edge of the region, an area explored heavily for mineral deposits. Along the North Shore of Lake Superior, the youngest rocks in the region can be found where, 1.1 billion years ago, the continent started to split from northeastern Minnesota down to Kansas. Where the earth's crust spread, lavas welled up and spread out from the rift, forming the dark basalts that form the landscape features seen today. Three periods of glaciations, ending around 10,000 years ago, scoured away any sedimentary deposits and eroded material, exposing these ancient rocks. To the west and south of the region lie thick glacial deposits that cover the underlying Precambrian rocks.

Today northeastern Minnesota boasts a wealth of resources that are preserved and protected for recreation. The BWCAW is the only wilderness area in the United States set aside for canoe travel. There are also two long-distance hiking trails that traverse this remote wilderness area, the Border Route Trail and the Kekekabic Trail. A third long-distance trail, the Superior Hiking Trail, follows the scenic ridges along Lake Superior from Duluth to the Canadian border. North Shore Rivers provide focal points for a series of state parks along the same stretch. Voyageurs National Park is adjacent to the BWCAW and has hiking trails accessible only by water. Northeastern Minnesota has a national monument (Grand Portage) and an underground mine state park in addition to many other state parks, state forests, two national forests, and scientific and natural areas. Hikes in this region are all centered near lakes or rivers and have the remote feel of the Northwoods.

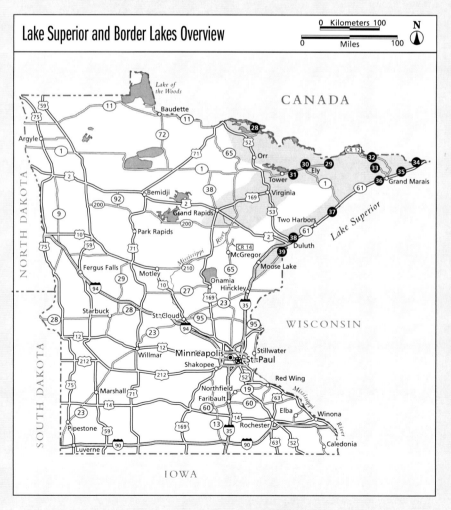

Lake Superior and Border Lakes Overview

28 Voyageurs National Park

Situated at the top of the state, Cruiser Lake Trail takes you over ridges and past beaver ponds, lakes, and several secluded hike-in camp spots. This magnificent, water-encircled hike crosses a section of the 75,000-acre, roadless Kabetogama Peninsula and goes by Cruiser Lake at its midpoint. The trail continues all the way to Rainy Lake at the Minnesota/Ontario border. To get to the trailhead, you'll have to take a boat across Kabetogama Lake into Lost Bay. You'll be floating on the historic water highway that transported the French voyageurs great distances to deliver their goods for trade.

Start: From the east end of Lost Bay on Kabetogama Lake

Distance: 7.8 miles out and back

Approximate hiking time: 4.5 hours

Difficulty rating: Moderate due to hiking over rocky ridges on well-maintained trails

Trail surface: A single footpath with roots, rocks, and dirt-covered trails

Lay of the land: A hike across the Kabetogama peninsula that separates Kabetogama and Rainy Lakes

Other trail users: Canoeists (who use the trail as a portage)

Canine compatibility: Dogs not permitted

Land status: National park

Nearest town: Kabetogama, MN

Fees/permits: The boat on Cruiser Lake can

be rented. There is a three-day/two-night limit. Use of the boat requires a key and a signed agreement to wear life jackets. Hikers have to carry in their life jackets if they plan to use the park boat.

Schedule: Open year-round. Rainy Lake Visitor Center is open year-round with limited winter hours. Kabetogama Lake and Ash River visitor centers are open seasonally, May through September.

Maps: USGS maps: Ash River, MN; Lake States Interpretive Association sells maps at all visitor centers.

Trail contacts: Voyageurs National Park, International Falls, MN; (218) 283-9821; www.nps .gov/voya

Finding the trailhead: From Orr: If hikers have a canoe or boat, the best park entrance to use is the Ash River Visitor Center. To get there, drive north on U.S. Highway 53. Turn east on CR 129 (Ash River Trail). Turn north on the Ash River Visitor Center entrance road.

The Cruiser Lake Trail is only accessible by water. Hikers need to travel by canoe or boat to the trailhead. There is a dock at the trailhead where watercraft can be tied up for the day. Hikers without watercraft must arrange for a water taxi from Kabetogama or Ash River. To travel to the trailhead by canoe, start at the Ash River boat landing and paddle north into a narrow channel (about a mile) to a quarter of a mile portage between Lost Lake and Long Slough Bay. Paddle 1 mile north on Long Slough to Lost Bay, then 2 miles east to the large dock at the eastern end of Lost Bay. To travel to the trailhead by boat, start at the Ash River boat landing and motor west/northwest past Round Bear Island. Then head east into Lost Bay and travel to the eastern end (5.5 miles total). *DeLorme: Minnesota Atlas & Gazetteer.* Page 87 A6

The Hike

Establishing a national park in Minnesota was nearly a century-long project involving public hearings, intensive studies, heated debate, and government delays. It all began in 1891, when a proposal was made to the Minnesota Legislature to establish a national park along the Canadian border from Lake Vermilion to Lake of the Woods. After some minor revisions, the bill passed and was sent up to the federal level, where it was ignored. The story from there is one of conflicting interests, red tape, and seeming disinterest by the federal government. The logging industry, paper mills, and hunters all took issue with the project, and the conflicts took years to resolve. Soon after Elmer L. Andersen took over the governorship in 1960, the national park proposal was revisited, and, from that point on, Andersen pushed persistently, pulling other influential people in with him until the federal government finally authorized Voyageurs National Park in 1971. After the state of Minnesota donated land, the park was formally established in April of 1975. Dominated by water—one-third of the park is covered by water—Voyageurs stretches 218,054 acres, encompassing four major lakes (Rainy, Kabetogama, Namakan, and Sand Point), plus more than thirty minor lakes.

Each continent has a shield (or continental nucleus) of Precambrian rock in which its whole history is documented. North America's nucleus is called the Canadian

Crossing Cruiser Lake

Shield—which, in its southern portion, embraces Voyageurs National Park. The shield tells the continent's history from 3,600 million to 600 million years ago. Voyageurs' wet landscape was formed when 2-mile-thick ice sheets, applying 150 tons of pressure per square foot, gouged out holes and depressions in the northern landscape. Then the glaciers melted, filling the holes with water, resulting in lakes, ponds, streams, and riverbeds. They also removed rock and other debris, leaving some of the oldest exposed rock formations found anywhere in the world. Scrape marks on the rocks, evidence of glacial scouring, are still visible today in Voyageurs National Park. What dry land there was soon became vegetated with vast forests, grasses, and other plant life, which offered food to the wildlife and humans who eventually followed.

This vast northern watershed that drains north into the Hudson Bay was once a transportation paradise for Native Americans and, later, French and British fur traders. For hundreds of years, Native Americans and Europeans (called *voyageurs*) paddled the lengthy system of connected waterways, their goods neatly packed in fragile birch bark canoes. The voyageurs, for whom the park is named, lived rough, often dangerous lives. They paddled up to sixteen hours a day, risking threatening confrontations with rivals in the fur trade or nature's more dangerous moments. They were generally a happy lot in spite of their rugged adventures, and the sounds of their voices raised in song echoed through the wilderness as they paddled. So well worn was their route along this extensive northern waterway that it became the international boundary between the United States and Canada. Through the years, the fur trade, gold mining, logging, and commercial fishing thrived along this section of valuable water highway, which was destined to become Voyageurs National Park.

Water remains the park's focal point today. Most of the trails and campsites are accessible only by boating across a lake or river. Wetlands exist in many forms, including peat lands, inland freshwater marshes, and riparian wetlands. Peat lands consist of thick deposits of slowly decaying material. Bogs and fens are the major types and occur in old lake basins or other topographic depressions. Bogs are fairly low in nutrients, yet some plant varieties such as sphagnum moss, pitcher plants, Venus flytraps, and many orchid species thrive there. Richer in nutrients, fens are where sedges, willows, grasses, and reeds are present. Freshwater marshes form in prairie potholes, surround ponds and lakes, or occur as emergent wetlands. They support soft-stemmed plants such as rushes, cattails, and water lilies. Riparian wetlands form on floodplains of rivers and streams and often dry up for a while during the season.

Although it took a while for humans to realize it, wetlands play a crucial ecological role. Their vegetation prevents stream-bank erosion and flooding, purifies water, provides habitat and food for wildlife, and offers recreation opportunities for humans. Wetlands were not always regarded as necessary to the health of an environment. To many, they were smelly, bug-incubating environments in desperate need of filling or draining, or, at the very least, alteration. Unfortunately, thousands of acres of wetlands disappeared and, with them, many species of wildlife that depended on them for survival—species that biologists are attempting to restore.

The wetlands of Voyageurs National Park are alive with wildlife, especially in the spring when thousands of migrating birds return to their northern summer home. Osprey, eagles, and great blue heron nest within the park where a visitor might also see kingfishers, mergansers, loons, and cormorants.

Miles and Directions

0.0 Start from the east end of Lost Bay on Kabetogama Lake. (Note: Paddling a canoe from the Ash River Visitor Center takes about an hour and a half. There are also water taxi services and outfitters in the area communities.) At the far east end of Lost Bay, you will land at a large dock. The trailhead is clearly marked, and there are outhouses available. The narrow, rock- and root-covered trail heads east and north across the Kabetogama Peninsula.

0.1 Take a right at this intersection toward Agnes Lake. The trail ascends a granite ridge where it can be difficult to spot. Well-placed rock cairns help guide the way.

0.3 View Agnes Lake to your right. A spur trail leads to the campsite; stay left on the main trail.

0.6 A boardwalk and wooden planks lead the way over some low and wet spots as the trail skirts a black spruce swamp. (FYI: The forest consists of a mix of mature aspen, large jack pine, oaks, ash, and balsam fir. Look for moose and wolf sign along the trail.)

1.9 Take a right at this intersection and keep going north toward Cruiser Lake. A left heads west to Ek Lake. On the right, a boardwalk crosses a stream below an 8-foot-high beaver dam. Walk through dense stands of paper birch and maple.

3.0 On the left, a swiftly moving, singing creek drains a small valley and cascades down a 15-foot waterfall that drops into a black pool approximately 30 feet downstream. (**Option:** Taking a little side hike along the creek allows you to see this waterfall.) The trail crosses over the creek above the waterfall, and then begins a long, slow climb up a gentle ridge topped with large red pine, jack pine, and white cedar trees.

Iron ring from logging operations on Lost Bay

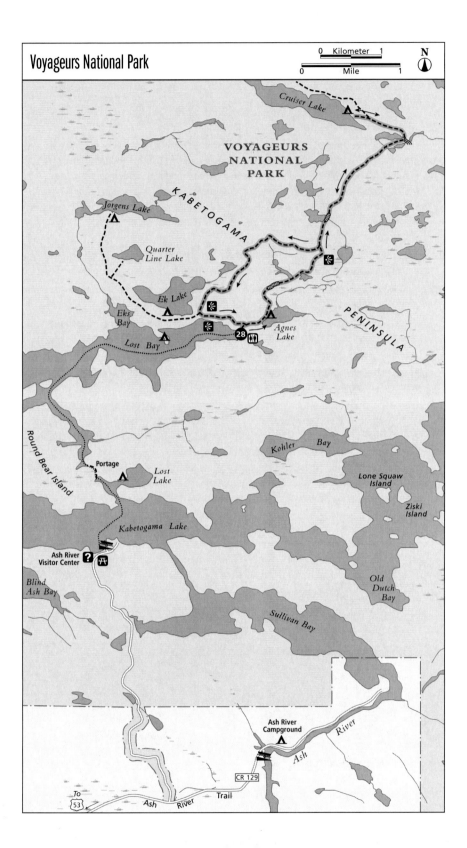

0 ___ Kilometer ___ 1

0 ___ Mile ___ 1

N

Cruiser Lake

VOYAGEURS
NATIONAL
PARK

KABETOGAMA

Jorgens Lake

Quarter
Line Lake

Ek Lake

Eks
Bay

Lost Bay

Agnes
Lake

28

PENINSULA

Kohler Bay

Round Bear Island

Portage

Lost
Lake

Lone Squaw
Island

Ziski
Island

Kabetogama Lake

Ash River
Visitor Center

Blind
Ash Bay

Old
Dutch
Bay

Sullivan Bay

Ash River
Campground

Ash River

Ash River Trail

CR 129

To
53

3.8 Turn left to take the spur trail to Cruiser Lake. A right continues toward the north shore of Cruiser Lake and then on to Rainy Lake.

3.9 The Cruiser Lake campsite is on a small island that can be accessed by a small footbridge. This is a scenic spot to picnic. (FYI: A canoe for paddling around on Cruiser Lake can be reserved no earlier than one week in advance at Kabetogama Lake Visitor Center. Hikers need to pick up a key at the visitor center prior to departing the mainland. Many people hike in and spend the night, then hike out again the next day.) Retrace your steps back to the main trail.

4.0 Back at the main trail, take a right to head back to Lost Bay.

5.9 After crossing the boardwalk below the 8-foot-high beaver dam, the trail goes left, back toward Agnes Lake. Take a right and turn to Ek Lake.

6.5 Take a left and proceed southwest at this unmarked intersection with an old trail, now closed, that heads north. In the future, you may not notice this trail as it will eventually be overgrown. Hike through a black spruce forest, and climb some small hills with scattered white pine.

7.0 The trail climbs a high, narrow, open ridge. Ek Lake is visible to the west.

7.2 A right at this intersection goes west and north toward Quarter Line and Jorgens Lakes. Take a left and head east toward Lost Bay. (FYI: There is another great snack and rest spot upon a high ridge overlooking Lost Bay.)

7.7 This intersection completes the loop. Take a right and proceed back to the dock; a left heads north to Agnes Lake.

7.8 Arrive back at the Lost Bay dock.

MAD AS A HATTER

Have you ever wondered where some of our antiquated sayings come from? Mad as a hatter is one that dates back to voyageur days when furs were in high demand for making fashionable hats. Madness was the resulting occupational disease of European hatters who breathed the mercury-saturated microscopic fibers released in the process of converting the furs to felt.

More Information

Local Information

Ash River Tourism Association: Ash River, MN; (800) 950-2061; www.ashriver.com

Kabetogama Lake Tourism Bureau: Lake Kabetogama, MN; (218) 875-2621 or (800) 524-9085; www.kabetogama.com

International Falls, Rainy Lake, and Ranier Convention and Visitors Bureau: International Falls, MN; (218) 283-9400 or (800) 325-5766; www.rainylake.org

Crane Lake Visitor and Tourism Bureau: Crane Lake, MN; (800) 362-7405; www.visitcranelake.com

Local Events/Attractions

Boat tours and naturalist programs have been offered on Rainy and Kabetogama Lakes in the past from mid-June through Labor Day. These may not be offered every year, so be sure to call or check the Web site for a schedule.

Historic Gold Mines: International Falls, MN

Ranier Summer Festival: August, Ranier, MN; (218) 286-5699. Includes street dance, art exhibits, food, and traditional Native powwow

Northern Minnesota District Fair: July, Littlefork, MN; (218) 278-6710

Accommodations

Ash Trail Lodge: Ash River, MN; (218) 374-3131 or (800) 777-4513 (reservations); www.ashtrail lodge.com

Anderson Motel: Orr, MN; (218) 757-3272

North Country Inn: Orr, MN; (218) 757-3778; www.northcountryinn.com

Rambler Motel: International Falls, MN; (218) 283-8454 or (800) 273-0464 (reservations)

Budget Host Inn: International Falls, MN; (218) 283-2577 or (800) 880-2577; www.budget hostinn.net

Thunderbird Lodge: International Falls, MN; (218) 286-3151 or (800) 351-5133; www.thunder birdlodge.info. Check the tourism bureaus listed above for more options.

Restaurants

Grandma's Pantry: Ranier, MN; (218) 286-5584 or (800) 391-3760

Billy's Spot Supper Club: International Falls, MN; (218) 283-2440 or (888) 208-1971

Chocolate Moose Restaurant: International Falls, MN; (218) 283-8888

Hike Tours

There are several naturalist programs and boat tours available.

Organizations

Friends of Voyageurs National Park and Lake States Interpretive Association: 3131 Highway 53, International Falls, MN; (218) 283-2103

Other Resources

Rendezvous–Voyageurs National Park **visitor guide** (published annually)

Voyageurs National Park: Water Route Footpath and Ski Trails by Jim DuFresne

Local Outdoor Retailers

Rainy Lake One Stop: Ranier, MN; (218) 286-5700; www.rainylakeonestop.com

29 Secret-Blackstone–Ennis Lake Trail

Located in the Superior National Forest on the edge of the Boundary Waters Canoe Area Wilderness, the Secret-Blackstone–Ennis Lake Trail ascends rocky, glacier-carved ridges that overlook small pothole lakes left by glacial meltwater. This area is known for fishing, rock climbing, and scenic vistas. Although this is a short hike, take time to catch your breath and linger at some of the beautiful overlooks on this rugged trail.

Start: From the Secret-Blackstone parking off the Moose Lake Road
Distance: 3.5-mile loop, with additional loop options available
Approximate hiking time: 2 hours
Difficulty rating: Moderate due to up and down, rocky terrain
Trail surface: Forested trails
Lay of the land: Aspen-birch-white pine forest with balsam fir present throughout, maple, spruce and black ash in low-lying areas
Other trail users: Anglers, overnight campers, and rock climbers

Canine compatibility: Dogs permitted
Land status: National forest
Nearest town: Ely, MN
Fees/permits: Self-issuing permit stations
Schedule: Open year-round, used by snowshoers in the winter
Maps: USGS maps: Snowbank Lake, MN, Ojibway Lake, MN
Trail contacts: U.S. Forest Service, Kawishiwi Ranger District, Ely, MN; (218) 365-7600

Finding the trailhead: From Ely, drive east on Highway 169 and in 2 miles pass through the town of Winton. Proceed east and in 2 more miles you will cross a bridge over Garden Lake (unmarked). Here, Highway 169 becomes CR 18 (also known as Fernberg Trail). Drive east on Fernberg Trail for 14 miles and take a left onto FS 438 (Moose Lake Road) and go 2 miles to a parking area on the right. *DeLorme: Minnesota Atlas & Gazetteer:* Page 89 E8

The Hike

Located 20 miles east of Ely, where the Superior National Forest borders the BWCAW, is a great little hiking area. The Secret-Blackstone–Ennis Lake Trail offers a variety of scenery, terrain, and recreation. The trail encircles Secret and Blackstone Lakes, traverses the cliffs on the north shore of Ennis Lake, and skirts two glacial pothole lakes.

As you hike this trail you will see evidence of an incredible force of nature and the earth's capacity to regenerate. On July 4, 1999, a record storm, with straight-line winds reaching 80 to 100 mph, blew through northeastern Minnesota damaging an estimated 380,000 acres, including 130 miles of hiking trails. An estimated twenty to twenty-five million trees were blown down or snapped off. One-third of the BWCAW was affected—the most extensive damage visited on the area since European settlement.

The heaviest hit areas were on the hilltops and ridges, with low areas generally left untouched. The trail was rerouted in some places to dodge large root balls of blow-downs. Birch, aspen, and balsam fir stands were completely leveled like swamp grass in some areas with only a few scattered majestic pines left standing. Even some of these sturdier trees were snapped off halfway up their trunks. Now, ten years later, Secret-Blackstone–Ennis Lake Trail allows many opportunities to count growth rings on giant pines, birch, and black ash trees more than one hundred years old and see new plant and tree growth.

As you follow the first part of the trail, Blackstone Lake appears to the left. This quiet lake has a campsite with a fire grate and a latrine for overnight use. The trail ascends a series of ridges after passing Blackstone Lake. As you begin climbing the first ridge, a view of Moose Lake appears to the north. Follow the steep rises to cliffs looking down onto pothole lakes surrounded by bogs or marshes. Pause to view the evidence of succession as black spruce and other vegetation proceed to fill in the depressions. The trail then drops into a mixed hardwood forest with scattered pines along the ridges.

As the trail nears the Ennis Lake overlook, the lake appears, stretched out 200 feet below for a spectacular view. Rock climbers frequent this spot during the summer to take advantage of 100-foot cliffs that have fractured into long vertical cracks and blocky ledges. If the area is clear, you can scramble down an unmarked fourth-class

View of Ennis Lake

trail to the right for a view of the overhanging cliffs from below. Watch out for poison ivy growing alongside the base of this trail.

The main trail meanders along the north shore of Ennis Lake with other great views. Blueberries line the north shore of the lake and are usually ripe around late July. Also here are scenic views of the lake, picnic spots, and refreshing swimming holes. Anglers hike in and fish these spots for small-mouth bass.

A section of the Secret-Blackstone–Ennis Lake Trail constructed in 1999 departs Ennis Lake and winds north into the woods past the east end of Secret and Blackstone Lakes. The new section joins the old loop around Blackstone Lake and crosses an unmapped portage trail that connects Blackstone Lake to Flash Lake.

This spectacular trail offers opportunities in every season for birding, viewing wildlife, and reflecting in peaceful solitude.

Miles and Directions

0.0 Start by going south from the parking area, under a power line, and across a boardwalk with a marsh on the right.

0.1 The trail meets the portage to Flash Lake. Stay to the right. The trail crosses a stream with a small waterfall and calm pool below.

0.3 A left turn follows the north loop around Blackstone Lake. Stay to the right. Blackstone Lake will come into view.

Overlooking a great swimming hole and campsite

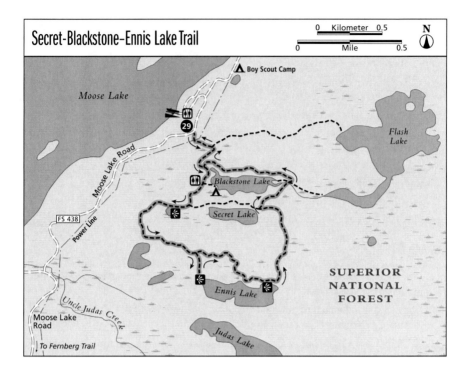

0   Kilometer   0.5

0   Mile   0.5

N

▲ Boy Scout Camp

Moose Lake

29

Flash Lake

Blackstone Lake

Moose Lake Road

Secret Lake

FS 438

Power Line

SUPERIOR
NATIONAL
FOREST

Ennis Lake

Uncle Judas Creek

Moose Lake
Road

Judas Lake

To Fernberg Trail

0.4   A spur trail to the left (390 feet) leads to a rather nice campsite on Blackstone Lake. (It is located far enough off the main trail to allow for privacy. Hikers, climbers, and anglers have all been known to use this site.) The trail to the right leads to the pit latrine. Continue straight ahead.

0.5   Turn right to continue toward Ennis Lake. A left heads east along a narrow ridge between the south shore of Blackstone Lake and the north shore of Secret Lake.

0.6   Climb up an overlook from a rocky ledge of a small pothole lake.

1.3   A spur trail to the right leads to the climbing area and overlook at the northwest end of Ennis Lake. Turn right. Straight ahead, the trail follows the north shore of the lake.

1.4   Walk out on the top of scenic 100-foot cliffs overlooking Ennis Lake. (FYI: During the summer months climbers often occupy this spot. This is also a great picnic stop.) From here go back and take the trail to the right to descend along the north shore of the lake.

1.8   The trail meets the lake edge and offers a series of scenic views as well as fishing, swimming, and picnicking spots.

1.9   The trail leaves Ennis Lake and heads north, meandering through more storm-damaged forest on its way toward Secret Lake.

2.5   A left turn follows the trail west that passes between the south shore of Blackstone Lake and the north shore of Secret Lake, along a narrow ridge. Stay to the right to skirt the east end of Blackstone Lake.

2.7   A portage trail between Blackstone and Flash Lakes crosses the trail. Continue straight ahead. The main trail joins a portage between Blackstone (to the left) and Flash (to the right) Lakes. You will follow this portage trail for about 40 feet, then keep left to stay on the main trail just before the portage trail reaches Flash Lake.

3.2 This intersection completes the loop around Blackstone Lake. Turn right to retrace your steps back to the parking area.

3.4 The trail meets the Flash Lake portage trail. Stay to the left to return to the trailhead.

3.5 Arrive back at the trailhead and parking lot.

More Information

Local Information
Ely Chamber of Commerce: Ely, MN; (218) 365-6123 or (800) 777-7281; www.ely.org
Boundary Waters Broadcasters: WELY Radio 94.5 FM, 1450 AM; Ely, MN; (218) 365-4444; www.wely.com

Local Events/Attractions
Blueberry Arts Festival: Late July, Ely, MN
Watercolor Show: July, Ely, MN; (218) 365-6123
Embarrass Fair: Late August, Embarrass, MN; (218) 365-6123
Harvest Moon Festival: Early September, Ely, MN; (218) 365-6123
Brandenburg Gallery: Ely, MN; (218) 365-6563 or (877) 493-8017; www.jim brandenburg.com
International Wolf Center: Ely, MN; (218) 365-4695; www.wolf.org
Ely-Winton Historical Society: Ely, MN; (218) 365-3226
North American Bear Center: Ely, MN; (218) 365-7879; www.bear.org

Ennis Lake Trail

Accommodations

The Blue Heron Bed & Breakfast & Dining Room at Blue Heron: Ely, MN; (218) 365-4720; www.blueheronbnb.com
Log Cabin Hideaways: (218) 365-6045; logcabinhideaways.com
Smitty's on Snowbank: Ely, MN; (218) 365-6032; www.smittys-on-snowbank.com
Fall Lake Campground: U.S. Forest Service, Ely, MN; (218) 365-2963 or (877) 444-6777
Birch Lake Campground: U.S. Forest Service, Ely, MN; (218) 365-4966

Restaurants

The Boathouse Brewpub: (218) 365-4301
The Moose: Ely, MN; (218) 365-6343
Grand Ely Lodge: Ely, MN; (218) 365-6565
Stony Ridge Café: Ely, MN; (218) 365-6757
The Front Porch Coffee and Tea House: Ely, MN; (218) 365-2326
Burntside Lodge: Ely, MN; (218) 365-3894; www.burntside.com

Local Outdoor Retailers

Piragis Northwoods Company: Ely, MN; (800) 223-6565; www.piragis.com
Ely Surplus Store: Ely, MN; (218) 365-4653
Wilderness Outfitters: Ely, MN; (218) 365-3211; www.wildernessoutfitters.com

30 Bass Lake Trail

Bass Lake is a spectacular recreation area that offers day hiking, overnight camping, canoeing, swimming, fishing, and snowshoeing. The hike circumnavigates the lake and covers a variety of terrain, traversing an old lakebed, streams, waterfalls, rocky overlooks, and sandy beaches. More than a beautiful hike, Bass Lake is unique in its geology, history, and ecology. Its story unfolds as you follow the trail.

Start: From the parking lot on CR 116 (Echo Trail) on the right
Distance: 5.9-mile loop
Approximate hiking time: 2.5 hours
Difficulty rating: Moderate due to mostly flat, smooth terrain with two slightly steep up- and downhill climbs over moderate elevation gain.
Trail surface: Forested trail over rock, dirt, and sand surfaces
Lay of the land: Trail circumnavigates Bass Lake on old lakebed and high rock ridges
Other trail users: Anglers, overnight campers,

and canoeists (who use the trail as a portage)
Canine compatibility: Dogs permitted
Land status: National forest
Nearest town: Ely, MN
Schedule: Open year-round, used by snowshoers and anglers in the winter
Maps: USGS maps: Ely Quadrangle, MN, Shagawa Lake Quadrangle, MN
Trail contacts: U.S. Forest Service, Kawishiwi Ranger District, Ely, MN; (218) 365-7600; www.fs.fed.us/

Finding the trailhead: From Ely, take Highway 169 east about a mile to CR 88 (McMahon Boulevard). Turn left onto CR 88. Drive just over 2 miles and turn right on CR 116 (Echo Trail). The Bass Lake Trailhead and parking area is 3 miles up the Echo Trail on the right. *DeLorme: Minnesota Atlas & Gazetteer.* Page 88 E5

Pink moccasin

The Hike

Bass Lake underwent a major transformation in the spring of 1925. At that time Bass Lake and nearby Low Lake were separated by a large glacial ridge that held Bass Lake 60 feet higher than Low Lake. A logging company cut into this natural dam, which had stood for thousands of years, to make a sluiceway that enabled the movement of logs downstream from Bass to Low, and on to the Range River.

In the spring of 1925 the ridge gave way, and Bass Lake drained at a phenomenal rate. Approximately 18 million gallons of water discharged from the lake over a ten-hour period, washing out a 250-foot valley where the glacial wall once stood. Bass Lake's surface dropped 55 feet, exposing 250 acres of lakebed. What was once one lake now became three. The drop created two smaller lakes, Little Dry and Dry Lakes, plus a small stream and waterfalls that drain Dry Lake into Bass Lake.

Hiking in a clockwise direction, you first drop into a shallow, narrow valley that was once the old lakebed. Here the tree cover is dense, with balsam, aspen and paper birch the predominate species. A tiny stream flows in this valley draining Little Long Lake to the west. Hike up a steep rocky ridge from the stream and ascend off of the old lakebed into an open stand of white and red pines with a multitude of large-leafed aster covering the forest floor. An overlook reveals the marsh-covered valley and stream that were once under water.

Follow this ridge and descend slightly to arrive at the stream that flows out of Dry Lake and cascades into Bass Lake via Dry Falls. Standing atop this falls, it's hard to fathom the old lake surface over your head. Gulp! This is a popular spot for swimming, picnicking, and taking in a wonderful view of Bass Lake.

After you cross the bridge, there is a short trail leading to Dry Lake, a managed trout lake. This trail now circumnavigates Dry and Little Dry Lakes, adding a loop to the hike around Bass Lake. The U.S. Forest Service constructed this loop in the fall of 1999. Just beyond this is another intersection marking an access to Dry Lake 50 feet to the left, and two Forest Service campsites to the right. Both campsites are on the lake and far enough from the main trail to offer some solitude.

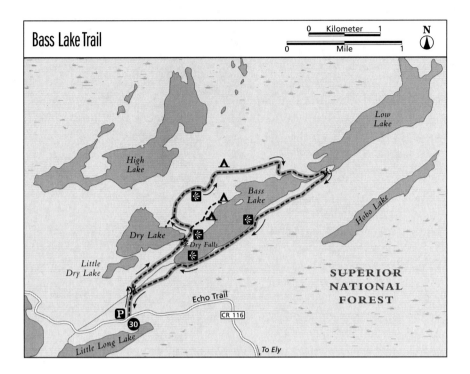

Bass Lake Trail

0 Kilometer 1

0 Mile 1

N

Low Lake

High Lake

Bass Lake

Hobo Lake

Dry Lake

Dry Falls

Little Dry Lake

SUPERIOR NATIONAL FOREST

Echo Trail

CR 116

P

30

Little Long Lake

To Ely

The trail continues to climb, offering a striking view of the north end of Bass Lake, and meanders along rocky, open ridges marked with waist-high rock cairns. The trail once again descends onto the old lake bottom, which is noticeably flat. Here grasses, lichens, and jack pines are pioneer species in the newly exposed sandy soil. After passing a campsite/picnic area to the right of the trail, you approach the edge of the old glacial wall (or moraine). The trail turns to cobbles and then to sand as you walk along the edge of the washout. Looking up to your left you can see the remains of the wall—so rocky and steep that little vegetation has been able to take hold.

Along the washout area of the trail, sandy beaches invite you to swim (watch out for poison ivy). Cross two small bridges that span the flow of water into Low Lake. From here the trail heads back along the south shore of Bass Lake. The trail follows the old lakebed for a short distance until you climb the ridge into a mature pine forest. There is one particularly scenic overlook on a cliff high over Bass Lake looking through a stand of large red pines.

The trail descends gradually, still following the old shoreline hemmed in cedars. Keep walking through the woods, crossing a wet-weather stream until you come to a picturesque view of Dry Falls. On calm days you can hear the tumbling water before you see it. The trail then drops down to the west end of the lake to meet the canoe launch and portage trail, then continues on to complete the loop. Go left to return to the trailhead and parking lot.

Miles and Directions

0.0 Start at the west end of the parking lot.

0.1 The trail splits into the loop around Bass Lake. This hike will go around the lake in a clockwise direction. Turn left to proceed to Dry Falls. A right heads east to access Bass Lake via the portage trail and follow the south shore.

0.2 Cross a bridge over a small stream that flows from Little Long Lake to Bass Lake. The trail winds through a forest consisting mostly of birch, aspen, and balsam trees on the old lakebed. Trail climbs a ridge with red and white pines in an open forest floor lined with asters, blueberries, and ferns.

0.8 A spur trail to the right gives a good view of the stream feeding into Bass Lake from Little Long Lake.

1.1 There is a bridge crossing above Dry Falls, a scenic picnic and swimming spot. Just past the bridge a spur trail to the left leads to Dry Lake, a managed trout lake.

Bass Lake

1.2	Come to a four-way intersection. A right leads to two campsites (first one 200 feet, second 300 feet), the left brings you to the shore of Dry Lake (50 feet). Continue straight ahead.
1.5	Trail ascends onto a rocky ridge that parallels the lake and is marked with rock cairns.
1.9	View of the north end of Bass Lake. Trail descends into an old lakebed, which is flat and sandy with lots of grasses.
2.5	Pass a campsite, fire grate, and picnic table.
2.8	The trail turns to cobbles as you start to cross the glacial ridge that washed out in 1925.
3.2	Come to sandy swimming beaches on your left. Watch out for poison ivy.
3.5	The trail crosses a bridge between Bass and Low Lakes.
4.3	The trail climbs a high ridge with a good view of the lake through a stand of red pines.
4.8	The trail crosses a wet weather stream.
5.2	There is a view of Dry Falls across Bass Lake.
5.3	The trail descends to the lake and the canoe launch.
5.8	This trail intersection completes the loop. Stay left to return to the parking lot.
5.9	Arrive back at the trailhead and parking lot.

More Information

Local Information
Ely Chamber of Commerce: Ely, MN; (218) 365-6123 or (800) 777-7281; www.ely.org
Boundary Waters Broadcasters: WELY Radio 94.5 FM, 1450 AM; Ely, MN; (218) 365-4444; www.wely.com

Local Events/Attractions
Blueberry Arts Festival: Late July, Ely, MN
Watercolor Show: July, Ely, MN; (218) 365-6123
Embarrass Fair: Late August, Embarrass, MN; (218) 365-6123
Harvest Moon Festival: Early September, Ely, MN; (218) 365-6123
Brandenburg Gallery: Ely, MN; (218) 365-6563 or (877) 493-8017; www.jim brandenburg.com
International Wolf Center: Ely, MN; (218) 365-4695; www.wolf.org
Ely-Winton Historical Society: Ely, MN; (218) 365-3226
North American Bear Center: Ely, MN; (218) 365-7879; www.bear.org

Accommodations
Fenske Lake Campground, Fall Lake Campground, Birch Lake Campground: Ely, MN; (218) 365-7600; www.fs.fed.us
Shagawa Inn: Ely, MN; (218) 365-5154
A Stay Inn Ely: Ely, MN; (888) 360-6010; www.stayinnely.com
The Blue Heron Bed & Breakfast & Dining Room at Blue Heron: Ely, MN; (218) 365-4720; www.blueheronbnb.com
Log Cabin Hideaways: (218) 365-6045; logcabinhideaways.com
Smitty's on Snowbank: Ely, MN; (218) 365-6032; www.smittys-on-snowbank.com
Fall Lake Campground: U.S. Forest Service, Ely, MN; (218) 365-2963 or (877) 444-6777
Birch Lake Campground: U.S. Forest Service, Ely, MN; (218) 365-4966

Restaurants
Stony Ridge Café: (218) 365-6757
The Boathouse Brewpub: (218) 365-4301
The Moose: Ely, MN; (218) 365-6343
Grand Ely Lodge: Ely, MN; (218) 365-6565
Stony Ridge Café: Ely, MN; (218) 365-6757
The Front Porch Coffee and Tea House: Ely, MN; (218) 365-2326
Burntside Lodge: Ely, MN; (218) 365-3894; www.burntside.com

Local Outdoor Retailers
Wilderness Outfitters: Ely, MN; (218) 365-3211; www.wildernessoutfitters.com
Piragis Northwoods Company: Ely, MN; (800) 223-6565; www.piragis.com
Ely Surplus Store: Ely, MN; (218) 365-4653
Wilderness Outfitters: Ely, MN; (218) 365-3211; www.wildernessoutfitters.com

31 Bear Head Lake State Park

Bear Head Lake State Park is located in Minnesota Northwoods lake country. Bald eagles and osprey nest high in the pines, while deer, black bear, and moose sip from the water's edge. Several miles of hiking trails loop through Bear Head Lake State Park. One of the trails even hooks up with the multi-use Taconite State Trail that extends 165 miles from Grand Rapids to Ely. The hike featured here consists of two connected loops. It passes through white and red pine–covered hills and valleys. The west loop encircles tiny Norberg Lake and skirts the shore of Bear Head Lake's east bay, while the east loop encircles even tinier Becky Lake.

Start: From the picnic area parking lot and trailhead
Distance: 6.1-mile loop
Approximate hiking time: 2.5 hours
Difficulty rating: Moderate, due to some hills and rocky trails, particularly on the Becky Lake loop
Trail surface: Dirt and rock trails
Lay of the land: A combination of ancient volcanic rocks and glacial deposits covered by mixed forest, including old pines along the shoreline of Bear Head Lake
Other trail users: Hikers only

Canine compatibility: Leashed dogs permitted
Land status: State park
Nearest town: Tower, MN
Fees/permits: State park vehicle permit required. Annual or day permits are available at the park office. Camping fees are separate.
Schedule: Open year-round
Maps: USGS maps: Eagles Nest, MN; state park map
Trail contacts: Bear Head Lake State Park, Ely, MN; (218) 365-7229; Department of Natural Resources, St. Paul, MN; (651) 296-6157 or (888) 646-6367; www.dnr.state.mn.us/parks

Finding the trailhead: From Tower, drive east on Highway 169 to CR 128. Take CR 128 south 6 miles to the park entrance. *DeLorme: Minnesota Atlas & Gazetteer.* Page 76 A3

The Hike

A walk through Bear Head Lake State Park is a journey deep into the earth's turbulent geologic history. Here, rocks from a much younger Earth lie exposed to the elements in the park and along roadcuts. Bedrock, scoured clean by glaciers, cradles Bear Head and other nearby lakes. Among these ancient rocks are Giants Range Granite and older Precambrian Ely Greenstone (2,700 million years old). The Giants Range Granite, which underlies the eastern half of Bear Head Lake State Park's total area, is part of a large body of rock that extends approximately 200 miles from Wadena, in the center of the state, to Ely. Greenstone was formed from underwater lava flows that cooled underwater and then were subjected to heat and pressure. Greenstone belts around the world, all from the same time period, are major sources of gold, silver, chromium, nickel, copper and zinc. The main mineral in Ely Greenstone, however, is iron.

Iron ore has ancient origins, formed from ferrous oxide extruded in lava from deep within the earth when underwater volcanoes erupted. At that time, plant life and oxygen were minimal and sea-bound. Eventually, plant life became prolific, expanding to land and releasing large amounts of oxygen into an otherwise carbon dioxide–dominated atmosphere. Oxygen was the key ingredient for turning ferrous oxide into the solid minerals of magnetite and hematite.

Rumors of gold near Lake Vermilion lured the adventuresome into the northeastern Minnesota wilderness in the mid-1800s to seek their fortunes among the ancient rocks. But their dreams of quick and easy strikes followed by long, carefree lives

East Bay of Bear Head Lake

spending the rewards soon evaporated, replaced by the reality of hard labor excavating iron ore. Soon, the towns of Soudan and Tower sprang up to support the miners, who labored long hours in open pits. Eventually, the pit walls became too steep, and the switch was made to an underground mine. The Soudan Mine's shaft extends 2,500 feet, making it the deepest mine in the state and eventually the largest of the Iron Range mines in Minnesota.

The Soudan Mine, part of a designated state park 8 miles west of Bear Head Lake State Park, lies in the Vermilion Iron Range, the oldest of Minnesota's three iron ore ranges. At its peak, the Soudan Mine employed 1,800 men and produced a total of fourteen million metric tons of ore containing 63 to 66 percent iron. But by the mid twentieth century, although the ore had not been exhausted, keeping the mine operational had become too expensive. U.S. Steel Corporation sold the mine and surrounding land to the state in 1963 for one dollar, and the mine and its accompanying historic buildings were opened for tours. The headframe (constructed in the 1920s) originally used to haul ore out of the ground is now used to transport tourists into and out of the mine's half-mile depths, where the temperature hovers around 50 degrees F.

Timber was another of the area's rich resources that people came to harvest. Once covered with stately pine, the area surrounding Bear Head Lake was heavily logged beginning in the late 1800s, but resources there soon became exhausted, and in a few years the mill constructed on the south side of the lake was dismantled and shipped to another location. Still remaining is the railroad grade, built so horses could pull logs along it down to the lake to be floated to the sawmill. Several fires in the early 1900s destroyed much of the forest within the 4,000-acre park, leaving remnant burned stumps scattered through the replacement forest of hardwoods and red and white pine. Some of the old trees can be seen along the shoreline, and the mixed forest is excellent habitat for a wide variety of birds and wildlife.

Red and white pines

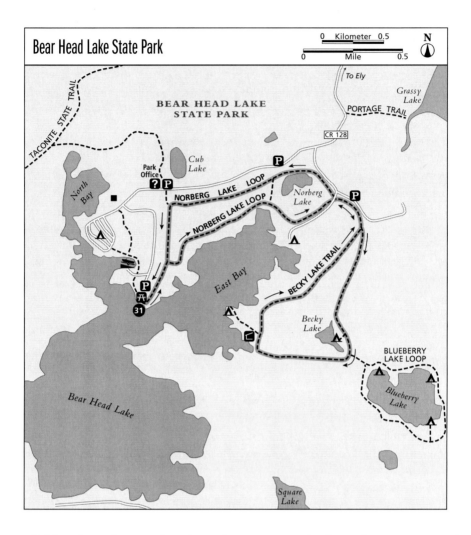

0   Kilometer   0.5

0   Mile   0.5

N

To Ely

Grassy
Lake

BEAR HEAD LAKE
STATE PARK

PORTAGE TRAIL

CR 128

TACONITE STATE TRAIL

Cub
Lake

Park
Office

North
Bay

NORBERG   LAKE   LOOP

NORBERG LAKE LOOP

Norberg
Lake

31

East Bay

BECKY LAKE TRAIL

Becky
Lake

BLUEBERRY
LAKE LOOP

Blueberry
Lake

Bear Head Lake

Square
Lake

Bald eagles and osprey have been known to nest in the park most years, and you can look for their nests in the tops of the tall pines. Frequently, bald eagles have nested near the picnic area, near the start of the featured hike. The park staff can tell you where birds may be nesting when you visit. People are asked to observe from a distance as the birds are sensitive and will abandon their nests if disturbed. Swimmers frequent the beautiful sand beach near the pine-shaded picnic area.

The featured hike follows the large east bay of Bear Head Lake over hilly terrain and through white and red pines and mixed woods, circling around Norberg and Becky Lakes. An additional loop around Blueberry Lake can be added to lengthen this scenic hike. While the terrain is gentle around Norberg Lake, the hiking is more difficult around Becky and Blueberry Lakes. Away from the bustle of the lake activity on Bear Head, the trail feels quite remote. Beautiful hike-in campsites are located on

Becky and Blueberry Lakes along the more rugged section of trail. These excellent hiking trails are also maintained for skiing in the winter.

Miles and Directions

0.0 Start from the picnic area parking lot. (FYI: Before beginning the hike, visit the beach and picnic area and look for an eagle's nest. Some years, the birds may be nesting at Grassy Lake or somewhere else nearby so there may not be a nest.) Start the hike at the north side of the parking lot. Follow the Hiking Club Trail sign and walk north on a wide ski/hiking trail.

0.1 This intersection begins the Norberg Lake loop. Take a right (east) and follow the narrower trail as it hugs the East Bay of Bear Head Lake. The rocky, pine needle–covered trail winds through large red pines and offers great views of East Bay.

0.5 Enter a stand of birch away from the lake.

0.8 See the end of East Bay and proceed uphill.

0.9 A spur goes down to the East Bay of Bear Head Lake on the right for a beautiful view. Proceed left to stay on the trail. Continue to ascend a ridge between Norberg and Bear Head Lakes and get glimpses of the East Bay of Bear Head Lake through red and white pine.

1.0 A left follows the west side of Norberg Lake; continue right on the Hiking Club Trail and head toward the group camp.

1.1 Come to the park road that leads to the primitive group camp, which is to the right. Turn left and follow the park road to the next intersection.

1.3 Take a right here to follow the park road toward the backpack parking area. A left takes you back around Norberg Lake.

1.5 Come to the sign that marks the Becky Lake Trail. Take a left. (FYI: This is a one-way trail during ski season.) Ascend and descend a series of hills.

2.2 Pass a spur trail on the right that leads to backpack campsite 1.

2.6 Take a right at the intersection with Blueberry Lake loop and head west toward Bear Head Lake. A left takes you to Blueberry Lake.

3.2 Pass a ski shelter on the left and a spur trail on the left that leads to backpack campsite 5.

3.6 Come into view of the East Bay of Bear Head Lake.

4.2 Return to the park road, completing the Becky Lake loop. Take a left toward the parking area. Follow the park road past the parking area.

4.4 Take a right to head back around the north side of Norberg Lake.

4.5 Stay left and hike west (the trail parallels the park entrance road at this point).

4.6 You can see Norberg Lake on the left through large red pines. The trail departs from the park road here.

4.8 The parking area for Norberg Lake is on the right. The spur trail on the left circles back around Norberg Lake; stay right to follow Hiking Club Trail. Depart from Norberg Lake through a stand of aspen.

5.4 The park office and registration parking come into view straight ahead.

5.5 Take a left to head south back to the picnic parking area. A right leads to the park office.

5.9 Return to the beginning of the Norberg Lake loop. Continue right (south) to head back to parking.

6.1 Arrive back at the parking area.

More Information

Local Information

Ely Chamber of Commerce, Ely, MN Vacation Hotline: (218) 365-6123 or (800) 777-7281; www.ely.org

Lake Vermilion Area Chamber of Commerce: Tower, MN; (218) 753-2301 or (800) 869-3766

Local Events/Attractions

Soudan Underground Mine Tour: Soudan, MN; open daily in summer from 9:30 a.m. to 5:30 p.m.; (218) 753-2245

Lake Vermilion Mailboat Tour: Tower, MN; departure 9 a.m. Monday through Saturday; (218) 753-4190. This is a 3.5-hour tour of Lake Vermilion.

Pike River Fish Hatchery: Tower, MN; open April 15 through May 15; (218) 753-5692. Located by the Pike River dam on Lake Vermilion.

International Wolf Center: Ely, MN; (218) 365-4695; www.wolf.org

BALD EAGLES

One of the state's most magnificent raptors makes its home within the beauty of Bear Head Lake State Park and nearby Eagles Nest Lake Number 3. It nests among the red and white pine, spruce, fir, and paper birch, fishes the lakes, and soars high overhead in the summer sunshine. The highly respected bald eagle seems to enjoy its boreal habitat where tamarack, black spruce, and white cedar thrive among lowland vegetation. Once common throughout the United States, the bald eagle population is estimated to have approached upward of 500,000 at its peak. But as the human population grew, so did the bird's enemies. Farmers complained about loss of livestock to eagle predation, and bounty hunters were hired to eliminate them. Logging and pesticides took their toll until extinction threatened this regal bird, our national emblem. With fewer than 1,000 breeding pairs in the Lower 48, efforts were initiated to restore bald eagle populations. Their numbers have since risen to 12,000 in Minnesota with more than 70,000 in the Lower 48. Their status was upgraded from endangered to threatened in 1994 but that status has since been removed. The largest populations in the United States, outside of Alaska, are in Minnesota and Wisconsin.

Bald eagles mate for life, often returning to the same nest, building additions each year. Although fairly compatible with humans, eagles will abandon their nests and their young if disturbed by human activity. At 6 to 8 feet across and made of twigs, their nests are easy to spot, and in early spring, they house one to three eggs. Adult females weigh ten to fourteen pounds and grow as big as 3.5 feet from beak to tail, with a wingspread of up to 7.5 feet. It's not unusual for these raptors to live twenty-five to thirty years.

Accommodations
Tower Café and Hotel: Tower, MN; (218) 753-2710
Bay View Lodge: Tower, MN; (218) 753-4825 or (800) 628-1607; www.bayviewlodge.com
Fortune Bay Resort Casino: Tower, MN; (218) 753-3606 or (800) 992-7529; www.fortunebay.com

Restaurants
Bay View Lodge: Tower, MN; (218) 753-4825; www.bayviewlodge.com
Black Bear Café: Tower, MN; (218) 749-2460
Tamarack, Fortune Bay Resort Casino: Tower, MN; (218) 753-6400

Local Outdoor Retailers
Piragis Northwoods Company: Ely, MN; (800) 223-6565; www.piragis.com
Ely Surplus Store: Ely, MN; (218) 365-4653

32 Border Route-Caribou Rock Trail

Caribou Rock Trail rewards the hiker with overlooks of Bearskin Lake, Duncan Lake, Moss Lake, Stairway Portage, and Rose Lake. At Stairway Portage, you'll enjoy a spectacular waterfall and see Canada's steep 300-foot Arrow cliffs on Rose Lake's north shore. Experience the rugged beauty of northern Minnesota's border country on this remote Boundary Waters Canoe Area Wilderness hike. Caribou Rock Trail is not heavily used or regularly maintained and may occasionally disappear in overgrowth. Therefore, it's wise to carry a compass and topographical map. Day-use permits are available at trailheads. If you plan to camp overnight in the BWCAW, you'll need to purchase an entry point permit.

Start: From the trailhead across from the parking area off CR 65
Distance: 7.6 miles out and back
Approximate hiking time: 5–7 hours
Difficulty rating: Difficult due to rugged, rocky trail with steep elevation and challenging route finding
Trail surface: Dirt and rock trail with tree roots and overgrown with plants in some areas
Lay of the land: Rugged trail with many steep hills. Ascends and descends ridges overlooking lakes in the Boundary Waters Canoe Area Wilderness (BWCAW).
Land status: National forest
Nearest town: Grand Marais, MN
Other trail users: Hikers only
Canine compatibility: Dogs permitted

Fees/permits: Wilderness permits are required for entry into and camping in the BWCAW. For day use, self-permitting is available at the trailhead or at any U.S.F.S. office. There is a user fee per person per trip. Overnights require obtaining a permit reservation. There is a reservation fee and a per-person per-night camping fee. Reservations can be made by calling (877) 550-6777 or online at www.bwcaw.org.
Schedule: Open year-round
Maps: USGS maps: Hungry Jack Lake, MN; Border Route Trail map
Trail contacts: Superior National Forest, Duluth, MN; (218) 626-4300; www. fs.fed .us/r9/superior.com; Gunflint District Ranger, Grand Marais, MN; (218) 387-1750

Finding the trailhead: From Grand Marais, take CR 12 (Gunflint Trail) north 28 miles to CR 65. Take a right on CR 65 and proceed north 2 miles to the trailhead sign. There is a small parking area on the right, and the trail begins on the left side of the road. *DeLorme: Minnesota Atlas & Gazetteer.* Page 79 B6

The Hike

There's no way to completely describe the magnificence of the Superior National Forest, BWCAW, and the Gunflint Trail. It's best to experience them, taking the wilderness in with all of your senses. It's here that you can journey back to the time when only bare feet and moccasins touched the earth, birch bark canoes plied its pure waters, and no roads disturbed the landscape. Known for centuries to Native Americans, the land lay undisturbed as they made their living off of its plants and animals. In recent history, the Dakota lived among its virgin pine, but in the 1600s the Ojibwe moved into the area from the eastern shores of Lake Superior, pushing the Dakota west. It was the Ojibwe who dominated the region when the first Europeans arrived in the early 1700s and established a mutually beneficial trade relationship.

Between 1670 and 1850, there was a large supply of fur-bearing animals in North America and a high demand for furs in Europe. Among Native Americans, there was a high demand for European trade goods: metal objects such as knives, axes, pots, sewing needles, and other goods such as cloth, decorative glass beads, and firearms. So they collected furs and traded them to French-Canadian voyageurs for durable goods. The voyageurs moved the furs to the coastal areas by canoe, where they were transported to Europe by ship for making high fashion items such as hats and coats. For a while, everyone profited from this ideal market economy, except for the fur-bearing animals that were trapped to near extinction. The main travel route used by

Looking eastward to Bearskin Lake from atop Caribou Rock

the voyageurs to haul many tons of trade goods in and numerous furs out went across Rose Lake on what is now called the Voyageur's Highway, or the international border between Minnesota and Ontario.

As Europeans settled the area in larger numbers, the landscape and its resources were dramatically changed. They viewed its dense forests, rushing streams, fur-bearing animals, and mineral deposits as an endless supply of goods that would not only give them sustenance but would make them wealthy as well. Gold seekers appeared in hopes of making fortunes in mining, and an east-to-west wagon road (now part of the Gunflint Trail) that led to the mines was created. Logging of coveted red and white pine was next, but this only lasted a few decades until the supply ran out.

It wasn't until the late 1800s that efforts began to preserve this rich Minnesota wilderness enjoyed by millions today. The history of its establishment is long and turbulent. Those with hydropower, logging, mining, and private land interests had other ideas for the area's rich resources. Nevertheless, efforts for public use persevered and eventually succeeded. Beginning with a small amount of acreage and followed by years of acquisitions (some through eminent domain), the Superior National Forest was eventually born.

In later years, improved access heightened interest in outdoor recreation, and the need arose for management of recreation resources. The first regulations for the new Superior National Forest, set down in 1927, addressed road building, retaining of wilderness, and management of timber cutting. These regulations were expanded in 1930 to further define the roadless area within the Superior National Forest. In

Overlook at Rose Lake looking north to the Canadian shore

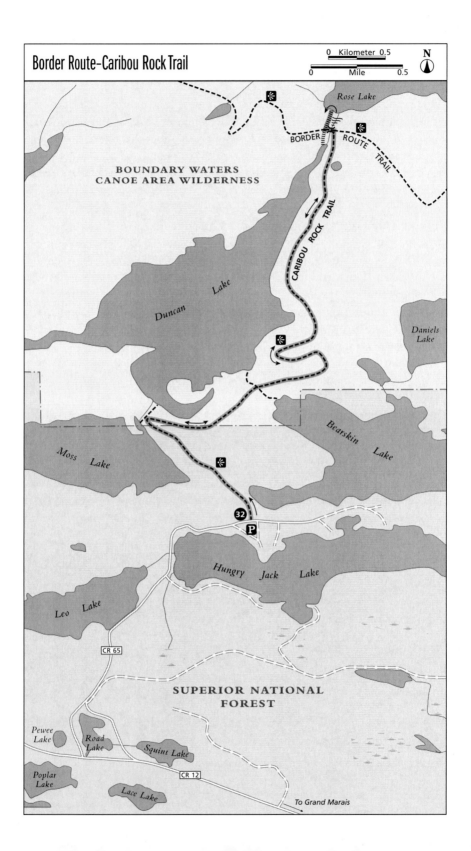

Border Route-Caribou Rock Trail

0   Kilometer   0.5

0   Mile   0.5

N

Rose Lake

BORDER   ROUTE   TRAIL

**BOUNDARY WATERS
CANOE AREA WILDERNESS**

CARIBOU ROCK TRAIL

Duncan   *Lake*

*Daniels
Lake*

Bearskin   Lake

*Moss
Lake*

32

P

Hungry   Jack   Lake

Leo   Lake

CR 65

**SUPERIOR NATIONAL
FOREST**

*Pewee
Lake*

*Road
Lake*

Squint Lake

*Poplar
Lake*

Lace Lake

CR 12

To Grand Marais

1964, the forest was designated a unit of the National Wilderness Preservation System, which provides special management considerations. In 1978 the BWCAW, a part of the Superior National Forest, was established. Visits to the area increased so significantly over the years that it became necessary to control numbers entering the BWCAW with a permit system. Today, the BWCAW consists of more than one million acres of lakes, rivers, streams, and rugged landscape preserved for wildlife and controlled public use.

The Caribou Rock Trail is an access trail to the beautiful and challenging Border Route Trail, a 95-mile trail that follows the Minnesota/Ontario border and connects the Grand Portage Trail and the Superior Hiking Trail to the east with the Kekekabic Trail, which stretches to Ely and the western edge of the BWCAW. The Minnesota Rovers Outing Club in Minneapolis began to create and maintain the Border Route Trail in 1972. Nine years later, more than 75 miles were completed, linking the eastern Grand Portage Trail to the Gunflint Trail. The Border Route Trail and Caribou Rock Trail follow high, erosion-resistant ridges some 500 feet above border lakes for spectacular views, descend into stream valleys, and climb back up steep ridges. The trails are almost entirely in the BWCAW, where federal regulations apply, and are maintained by the U.S. Forest Service, Minnesota Outdoors Club, Gunflint Lake resorts, and various groups of volunteers. Caribou Rock and Border Route Trails are rough, remote, and some of the wildest and most primitive trails in the state. These trails aren't designed for casual day-hikes, and even accessing the trails can be a challenge. A good map and compass and backcountry skills are necessary.

Miles and Directions

0.0 Start at the trailhead across from the parking area on CR 65. There is a self-permit station at the trailhead. Be sure to fill out a day-use permit. If you plan to camp overnight, you must reserve a permit in advance and have it with you. Begin hiking north. You will ascend a ridge between Bearskin and Moss Lakes.

0.2 Reach the first of the many breathtaking overlooks on this hike; this one is of Bearskin Lake to the east. The trail continues northwest as it follows along the length of the ridge.

0.5 Come into view of Moss Lake to the left. Continue along the ridge.

0.7 Cross into the Boundary Waters Canoe Area Wilderness.

0.8 At this point, instead of descending into the valley between Moss and Duncan Lakes to join the portage trail, take a sharp right (east) to follow the other side of the ridge. If you find yourself down at the portage trail by mistake, retrace your steps back to the main trail. (The portage and hiking trails are connected by a short spur trail.)

1.2 Begin a steep descent off the ridge and into the valley between Duncan and Bearskin Lakes. You will be hiking north. (Note: There is serious erosion on this section of trail and the footing is poor, so exercise caution.)

1.4 Here is an area with lots of blown-down trees. Look carefully for the trail around large rocks and tree roots.

1.6 Cross the portage trail between Bearskin and Duncan Lakes. Continue straight ahead (north). Begin ascending a steep knob. The climb is gradual as the trail circles the south side toward the east, and then becomes steep up to the top. Route finding here can be challenging, and the trail can be difficult to find in places. Be sure to use your map and compass.

2.3 At the top of the knob, view Duncan Lake to the left (west).

2.4 Begin a steep descent into another valley between Duncan and Bearskin Lakes.

2.7 Ascend the ridge that runs along the west side of Duncan Lake. As you continue north along this ridge, the lake will narrow to a stream before the stairway portage. You will see BWCAW campsites across on the west shore. There are a few fantastic views of the lake high up on this ridge.

3.5 Begin to descend the ridge toward Stairway Portage. This section is shaded and cool, with many cedars.

3.7 Turn left onto Border Route Trail and cross the bridge over the stream that flows from Duncan to Rose Lake as it begins a series of cascades. A right follows the Border Route Trail east to the town of Grand Portage.

3.8 Turn right to descend the ninety-one steps of the Stairway Portage and view the falls. A left follows the Border Route Trail west. The Stairway Portage is shaded and cool, and there are places to sit and take in the view along the descent. From this point, retrace your steps back to the trailhead.

7.6 Arrive back at the trailhead and parking lot.

More Information

Local Information

Grand Marais Chamber of Commerce: Grand Marais, MN; (218) 387-9112 or (888) 922-5000 or www.grandmaraismn.com

Grand Marais Visitor Center: (218) 387-9112 or (888) 922-5000; www.grandmarais.com

Local Events/Attractions

Antique Car Show: Mid-May, Grand Marais, MN

Cook County Fair: Mid-August, Community Center, Grand Marais, MN

Grand Marais Fisherman's Picnic: First weekend in August, Grand Marais, MN

Grand Marais Playhouse: Grand Marais, MN; (218) 387-1284, extension 5; www.grandmarais playhouse.com

Minnesota Shakespeare Festival: June, Grand Marais, MN

North House Folk School: Grand Marais, MN; (218) 387-9762 or (888) 387-9762; www.north house.org

Sivertson Gallery: Grand Marais, MN; (218) 387-2491 or (888) 880-4369; www.sivertson.com

Grand Portage Rendezvous Days: Second weekend of August, Grand Portage, MN

Accommodations

Dream Catcher B&B: Grand Marais, MN; (218) 387-3119 or (800) 682-3119; www.dream catcherbb.com

Gunflint Motel: Grand Marais, MN; (218) 387-1454 or (800) 439-1311; www.gunflintmotel.com

MacArthur House Bed & Breakfast: Grand Marais, MN; (218) 387-1840 or (800) 792-1840; www.boreal.org/macarthur

Naniboujou Lodge: Grand Marais, MN; (218) 387-2688; www.naniboujou.com

Nelson's Travelers Rest Cabins & Motels: Grand Marais, MN; (218) 387-1464 or (800) 249-1285; www.travelersrest.com

Outpost Motel: Grand Marais, MN; (218) 387-1833 or (888) 380-1833; www.outpostmotel.com

Seawall Motel & Cabins: Grand Marais, MN; (218) 387-2095 or (800) 245-5806

Snuggle Inn Bed & Breakfast: Grand Marais, MN; (218) 387-2847 or (800) 823-3174; www.snuggleinnbb.com

Restaurants

Angry Trout Café: Grand Marais, MN; (218) 387-1265 (seasonal)

Birch Terrace Supper Club: Grand Marais, MN; (218) 387-2215

Blue Water Café: Cascade Lodge, Grand Marais, MN; (218) 387-1597 or (800) 322-9543; www.cascadelodgemn.com

Gunflint Tavern: Grand Marais, MN; (218) 387-1563

Harbor Inn Restaurant & Motel: Grand Marais, MN; (218) 387-1191 or (800) 595-4566 (seasonal)

Ryden's Border Store: Grand Portage, MN; (218) 475-2330

Organizations

Minnesota Outdoors Club: Minneapolis, MN; www.mnrovers.org

Hike Tours

Boundary Country Trekking: Grand Marais, MN; (218) 388-4487 or (800) 322-8327; www.boundarycountry.com

Local Outdoor Retailers

Joyne's Department & Ben Franklin Store: Grand Marais, MN; (218) 387-2233

Lake Superior Trading Post: Grand Marais, MN; (218) 387-2020

33 Eagle Mountain

See the great expanse of Minnesota wilderness from this, the state's highest point. Eagle Mountain rises more than 500 feet from the surrounding landscape to present spectacular views of the marshy headwaters of the Cascade River and the surrounding wilderness. The solid granite that makes up Eagle Mountain is part of a large volcanic formation called the Duluth Complex, formed 1.1 billion years ago. The landscape is rocky, steep, root covered, and often wet. If you haven't had enough solitude when you return to the base of the mountain, head 6 miles north on the Brule Lake Trail, or camp at one of two secluded sites near Whale Lake. Here, you're likely to hear the loon's distinctive cry. Remember, permits are necessary. The trail begins in the Superior National Forest at an elevation of 1,800 feet and climbs 500 feet over 3.5 miles to the top of Eagle Mountain.

Start: From the east end of the parking lot

Distance: 6.8 miles out and back

Approximate hiking time: 3–4 hours

Difficulty rating: Moderate due to rocky, rough trail and steep climbing in the last half mile

Trail surface: Rough, rock and dirt trail

Lay of the land: Travel over marshy areas and up a granite mountain

Other trail users: Hikers only

Canine compatibility: Controlled dogs permitted (must be under verbal or leash control)

Land status: National forest and wilderness area

Nearest town: Grand Marais, MN

Fees/permits: Wilderness permits are required for entry into and camping in the BWCAW. For day use, self-permitting is available at the trailhead or at any U.S.F.S. office. There is a user fee per person per trip. Overnights require obtaining a permit reservation. There is a reservation fee and a per-person per-night camping fee. Reservations can be made by calling (877) 550-6777 or at www.bwcaw.org.

Schedule: Open year-round

Map: USGS map: Eagle Mountain, MN

Trail contacts: Superior National Forest, Duluth, MN; (218) 626-4300; www.fs.fed.us/r9/superior.com; Gunflint District Ranger; Grand Marais, MN; (218) 387-1750

Finding the trailhead: From Grand Marais, drive north on the Gunflint Trail (CR 12) for 3.7 miles to CR 8. Go west 5 miles on CR 8 then, as the road bends and turns into CR 27, go north on CR 27 for 5 more miles to FS 170. Take a left on FS 170 and travel west for 5 miles. Follow forest service signs to the Eagle Mountain trailhead, which will be on the right. *DeLorme: Minnesota Atlas & Gazetteer.* Page 78 C5

The Hike

Every state has its high and low points. In Minnesota, they're roughly 13 miles apart. So, in one day, you can visit them both. Fill a water bottle from Lake Superior at 600

feet above sea level, and pour it out atop Eagle Mountain at 2,301 feet. Imagine it flowing down the Cascade River back to the big lake.

Not too many people think of relatively flat Minnesota as having mountains, and it doesn't—at least not the 7,000 to 20,000-foot peaks the word generally conjures up. Instead, Minnesota has a worn–down remnant of an ancient mountain range—the Sawtooth Range formed more than a billion years ago by the earth's internal pressures and resulting upheavals. State geologists in the late 1800s set out with a simple aneroid barometer to determine the state's highest point. They ended up at the edge of Winchell Lake and climbed to the top of the 2,230-foot-high Misquah Hills, which they claimed as their objective. It wasn't until the 1960s that their mistake was discovered by aerial photography, and Eagle Mountain at 2,301 feet, just 6 miles south of Misquah Hills, claimed its rightful place as Minnesota's highest point.

In more recent geologic history (roughly 10,000 years ago), glaciers shaped the landscape and left behind lakes, bogs, hills, polished and striated bedrock outcroppings, moraines, drumlins, and eskers as a setting for a beautiful boreal forest—the only one in the Lower 48. One of the world's three great forest ecosystems, the northern boreal forest covers 3.7 billion acres and supports a vast wildlife and plant ecosystem. As the word boreal (meaning of or pertaining to the north, or north wind) implies, this forest contains species highly adapted to cool climates, including spruce, pine, fir, larch, birch, and poplar. The future of boreal forests is vulnerable to the continued threat of global warming, as even minor temperature fluctuations can affect the growth and regeneration of many plant and ultimately animal species.

The Eagle Mountain Trail, which lies in the Superior National Forest and the BWCAW, is often wet on the lower section of trail before Whale Lake, crossing water-filled bogs and streams over boardwalks. It begins as a fairly level trail, then changes dramatically. From Whale Lake, the trail climbs 600 feet in less than a mile, where Eagle Mountain's 2,220-foot-high sister peak, Misquah Hills, is visible below, mirrored in calm water. Near the summit, there are three main overlooks that offer panoramic vistas of the surrounding landscape, where the north branch of the Cascade River, the Sawtooth Mountains, the Misquah Hills, and several lakes, hidden at lower elevations within the vast forest, are now visible. The Superior National Forest is one of the largest federal forests in the Lower 48, containing three million acres and more than 2,000 lakes; dense moss-carpeted forests of pine, spruce, aspen, birch, cedar,

Top of Eagle Mountain

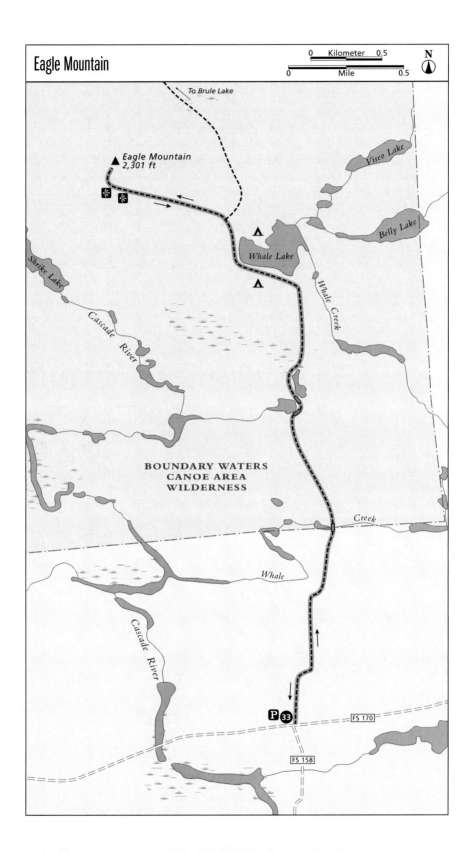

Eagle Mountain

To Brule Lake

Vireo Lake

▲ Eagle Mountain
2,301 ft

Belly Lake

Shrike Lake

Whale Lake

Whale Creek

Cascade River

**BOUNDARY WATERS
CANOE AREA
WILDERNESS**

Creek

Whale

Cascade River

P 33

FS 170

FS 158

and tamarack; as well as vast bogs and swamps. There are 400 miles of designated hiking trails and more than 1,500 miles of canoe routes through the BWCAW, as well as more than 2,700 miles of roads outside the BWCAW.

Miles and Directions

0.0 Start from the east end of the parking lot. You'll see a large Forest Service bulletin board and a self-issuing permit station. Be sure to fill out a permit before continuing. The trail begins as a narrow dirt footpath with some exposed rocks and roots. (FYI: The elevation is 1,800 feet above sea level.)

1.0 Cross over Whale Creek on a boardwalk, enter the Boundary Waters Canoe Area Wilderness, and see large white pines, mature paper birch, and very tall black spruce.

1.4 Cross a boardwalk over a large bog with Labrador Tea, black spruce, white cedar, and bog rosemary. This wetland drains into the Cascade River.

1.5 Cross another small boardwalk.

2.2 Arrive at Whale Lake where there are two hike-in campsites. From here you can see a granite knob rising over the lake. Eagle Mountain is to the left (west) of this knob.

2.5 Go left at this intersection. (**Option:** A right will take you six miles to Brule Lake.) Until this point, the trail has been relatively flat. Now you will start climbing the large granite knob that is Eagle Mountain.

3.1 Come to an overlook facing south.

3.3 This is the main overlook area, with beautiful views facing south and west. To get to the top and USGS marker, continue to walk up the trail on the right (look for a rock cairn) and follow the cairns.

3.4 Reach the USGS marker and Minnesota historical society plaque, elevation 2,301 above sea level.

3.5 Back at the main overlook, turn left to return down the mountain.

3.7 Pass the south-facing overlook to your right.

4.3 Take a right to head back to Whale Lake. A left leads to Brule Lake.

4.6 Back at Whale Lake continue south.

5.3 Cross over a small boardwalk.

5.8 Cross the boardwalk over Whale Creek and exit the BWCAW.

6.8 Arrive back at the parking area.

More Information

Local Information

Grand Marais Chamber of Commerce: Grand Marais, MN; (218) 387-9112 or (888) 922-5000 or www.grandmaraismn.com

Grand Marais Visitor Center: (218) 387-9112 or (888) 922-5000; www.grandmarais.com

Local Events/Attractions

Antique Car Show: Mid-May, Grand Marais, MN
Cook County Fair: Mid-August, Community Center, Grand Marais, MN

Grand Marais Fisherman's Picnic: First weekend in August, Grand Marais, MN

Grand Marais Playhouse: Grand Marais, MN; (218) 387-1284, extension 5; www.grandmarais playhouse.com

Minnesota Shakespeare Festival: June, Grand Marais, MN

North House Folk School: Grand Marais, MN; (218) 387-9762 or (888) 387-9762; www.north house.org

Sivertson Gallery: Grand Marais, MN; (218) 387-2491 or (888) 880-4369; www.sivertson.com

Grand Portage Rendezvous Days: Second weekend of August, Grand Portage, MN

Accommodations

Cascade Lodge and Restaurant: Lutsen, MN; (218) 387-1112 or (800) 322-9543 or www.cascadelodge.com

Dream Catcher B&B: Grand Marais, MN; (218) 387-3119 or (800) 682-3119; www.dream catcherbb.com

Gunflint Motel: Grand Marais, MN; (218) 387-1454 or (800) 439-1311; www.gunflintmotel.com

MacArthur House Bed & Breakfast: Grand Marais, MN; (218) 387-1840 or (800) 792-1840; www.boreal.org/macarthur

Naniboujou Lodge: Grand Marais, MN; (218) 387-2688; www.naniboujou.com

Nelson's Travelers Rest Cabins & Motels: Grand Marais, MN; (218) 387-1464 or (800) 249-1285; www.travelersrest.com

Outpost Motel: Grand Marais, MN; (218) 387-1833 or (888) 380-1833; www.outpostmotel.com

Seawall Motel & Cabins: Grand Marais, MN; (218) 387-2095 or (800) 245-5806

Snuggle Inn Bed & Breakfast: Grand Marais, MN; (218) 387-2847 or (800) 823-3174; www.snuggleinnbb.com

Restaurants

Angry Trout Café: Grand Marais, MN; (218) 387-1265 (seasonal)

Birch Terrace Supper Club: Grand Marais, MN; (218) 387-2215

Blue Water Café: Cascade Lodge, Grand Marais, MN; (218) 387-1597 or (800) 322-9543; www.cascadelodgemn.com

Gunflint Tavern: Grand Marais, MN; (218) 387-1563

Harbor Inn Restaurant & Motel: Grand Marais, MN; (218) 387-1191 or (800) 595-4566 (seasonal)

Ryden's Border Store: Grand Portage, MN; (218) 475-2330

Local Outdoor Retailers

Joyne's Department & Ben Franklin Store: Grand Marais, MN; (218) 387-2233

Lake Superior Trading Post: Grand Marais, MN; (218) 387-2020

34 Grand Portage State Park

This park, which contains some of the most spectacular scenery in Minnesota, lies within the Grand Portage Band of the Chippewa Indian Reservation. It is located along the historic Pigeon River, which is the largest stream along the North Shore and an international boundary. Boreal forest covers the park. The paved, wheelchair-accessible trail follows the river to High Falls. From there, the trail becomes more challenging, climbing steadily on a difficult, rocky footpath where switchbacks are common. This exceptionally rugged 3.5-mile trail to Middle Falls, a three-to-four-hour extension of the High Falls Trail, will reward you with spectacular views.

Start: From the parking area off Highway 61 at the park entrance
Distance: 1.0-mile out to High Falls and back
Approximate hiking time: 1 hour (including time to enjoy the falls)
Difficulty rating: Easy due to very wide paved and packed gravel trails that are wheelchair accessible
Trail surface: Wide, flat paved and packed gravel
Lay of the land: The border of Minnesota and Ontario along the Pigeon River
Other trail users: Wheelchair users
Canine compatibility: Leashed dogs permitted
Land status: State park (The land is owned by the Grand Portage Ojibwe and is part of the Grand Portage Indian Reservation. It is the only state park in Minnesota on Indian land.)
Nearest town: Grand Marais, MN
Fees/permits: State park vehicle permit required. Annual or day permits are available at the park office. Camping fees are separate.
Schedule: Open year-round. (The park is closed from 10:00 p.m. until 8:00 a.m.)
Map: USGS map: Grand Portage, MN
Trail contacts: Grand Portage State Park, Grand Portage, MN; (218) 475-2360; Department of Natural Resources, Information Center, St. Paul, MN; (651) 296-6157 or (888) 646-6367 (only in MN); www.dnr.state.mn.us/parks

Finding the trailhead: From Grand Marais, drive 36 miles north on Highway 61 to the town of Grand Portage. The park entrance is 7 miles north of the town of Grand Portage off Highway 61 on the left. *DeLorme: Minnesota Atlas & Gazetteer:* Page 79 E10

The Hike

The remote triangle of Minnesota wilderness wedged between the Canadian border and Lake Superior was once the gathering place for a lucrative fur trade business. Native Lakota, Cree, and Ojibwe (Anishinaabe) people used it as a trading base for hundreds of years before the French arrived in the 1700s. They traveled along the Pigeon River and into Canada for wild rice and to trade goods. The Pigeon River, which today forms the international border, proved an ideal highway for traveling and transporting goods great distances because it connected Lake Superior to a vast

Kilometer 0.5

Mile 0.5

N

Middle Falls

GRAND
PORTAGE
STATE PARK

TRAIL

CANADA
ONTARIO

Pigeon River

High Falls

UNDER
CONSTRUCTION

UNITED STATES
MINNESOTA

34 P Park
Entrance

To Grand Marais 61

Port of
Entry

system of inland waterways. But the river wasn't without its obstacles. In one particularly difficult 20-mile stretch of the river, traders had to face dangerous rapids, a 120-foot waterfall, high cliffs, and rocky terrain, making a long portage necessary. The Anishinaabe bundled their loads, then hauled them and their fragile birch bark canoes 9 difficult miles from Grand Portage to Fort Charlotte and the Pigeon's calmer waters. So indelible had this portage become that the Native Americans named it "the great carrying place," which the French later translated to "Grand Portage." This hiking trail, which is part of the Grand Portage National Monument, is a few miles from the state park. The featured hike follows the historic Pigeon River to the spectacular High Falls around which the travelers needed to portage.

When French fur traders arrived in the 1600s, natives at Grand Portage shared their centuries-old skills for travel and survival in the rugged northern Minnesota wilderness. French-Canadian voyageurs used these skills to transport furs and trade goods between the Native American trappers and European traders, who wanted beaver pelts for the booming felt hat fashion industry in Europe. Soon, a trading post was built on the site, and Grand Portage became the first European settlement in Minnesota. The Northwest Company was established by the French-Canadians at Grand Portage in the late 1700s. It eventually merged with the British Hudson's Bay Company in 1821. But the post at Grand Portage was abandoned in 1803 when the company relocated to Fort William. By the mid 1800s, the demand for furs had dwindled, and logging and commercial fishing had become the main industries on the North Shore by the late 1800s.

For centuries, the Pigeon River location served as a post for trade and exploration, but following the War of 1812, it gained new significance. The international boundary between the United States and Canada had long been disputed because the route of water travel on which it had formerly been established varied with time and lay in remote country. Two teams of British and American surveyors were assigned the task of establishing a boundary. They returned with three choices: Kaministikwia River (to the north); Pigeon River; and the St. Louis River (to the south). Fortunately for the United States, Lord Alexander Ashburton, heading the British team, saw little value in the wilderness region between the St. Louis River and the Pigeon. Daniel Webster, for the United States, settled the question by declaring the Pigeon the new international boundary.

Existing within the borders of the Grand Portage Indian Reservation, the state park owes its existence to a unique partnership. Although the park is leased and operated by the Department of Natural Resources, the Chippewa band of the Grand Portage Indians owns the land. The old trading post at Grand Portage, located 7 miles west of the state park, became a national monument in 1958, and buildings remaining from fur trading days were restored and furnished in 1797 style. Visitors can imagine those days by viewing the Great Hall fur press and a canoe warehouse that exhibits several historic items, including two traditional birch bark canoes.

Grand Portage State Park offers hiking trails that are both easy and difficult (the easiest and most difficult on the North Shore). The featured hike is an out-and back walk along a well-designed and maintained wheelchair-accessible interpretive trail that rewards the hiker with breathtaking views of High Falls. Here, as you take in the views, imagine what went through the minds of the Native American people as they thought about how to get their goods and canoes around these mighty falls. Beyond High Falls the Middle Falls Trail begins. This is a much more difficult section, comparable to the Superior Hiking Trail on other parts of the north shore. The trail makes the rocky, switchback climb to Middle Falls, then loops inland and rejoins the Middle Falls Trail, which returns along the same path to High Falls. At the Middle Trail's high point, several miles inland, Lake Superior is visible in the distance. Since the recent discovery of reindeer lichen on the trail between High Falls and Middle Falls, efforts are being made to protect this plant from trampling and other effects of human presence. Reindeer lichen normally grows in arctic conditions where it's the main staple of reindeer or caribou. Most common throughout the northern boreal forest belt, the plant requires high humidity, prefers open-canopy forests on well-drained, water-shedding sites, and often grows on rocks, stumps, and logs. Reindeer lichen is vulnerable to destruction by fire because it has an extremely long recovery rate.

Miles and Directions

0.0 Start from the parking area at the park entrance by the office. Walk past the office and take time to browse inside for interpretive information about the park. Continue past the office and follow the wide, paved High Falls Trail toward the river. Interpretive signs lead the way and describe the Ojibwe's way of life.

0.4 A right leads to an overlook of the High Falls just downstream from a set of wooden platforms. Be sure to take your camera. Stay left to reach a second overlook.

0.5 A set of benches and wooden steps lead the way to another overlook, higher than the first, and just below the falls. Hear the roar of the water and feel the power of the river at this point. From here, retrace your steps back to the parking area.

1.0 Arrive back at the parking area.

ROVE FORMATION

Several geological processes created the ruggedness of Lake Superior's shores. It took centuries for mud deposited by ancient seas to harden into a layer of shales and slates, which geologists call the Rove Formation. At two billion years old, these are some of the oldest sedimentary rocks in North America that have remained unchanged by heat or pressure (unmetamorphosed). These layered rocks are visible along the inside of the Pigeon River gorge below High Falls. Volcanic eruptions followed, intruding harder material (dikes) into the Rove Formation. Then, glaciers scoured away the softer slate and shale, leaving the more erosion-resistant rock seen today as High Falls.

More Information

Local Information

Grand Marais Chamber of Commerce: Grand Marais, MN; (218) 387-9112 or (888) 922-5000 or www.grandmaraismn.com
Grand Marais Visitor Center: (218) 387-9112 or (888) 922-5000; www.grandmarais.com

Local Events/Attractions

Antique Car Show: Mid-May, Grand Marais, MN
Cook County Fair: Mid-August, Community Center, Grand Marais, MN
Grand Marais Fisherman's Picnic: First weekend in August, Grand Marais, MN
Grand Marais Playhouse: Grand Marais, MN; (218) 387-1284, extension 5; www.grandmarais playhouse.com
Minnesota Shakespeare Festival: June, Grand Marais, MN
North House Folk School: Grand Marais, MN; (218) 387-9762 or (888) 387-9762; www.north house.org
Sivertson Gallery: Grand Marais, MN; (218) 387-2491 or (888) 880-4369; www.sivertson.com
Grand Portage Rendezvous Days: Second weekend of August, Grand Portage, MN

Accommodations

Dream Catcher B&B: Grand Marais, MN; (218) 387-3119 or (800) 682-3119; www.dream catcherbb.com
Gunflint Motel: Grand Marais, MN; (218) 387-1454 or (800) 439-1311; www.gunflintmotel.com
MacArthur House Bed & Breakfast: Grand Marais, MN; (218) 387-1840 or (800) 792-1840; www.boreal.org/macarthur
Naniboujou Lodge: Grand Marais, MN; (218) 387-2688; www.naniboujou.com
Nelson's Travelers Rest Cabins & Motels: Grand Marais, MN; (218) 387-1464 or (800) 249-1285; www.travelersrest.com
Outpost Motel: Grand Marais, MN; (218) 387-1833 or (888) 380-1833; www.outpostmotel.com
Seawall Motel & Cabins: Grand Marais, MN; (218) 387-2095 or (800) 245-5806

Snuggle Inn Bed & Breakfast: Grand Marais, MN; (218) 387-2847 or (800) 823-3174; www.snuggleinnbb.com

Restaurants

Angry Trout Café: Grand Marais, MN; (218) 387-1265 (seasonal)
Birch Terrace Supper Club: Grand Marais, MN; (218) 387-2215
Blue Water Café: Cascade Lodge, Grand Marais, MN; (218) 387-1597 or (800) 322-9543; www.cascadelodgemn.com
Gunflint Tavern: Grand Marais, MN; (218) 387-1563
Harbor Inn Restaurant & Motel: Grand Marais, MN; (218) 387-1191 or (800) 595-4566 (seasonal)
Ryden's Border Store: Grand Portage, MN; (218) 475-2330

Local Outdoor Retailers

Joyne's Department & Ben Franklin Store: Grand Marais, MN; (218) 387-2233
Lake Superior Trading Post: Grand Marais, MN; (218) 387-2020

35 Judge C. R. Magney State Park

Trout fishing is said to be productive along the Brule, where, of 9 total miles of hiking trails in the park, 1.4 miles take you to the popular Devil's Kettle and, you can join the much longer Superior Hiking Trail. You'll pass several waterfalls and cascades on this picturesque river hike that gradually climbs to a higher elevation over a wooded and rocky landscape. If you need a rest along the way, stop at a designated area and picnic to the pleasant tune of the Brule's rushing water.

Start: From the trail parking lot off Highway 61
Distance: 2.5 miles out and back
Approximate hiking time: 1.5 hours
Difficulty rating: Difficult due to steep ascents and descents, rocky trails and steep stairs near the falls
Trail surface: Dirt trail with rocks and roots. A set of long wooden stairs with handrails is located within a half mile of the falls.
Lay of the land: Rhyolite and basalt lava flows of the Brule River Valley
Other trail users: Hikers only

Canine compatibility: Leashed dogs permitted
Land status: State park
Nearest town: Grand Marais, MN
Fees/permits: State park vehicle permit required. Annual or day permits are available at the park office. Camping fees are separate.
Schedule: Open year-round, sunup to sundown
Maps: USGS maps: Marr Island, MN; state park map
Trail contacts: Judge C. R. Magney State Park, Grand Marais, MN; (218) 387-3039; www.dnr .state.mn.us

Finding the trailhead: From Grand Marais, travel 14 miles north on Highway 61. Located on the Brule River in the Arrowhead region of northeastern Minnesota, Judge C. R. Magney State Park is on the left. *DeLorme: Minnesota Atlas & Gazetteer.* Page 79 D9

The Hike

Minnesota's beautifully rugged landscape becomes more pronounced as the shore of Lake Superior draws closer to Canada's doorstep. Judge Magney State Park is a well-preserved gem located 25 miles from the Canadian border along Lake Superior's North Shore. The park's main highlight is the scenic Brule River, the third largest of North Shore streams, originating in Brule Lake that sits near Eagle Mountain, Minnesota's highest peak. Some people call this the Arrowhead River, and others know it as Bois Brule to distinguish it from Wisconsin's Brule River. The French-Canadian voyageurs named this river the Bois Brule or "burned forest," which apparently comes from an Ojibwe translation.

Waterfalls, cascades, and whitewater are typical of the Brule River, especially as it nears Lake Superior, where it unloads runoff collected from 282 square miles along its 40-mile run. This wild and undeveloped river's most spectacular and mysterious attraction is a dramatic pink rhyolite gorge that begins downriver at Upper Falls and terminates about a quarter mile farther upriver at Devil's Kettle where water seems to disappear into a bottomless pothole. At this spot, 1.5 miles from the Brule's mouth, a

Upper Falls

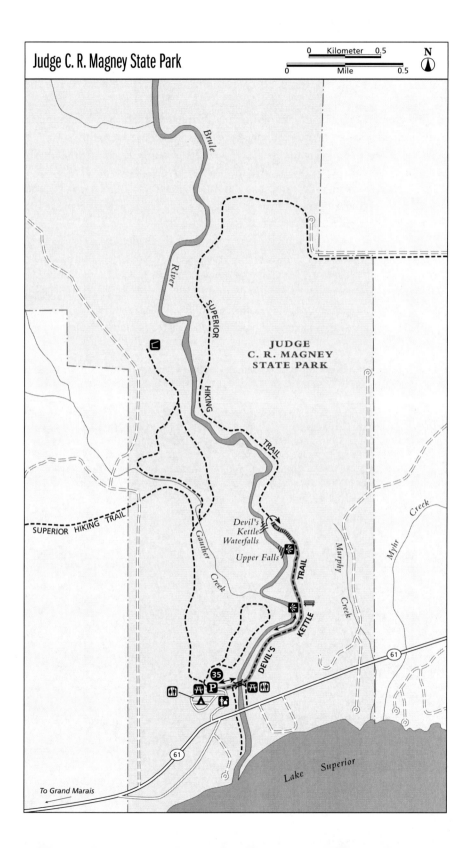

Judge C. R. Magney State Park

0 Kilometer 0.5
0 Mile 0.5

N

Brule

River

SUPERIOR

HIKING

TRAIL

JUDGE
C. R. MAGNEY
STATE PARK

SUPERIOR HIKING TRAIL

Gauthier

Creek

Devil's
Kettle
Waterfalls

Upper Falls

TRAIL

KETTLE

DEVIL'S

Murphy

Creek

Myhr

Creek

Creek

35

P

61

61

To Grand Marais

Lake   Superior

massive rhyolite knob divides the river, resulting in a 50-foot waterfall on one side and a shorter drop into Devil's Kettle on the other. This kettle, or pothole, resulted from the abrasive action of stones being constantly swirled by turbulent waters against riverbed rock. It began in a tiny hole or crack that continued to grow larger as the force of unrelenting water wore away the rock. While kettles like this one are common, this one appears to be bottomless. It's presumed that water falling into the kettle emerges somewhere along the stream to drain into Lake Superior, but no one knows for sure.

Judge C. R. Magney State Park got its start as a government-sponsored work camp for transients who needed income and lodging during the Depression. The men were kept busy for several years with public service work, logging, farming, and fire trail construction. Eventually, they established a small tourist park next to the Brule River. Today, remnants of concrete foundations left from the work camp can be found in the campground and picnic area. In 1957, 940 acres were designated state park land—then called Bois Brule State Park. It was renamed in 1963 in memory of Clarence R. Magney, former Duluth mayor, Minnesota Supreme Court justice, and nature advocate who was instrumental in establishing eleven state parks and waysides along Lake Superior. The park has since been expanded to approximately 4,500 acres.

In addition to forest fires that gave the Bois Brule its name, much of the original trees were cut in the late 1800s. Today, the forest is made up of boreal forest species such as balsam fir, paper birch, and black spruce. Large northern white cedars grow along the banks of the river, providing food for white-tailed deer and grouse. Large white pine, once abundant before logging days, can still be found in the park. The park, which is undergoing a white pine restoration project, has enclosed reseeded areas to protect them from white-tailed deer that would otherwise feed on the young seedlings. You will see these enclosures along the trail. This hike takes you along the east side of the Brule River, with elevation gains, steep descents, and spectacular scenery all within a very short distance. Even though the trail is steep and rugged in places, excellent trail engineering and maintenance has created safe and manageable access to an otherwise inaccessible canyon. For a short, easily accessible hike, this one is well worth the trip.

Miles and Directions

0.0 Start from the trail parking lot. From the east side of the parking lot, take the Devil's Kettle Trail toward the river. After crossing a bridge over a small drainage, look to the left and see the Judge C. R. Magney memorial. Then cross the bridge over the Brule River.

0.1 Pass the picnic area and toilets (on the right), and turn left to continue on the Devil's Kettle Trail. There is a sign here about the Brule being a designated trout stream.

0.3 Ascend a set of approximately twenty wooden stairs. You will be hiking alongside the river at the edge of the gorge.

0.4 Pass a bench on the right overlooking the river. There is a trail intersection here with a ski trail. Stay left to continue going up river.

0.8 Reach an overlook of the upper falls on the left. (FYI: This is a great place to rest, have a snack, and take in the view on the bench provided.)

0.9 Begin descending to the river's edge along a well-built wooden staircase (164 steps). A couple of landings with benches provide resting spots.

1.0 At the bottom of the stairs, follow the boardwalk. You'll hear the roar of the Upper Falls before they come into view.

1.1 A set of stairs goes down to the edge of the river and the bottom of the upper falls. This is a great spot for photos and for feeling the spray of the falls. Ascend another set of wooden stairs (made from squared-off logs) to get to the top of Devil's Kettle.

1.25 On the left is a bench and overlook of the Devil's Kettle, yet another great spot for photos. The trail continues along the river to the right, joining the Superior Hiking Trail. From this point, retrace your steps to return to the start.

2.5 Arrive back at the parking area.

More Information

Local Information
Grand Marais Chamber of Commerce: Grand Marais, MN; (218) 387-9112 or (888) 922-5000 or www.grandmaraismn.com
Grand Marais Visitor Center: (218) 387-9112 or (888) 922-5000; www.grandmarais.com

Local Events/Attractions
Antique Car Show: Mid-May, Grand Marais, MN
Cook County Fair: Mid-August, Community Center, Grand Marais, MN
Grand Marais Fisherman's Picnic: First weekend in August, Grand Marais, MN
Grand Marais Playhouse: Grand Marais, MN; (218) 387-1284, extension 5; www.grandmarais playhouse.com
Minnesota Shakespeare Festival: June, Grand Marais, MN
North House Folk School: Grand Marais, MN; (218) 387-9762 or (888) 387-9762; www.north house.org
Sivertson Gallery: Grand Marais, MN; (218) 387-2491 or (888) 880-4369; www.sivertson.com
Grand Portage Rendezvous Days: Second weekend of August, Grand Portage, MN

Accommodations
Dream Catcher B&B: Grand Marais, MN; (218) 387-3119 or (800) 682-3119; www.dream catcherbb.com
Gunflint Motel: Grand Marais, MN; (218) 387-1454 or (800) 439-1311; www.gunflintmotel.com
MacArthur House Bed & Breakfast: Grand Marais, MN; (218) 387-1840 or (800) 792-1840; www.boreal.org/macarthur
Naniboujou Lodge: Grand Marais, MN; (218) 387-2688; www.naniboujou.com
Nelson's Travelers Rest Cabins & Motels: Grand Marais, MN; (218) 387-1464 or (800) 249-1285; www.travelersrest.com
Outpost Motel: Grand Marais, MN; (218) 387-1833 or (888) 380-1833; www.outpostmotel.com
Seawall Motel & Cabins: Grand Marais, MN; (218) 387-2095 or (800) 245-5806
Snuggle Inn Bed & Breakfast: Grand Marais, MN; (218) 387-2847 or (800) 823-3174; www.snuggleinnbb.com

Restaurants

Angry Trout Café: Grand Marais, MN; (218) 387-1265 (seasonal)
Birch Terrace Supper Club: Grand Marais, MN; (218) 387-2215
Blue Water Café: Cascade Lodge, Grand Marais, MN; (218) 387-1597 or (800) 322-9543;
www.cascadelodgemn.com
Gunflint Tavern: Grand Marais, MN; (218) 387-1563
Harbor Inn Restaurant & Motel: Grand Marais, MN; (218) 387-1191 or (800) 595-4566
(seasonal)
Ryden's Border Store: Grand Portage, MN; (218) 475-2330

Local Outdoor Retailers

Joyne's Department & Ben Franklin Store: Grand Marais, MN; (218) 387-2233
Lake Superior Trading Post: Grand Marais, MN; (218) 387-2020

36 Cascade River

If it's a good workout you're looking for along with picturesque views of a tumbling whitewater river, climb the trail that follows the Cascade River inland from the North Shore. For spectacular views of Lake Superior, side hikes extend outside the park to Moose and Lookout Mountains, both of which rise 600 feet above the lake. Along the hike, the trail ventures close to the riverbank for views of waterfalls and then away from the river where the Cascade's rushing water can be heard far below. The hiking trail climbs more than 600 feet upstream along the west side, crosses over on a county road, and then journeys back down the east side. Portions of the trail are steep, and other portions cross wet areas on log bridges or boardwalks, so protective footwear is a must. This is a strenuous hike along a narrow, volcanic canyon that carries a rapidly moving river to Lake Superior, but it's well worth the effort.

Start: From the Trail Center parking area off Highway 61
Distance: 7.3-mile loop
Approximate hiking time: 4.5 hours
Difficulty rating: Difficult due to rugged trail with steep ascents and descents
Trail surface: Rock and dirt trails with exposed tree roots. Some portions are steep and cross wet areas on wooden bridges or boardwalks.
Lay of the land: Trace the Cascade River as it flows through a volcanic rock canyon over several falls on its way to Lake Superior.
Other trail users: Backpackers (on the Superior Hiking Trail)

Canine compatibility: Leashed dogs permitted
Land status: State park, national forest, and private land
Nearest town: Grand Marais, MN
Fees/permits: State park vehicle permit required. Annual or day permits are available at the park office. Camping fees are separate.
Schedule: Open year-round, but closed from 10:00 p.m. to 8:00 a.m., except to registered campers
Maps: USGS maps: Deer Yard Lake, MN; state park map
Trail contacts: Cascade River State Park, Lutsen, MN; (218) 387-3053; www.dnr.state

.mn.us; Superior National Forest, Duluth, MN; (218) 626-4300; www.fs.fed.us/r9/superior .com; Gunflint District Ranger, Grand Marais, MN; (218) 387-1750; Superior Hiking Trail Association, Two Harbors, MN; (218) 834-2700; www.shta.org

Finding the trailhead: From Tofte, drive northeast approximately 21 miles on Highway 61 to the park entrance, which is at mile marker 101. *DeLorme: Minnesota Atlas & Gazetteer.* Page 78 E5

The Hike

A beautiful rugged river, three creeks, the cliff-lined Lake Superior shoreline, and a hiking trail that hugs the Cascade River are the chief attractions of the North Shore's Cascade River State Park. In its 15-mile journey to Lake Superior, the Cascade River drains approximately 120 square miles. The Cascade's headwaters include many lakes, ponds, and marshes that create steady, even flows throughout the summer. Five miles into its journey high above Lake Superior, the river begins to drop over bedrock ledges in a series of cascades that continue to its mouth. The steepest drop is in the final 3 miles, where the river falls 900 feet—120 feet in just the last quarter mile through a steep, twisting gorge.

The Cascade River State Park encompasses the lower portion of the river gorge, where hikers can find a footbridge that spans the river. Your hike starts by crossing a small footbridge, with views of the spectacular cascades of the lower gorge. The Cascade River Trail then travels 600 feet up the west side of the river and journeys back down on the other side after crossing back over the river on a county road. The trail ventures out of the park through a section of private land on the east side and Superior National Forest land on both sides of the upper portion. The park has 18 miles of hiking trails, including part of this hike, which connects with the Superior Hiking Trail and the North Shore State Trail. On the west side of the river, Cascade River Trail joins Lookout Mountain Trail, which leaves the park boundaries and climbs to the top of Lookout Mountain in Minnesota's Sawtooth Range.

The landscape of Cascade River State Park and all along the North Shore reveals evidence of ancient volcanic activity from the Precambrian period. Late in the period (roughly 1.1 billion years ago), a huge rift formed in the continent, from the Lake Superior region down to south Kansas. A series of lava flows along this crack, when cooled, formed the dark basalt of the North Shore volcanic group. In some places from Duluth to Grand Portage, these flows are five miles thick. It's estimated that 15,000 feet of lava were deposited in layers within the area of the park. Interruptions in volcanic activity resulted in intermittent layers of softer sandstone, which was washed in by streams and deposited. A large mass of lava that formed the Duluth Complex—a large body of coarse-grained volcanic rock that cooled beneath the earth's surface and is visible for 150 miles from Duluth to the Canadian border—intruded inland and tilted the basalt and sandstone layers toward Lake Superior. Glacial scouring and meltwater followed, eroding the Cascade River gorge. The river's cascades result from varying degrees of erosion of the rock layers. The most prominent feature of the park resulted from the tilting and erosion of these lava flows and sandstone layers. The Terrace Point basalt flow that forms a ridge along the North Shore is the layer most resistant to erosion. Lookout Mountain, a point on this ridge, has a steep north-facing bluff and a long, gentle lakeward slope formed by the flow. This landform is called a *cuesta* (a long, low ridge with a relatively steep face on one side and a long, gentle slope on the other). These cuestas that you can see along the shore on a clear day are what give the visual imagery for the name Sawtooth Mountains. If your interest is piqued, *Geology on Display*, by John C. Green, is an excellent resource of information on the geology of Cascade River and other North Shore parks.

Cascade River waterfalls

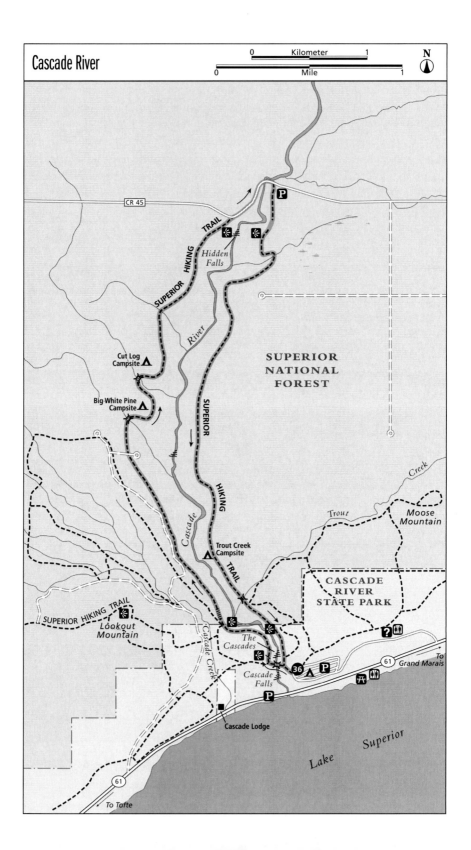

Cascade River

Kilometer
0   1
0   Mile   1

N

CR 45

SUPERIOR HIKING TRAIL

Hidden Falls

River

Cut Log Campsite

Big White Pine Campsite

SUPERIOR NATIONAL FOREST

SUPERIOR HIKING

Cascade

Creek

Trout

Moose Mountain

Trout Creek Campsite

TRAIL

CASCADE RIVER STATE PARK

SUPERIOR HIKING TRAIL

Lookout Mountain

Cascade Creek

The Cascades

36

Cascade Falls

61

To Grand Marais

Cascade Lodge

61

Lake Superior

To Tofte

The Terrace Point basalt flow is also a source of Thomsonite, a green, white, and pink-ringed mineral that was formed in gas cavities in the basalt. Thomsonite is a popular mineral of collectors, and commercial collecting and purchasing options are available nearby. It is most easily collected after it has been weathered and broken away from the basalt. Good Harbor Bay, northeast of Cascade River State Park on the North Shore, is a popular collecting spot, where it can be found washed up on the beaches. Remember, no collecting is permitted in Cascade River State Park.

Plant life along the Cascade River is lush, bathed in the spray of leaping water. Moss and fern cling to wet rock walls, and groves of white cedar inhabit the moist soils. Large stands of maple grace the higher, drier soil along with paper birch and white spruce, creating a diverse habitat that's inviting to all sorts of animal life, such as white-tailed deer, timber wolves, black bear, pine marten, and red fox. Bird life along the Cascade River is both diverse and prolific, with many songbirds nesting from mid-May to mid-July and hawks soaring overhead. As you pause at one of the many overlooks, listen to the melodic songs against the peaceful backdrop of the river tumbling its way to Lake Superior.

Miles and Directions

0.0 Start from the trail center parking lot next to the campground. The trailhead is right across from the trail center's door. Proceed north toward the river.

0.1 At this intersection, a right follows the river upstream on the east side. Take a left and cross the bridge over the Cascade River. On the west side of the bridge, an overlook and bench provide a place to enjoy the view of the lower gorge and its cascades. Then, a left goes back to Highway 61. Turn right and ascend the west bank of the river, heading north on the Superior Hiking Trail. Pass two ski trails on the left.

0.3 The trail forks. Take a right to follow the river. A left joins the trail again 300 feet ahead.

0.5 A bench and overlook of the river are to the right of the trail. Just past this point on the left are Lookout Mountain Trail and the Superior Hiking Trail. Lookout Mountain is 0.9 mile from this intersection. Turn right to follow the river, passing a ski trail on the left.

0.6 Descend ninety-six steps down to the river's edge. At the bottom, a spur trail goes right toward the river. Continue left on the Superior Hiking Trail.

1.4 Pass a scenic spot under a grove of cedars with a fire ring. The trail continues along the river.

1.5 A spur trail on the right leads to a waterfall on a tributary creek of the Cascade River in 0.3 mile. After viewing the falls, take a left and ascend a steep trail that can be slippery in wet weather. The trail then moves away from the river and passes the site of an old mine.

1.8 Cross a small bridge over a small stream. Pass a large white pine on the right.

1.9 Big White Pine Campsite is on the left. Stay right on the Superior Hiking Trail.

2.4 Cross a bridge over a tributary stream. The trail ascends along the creek.

2.5 Pass Cut Log Campsite on the left. Keep right to follow the Superior Hiking Trail and walk through beautiful stands of maple. The sounds of the river are muffled but still within hearing range.

3.6   A steep ascent leads to great views of Hidden Falls. Then pass above a landslide where a section of the steep riverbank has collapsed. Reach CR 45, turn right, and walk along the road to cross the bridge over the Cascade River.

3.9   Turn left and walk to an access parking area for the Superior Hiking Trail. Pass the Superior Hiking Trail on the right and walk underneath the bridge heading down river on the east side.

4.4   Hear the loud rushing of water and take in the spectacular view of Hidden Falls.

4.5   Notice small caves in the river canyon wall across the river.

4.7   The trail descends steeply to meet the river and then ascends steeply.

4.8   The trail enters private property for the next 1.5 miles. Please stay on the trail in this section.

5.1   Ascend a steep section of trail that is severely eroded on a log stairway. Pass through a grove of aspens and some large white pines on a ridge high above the river.

6.3   The trail leaves private property.

6.5   Pass a spur trail to the left. Keep right along the river.

6.6   Pass Trout Creek campsite on the right and ascend away from the river.

6.7   Cross a bridge over Trout Creek, a tributary of the Cascade River. (FYI: Notice evidence of flooding in this area from times of high water. Walk out to the river's edge and see the layered red sandstone.)

6.8   Ascend a steep ridge and pass a ski loop on the left. Stay right.

6.9   Enter the state park, leaving the Superior National Forest. Pass an overlook of the Cascade River on the right.

7.0   Pass a spur trail on the right. Continue left on the Superior Hiking Trail.

7.1   In the next tenth of a mile, pass two junctions with ski trails. Keep right and follow the trail along the river.

7.2   Reach the intersection at the east end of the bridge over the Cascade River. Take a left to head back to the trail center.

7.3   Arrive back at the trail center parking.

More Information

Local Information
Grand Marais Chamber of Commerce: Grand Marais, MN; (218) 387-9112 or (888) 922-5000 or www.grandmaraismn.com
Grand Marais Visitor Center: (218) 387-9112 or (888) 922-5000; www.grandmarais.com

Local Events/Attractions
Antique Car Show: Mid-May, Grand Marais, MN
Cook County Fair: Mid-August, Community Center, Grand Marais, MN
Grand Marais Fisherman's Picnic: First weekend in August, Grand Marais, MN
Grand Marais Playhouse: Grand Marais, MN; (218) 387-1284, extension 5; www.grandmarais playhouse.com
Minnesota Shakespeare Festival: June, Grand Marais, MN
North House Folk School: Grand Marais, MN; (218) 387-9762 or (888) 387-9762; www.north house.org

Sivertson Gallery: Grand Marais, MN; (218) 387-2491 or (888) 880-4369; www.sivertson.com
Grand Portage Rendezvous Days: Second weekend of August, Grand Portage, MN

Accommodations

Dream Catcher B&B: Grand Marais, MN; (218) 387-3119 or (800) 682-3119; www.dream
catcherbb.com
Gunflint Motel: Grand Marais, MN; (218) 387-1454 or (800) 439-1311; www.gunflintmotel.com
MacArthur House Bed & Breakfast: Grand Marais, MN; (218) 387-1840 or (800) 792-1840;
www.boreal.org/macarthur
Naniboujou Lodge: Grand Marais, MN; (218) 387-2688; www.naniboujou.com
Nelson's Travelers Rest Cabins & Motels: Grand Marais, MN; (218) 387-1464 or (800) 249-
1285; www.travelersrest.com
Outpost Motel: Grand Marais, MN; (218) 387-1833 or (888) 380-1833; www.outpostmotel.com
Seawall Motel & Cabins: Grand Marais, MN; (218) 387-2095 or (800) 245-5806
Snuggle Inn Bed & Breakfast: Grand Marais, MN; (218) 387-2847 or (800) 823-3174;
www.snuggleinnbb.com

Restaurants

Angry Trout Café: Grand Marais, MN; (218) 387-1265 (seasonal)
Birch Terrace Supper Club: Grand Marais, MN; (218) 387-2215
Blue Water Café: Cascade Lodge, Grand Marais, MN; (218) 387-1597 or (800) 322-9543;
www.cascadelodgemn.com
Gunflint Tavern: Grand Marais, MN; (218) 387-1563
Harbor Inn Restaurant & Motel: Grand Marais, MN; (218) 387-1191 or (800) 595-4566
(seasonal)
Ryden's Border Store: Grand Portage, MN; (218) 475-2330

Local Outdoor Retailers

Joyne's Department & Ben Franklin Store: Grand Marais, MN; (218) 387-2233
Lake Superior Trading Post: Grand Marais, MN; (218) 387-2020

37 Split Rock Lighthouse State Park

The hike up the Split Rock River, one of the state's most scenic, offers a water-carved gorge, a rigorous walk, waterfalls and rapids, quiet woods, and a marvelous view of Lake Superior—all in one hike. It takes you upriver along the west side of the beautiful, winding Split Rock River, crosses it, and returns down the east side. Along the way, sights include the magnificent gorge the river has cut into pink rhyolite flows and many rapids and falls that fill the canyon with their soothing sounds. The splendor of this North Shore river is punctuated by the sound of a number of songbirds. Either before or following your hike, visit the Split Rock Lighthouse and learn about the unique history of this breathtaking site.

Split Rock River overlook

Start: From the Department of Transportation wayside on Highway 61
Distance: 4.6-mile loop
Approximate hiking time: 3 hours
Difficulty rating: Moderate to difficult due to rugged, rocky terrain
Trail surface: Rugged dirt trail with rocks and tree roots, and mowed grass trail on the east side of the river
Lay of the land: The steep river valley of the Split Rock River, which flows into Lake Superior
Other trail users: Backpackers
Canine compatibility: Leashed dogs permitted
Land status: State park
Nearest town: Beaver Bay, MN

Fees/permits: State park vehicle permit required. Annual or day permits are available at the park office. Camping fees are separate.
Schedule: Open year-round, dusk to dawn
Maps: USGS maps: Split Rock Point, MN; state park map
Trail contacts: Split Rock Lighthouse State Park, Two Harbors, MN; (218) 226-6377; www.dnr.state.mn.us; Department of Natural Resources, Information Center, St. Paul, MN; (651) 296-6157 or (888) 646-6367 (only in MN); www.dnr.state.mn.us; Minnesota Historical Society Web site: www.mnhs.org; Superior Hiking Trail Association, Two Harbors, MN; (218) 834-2700; www.shta.org

Finding the trailhead: From Two Harbors, drive approximately 20 miles on Highway 61. Just after milepost 43, turn left at the Department of Transportation wayside at the Split Rock River. The park entrance is on the right in another 2.5 miles. Please note that wayside parking is free, but is limited to a maximum of six hours. Overnight parking and tent camping is available in the state park. *DeLorme: Minnesota Atlas & Gazetteer.* Page 67 A83

The Hike

The Lake Superior shoreline is a mix of quiet bays, steep rugged cliffs, and rocky beaches. These cliffs, though beautiful to look at, were once a threat to off-course ships that unintentionally ventured too close. There was nothing to fear when the waters were calm, but when the shore became curtained in fog, the wind gathered speed, waves became walls, and fingers of spray reached over the tops of the 90-foot cliffs, travel on this largest of the Great Lakes became treacherous. Even compasses were unreliable in preventing wrecks due to the magnetic properties of mineral deposits on shore that deflected compass needles eastward.

At the turn of the twentieth century, the iron ore industry was thriving, and cargo ships wore a highway across the Great Lakes where loads were picked up at Two Harbors, Duluth, Minnesota, and Superior, Wisconsin, and shipped to the steel mills in Cleveland. Lake Superior was already considered dangerous, but a November 1905 storm took a particularly large toll when icy winds raced in from the northeast at 60 mph, pushing helpless ships across the lake and into the treacherous shore. Several uninsured ships of the Pittsburgh Steamship Company (a subsidiary of the U.S. Steel Corp.) were damaged in the storm, which helped earn Lake Superior the reputation of being the most dangerous body of water in the world. Following the storm, the federal government agreed to appropriate $75,000 for the construction of a lighthouse and fog signal at Split Rock. Construction began in 1909, and the lighthouse became operational the following year. The light was so efficient and powerful that fishermen could see it as far away as Grand Marais, 60 miles up the shore.

Completion of the North Shore highway (Highway 61) in 1924 made it easier for the curious to visit Split Rock Lighthouse, and keepers added tour guide to their job descriptions. The site was so popular that by 1930, approximately 5,000 people were visiting the lighthouse each year. By 1938, the number had jumped to 27,591, according to an old visitor record book. The popularity of Split Rock Lighthouse prompted improvements over the years, such as safety fences and the addition of a gift shop and an access road. By 1969, more sophisticated navigation systems had diminished the need for lighthouses, and Split Rock Lighthouse was retired and closed. But public interest continued to grow, and visitor numbers reached 200,000 annually by the mid-1980s. By then, Split Rock Lighthouse belonged to the state, having been obtained from the Coast Guard in 1971. The site is now administered by the Minnesota Historical Society, which has preserved the light station as one of the state's historic sites and restored it to appear as it did in its pre-electricity era in the 1920s.

It isn't certain where the name Split Rock came from, but there are several possibilities. One is that it is named after the way the Split Rock River splits the rock

Overlook to Lake Superior

canyon through which it passes before emptying nearby into Lake Superior. Another is that the name came from the white streaks of anorthosite that run through the black, igneous rock on which the lighthouse sits, seeming to split it in two. Yet another possibility is that the name came from the cliffs northeast of the river known as Split Rock Point, because they appear as one rock split in two when viewed from the water. Some say it came from the split rock formation known as The Pillars on the west side of the river.

As you hike up the west side of the Split Rock River, it's easy to be moved by its power as it rushes and leaps over falls and rapids and cuts a deep gorge through dark basalt and pink rhyolite lava flows. Hikers' legs get a workout as they steadily climb, following the course of the river past rock formations like The Pillars (dramatic towers of pink and red rhyolite that were fractured due to the columnar jointing of the rhyolite as it cooled from 1,832 degrees F). Along the trail there are some beautiful riverside campsites (outside the park boundary on the Superior Hiking Trail) and a well-crafted bridge built by Superior Hiking Trail volunteers. On the east side, the trail remains above the river on a high bank, giving the hiker a panoramic perspective of the valley and Lake Superior.

Miles and Directions

0.0 Start from the Department of Transportation wayside on Highway 61. Look for signs marking Superior Hiking Trail and campsite mileage. Walk upriver, following the west side of Split Rock River.

0.1 The trail follows the hilly contours of the land and is above the thick, alder-choked river valley.

0.3 Two side trails lead down to dark pools below rapids or falls. Watch the white foam spin in eddies on the dark, tea-colored water.

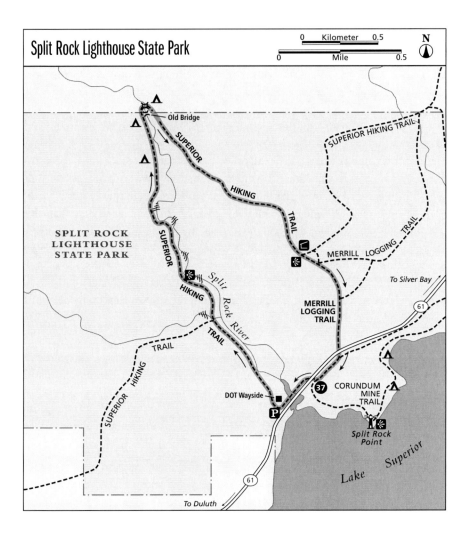

Split Rock Lighthouse State Park

0   Kilometer   0.5

0   Mile   0.5

N

Old Bridge

SUPERIOR HIKING TRAIL

SUPERIOR HIKING TRAIL

SPLIT ROCK LIGHTHOUSE STATE PARK

SUPERIOR HIKING

Split Rock River

MERRILL LOGGING TRAIL

MERRILL LOGGING TRAIL

To Silver Bay

61

TRAIL

SUPERIOR HIKING

DOT Wayside

P

CORUNDUM MINE TRAIL

37

Split Rock Point

Lake Superior

61

To Duluth

0.5   The main Superior Hiking Trail comes in from the left. (**Option:** This trail leads south toward Gooseberry Falls State Park in 6 miles.) Turn right and cross a small creek with a waterfall on the left. On the right, the river has carved an undercut channel into the solid rock wall. The trail climbs out of the creek valley and parallels Split Rock River.

1.6   The trail nearly touches the river's edge, and then climbs a steep, rocky path with a view of cascades, waterfalls, and rapids below.

1.9   Come to the "split rock" pillars between the trail and river's edge. As you look upstream, you can see a deep canyon.

2.0   Pass a Superior Hiking Trail campsite.

2.2   See remnants of an old Superior Hiking Trail bridge that used to cross the river.

2.3   Pass another campsite and come to the new bridge built by Superior Hiking Trail volunteers. A logbook provides a place for you to enter your thoughts. Cross the bridge and turn right to head downstream.

2.4 Come to a multi-group campsite. Stay close to the river to continue on the trail and glimpse spectacular views of the canyon.

2.9 Another campsite sits on the edge of the Split Rock River State Park boundary. Climb away from the river valley and enter a forest of aspen, ash, and paper birch.

3.9 Come out onto a knoll and catch a panoramic view of Lake Superior and its rocky shoreline. Pass a shelter built for hikers.

4.0 Here, the Superior Hiking Trail goes left, 10.8 miles to Beaver Bay. Take a right and walk downhill. This trail is marked as a Superior Hiking Trail spur trail. Fifty feet farther, come to a trail intersection. Stay right and continue to descend along a wide, mowed trail.

4.2 Another ski loop comes in from the left. Keep right and walk toward the lake and Highway 61.

4.3 Cross Highway 61 and walk southwest along the paved park road. View the mouth of the river where it empties into Lake Superior, the curving sandbar, and old pilings where an old logging railroad ended in 1906. A large logging camp was located on the east side of the rivermouth. This is also a great spot for a cool dip after your hike. This area is marked as day-use only.

4.5 Cross back over Highway 61 to go back to the Department of Transportation wayside and your car.

4.6 Arrive back at your vehicle.

More Information

Local Information
Two Harbors Area Chamber of Commerce: Two Harbors, MN; (218) 834-2600 or (800) 777-7384; www.twoharbors.com/chamber

Local Events/Attractions
Grandma's Marathon: June, Two Harbors to Duluth; (218) 727-0947
Summer Solstice: June, Lighthouse, Two Harbors, MN; (218) 834-4898
Two Harbors Folk Festival: July, Two Harbors Fairgrounds, Two Harbors, MN; (218) 834-4668

Accommodations
Split Rock Lighthouse State Park: Two Harbors, MN; (218) 226-6377
Bob's Cabins: Two Harbors, MN; (218) 834-4583; www.bobscabins.duluth.com/
Flood Bay Motel: Two Harbors, MN; (218) 834-4076
Castle Haven Resort: Two Harbors, MN; (218) 834-4303
J Gregor's Inn: Two Harbors, MN; (218) 226-4614 or (888) 226-4614
Cove Point Lodge: Beaver Bay, MN; (800) 598-3221; www.covepointlodge.com
Superior Shores Resort: Two Harbors, MN; (218) 242-1988; superiorshores.com

Restaurants
Betty's Pies: Two Harbors, MN; (218) 834-3367 or (877) 269-7494
Black Wood's Bar & Grill: Two Harbors, MN; (218) 834-3846
Louise's Place: Two Harbors, MN; (218) 834-2176
The Lemon Wolfe Café: Beaver Bay, MN; (218) 226-7225

Hike Tours

Lighthouse tours: hours vary, but are usually May 15 through October 15, from 10:00 a.m. to 6:00 p.m. From October 16 through May 14, only the history center is open from noon to 4:00 p.m. The visitor center is open until 7:00 p.m.

Local Outdoor Retailers

Beaver Bay Sport Shop: Beaver Bay, MN; (218) 226-4666
Central Sales II: Two Harbors, MN; (218) 834-4000

38 Park Point

Visitors come to Duluth for many reasons. Some are awed by the city, and the harbor lights as they descend into Duluth at night from a high ridge overlooking Lake Superior. Others look forward to birding on Park Point or Hawk's Ridge, while still others gather near shore to watch international ships enter the famous harbor. Park Point is a narrow, 9-mile-long, partially forested, sometimes grassy stretch of sand with a long, interesting, controversy-filled history. It's a walk along a sandy beach where unsalted waves become giants as they're pushed to shore by ambitious winds.

Start: From the City Park parking area adjacent to the Sky Harbor Airport
Distance: 4.2-mile loop
Approximate hiking time: 2 hours
Difficulty rating: Easy along the old road along the bay and moderate scrambling on rocks and walking on beach sand along Lake Superior
Trail surface: Sand, rocks, and old dirt road
Lay of the land: A 7-mile-long baymouth bar separating the St. Louis Bay from Lake Superior
Other trail users: Beachgoers, sea kayakers, and birders

Canine compatibility: Leashed dogs permitted
Land status: City park
Nearest town: Duluth, MN
Fees/permits: No fees or permits required
Schedule: Open year-round. Day use only.
Map: USGS map: Superior, MN
Trail contacts: Parks & Recreation Commission, Duluth, MN; (218) 723-3612; www.ci. duluth.mn.us; Duluth City Hall, Duluth, MN; (218) 730-5000

Finding the trailhead: From Duluth going north or south on Interstate 35: Take the Lake Avenue exit and proceed east. At the first stoplight, turn right (this is Lake Avenue). At the next stoplight (one block), take a left (still Lake Avenue). Cross the aerial lift bridge. On the other side, you will be on Minnesota Avenue. Follow this out past the Park Point recreation facilities and parking to the Sky Harbor Airport (about 4 miles). Park just outside the airport. *DeLorme: Minnesota Atlas & Gazetteer.* Page 66 E3

The Hike

Six-mile Park Point (formerly known as Minnesota Point) and 3-mile Wisconsin Point, together, form the longest baymouth bar in the world. The term baymouth bar refers to a deposit of sediments extending across the mouth of a bay, separating the bay from open water. Park Point and Wisconsin Point separate St. Louis Bay and the Nemadji River from the open waters of Lake Superior. It's estimated that this bar (or sand spit) was created 5,000 years ago at the tail end of a long geologic process. As miles-thick glaciers advanced southwestward, their tremendous weight compressed the land. When temperatures warmed and the ice began to melt, the glaciers retreated to the north and east, lifting the heavy weight off the southwestern part of the lake, where the relieved land began to spring back. It was this uplift that increased the St. Louis River's gradient in its final stretch to the lake. With the retreating glacial mass covering the northeastern part of the lake, pressing it down, the lake water shifted in that direction—as it would if you tilted a bowl full of water. When the weight was finally lifted from the northeast edge, and the land on that end rose, the resulting shift of the water back to the southwest caused the water to spill over into the mouth of the St. Louis River, drowning it in lake water and forming the St. Louis Bay. Gradually, suspended sediments transported by the St. Louis and Nemadji River currents settled out, providing much of the silt underlying the spit. In addition, prevailing winds and resulting wave action transported sand from eroding sandstone deposits westward across Wisconsin's south shore to combine with the river sediment, forming the long sand spit stretching from Duluth to Wisconsin.

Sand dunes on Park Point

Nature's forces continue to shape the land and water today, piling up more sand in some places and eroding it in others. Winds blowing shoreward blow sand along the ground's surface, and when that sand meets with vegetation, it's deflected and the grains drop. Over time, this sand builds up into small mounds. Wind continues to carry sand grains up the windward sides of the mound, and the grains move until they eventually roll down the steep backslope. Mound formation and the entrapment of sand are the beginning of dune formation. To develop into a large dune, sand must be trapped. To grow in height and breadth, sand must encounter vegetation, such as the dune-building marram grass (*Ammophila breviligulata*). This grass is the keystone plant species for dune formation on Minnesota and Wisconsin points. The hardy grass is able to withstand the cold winters and extreme heat (when sand temperatures reach 100 degrees F or higher). Burial by the blowing sands actually stimulates growth as the plant attempts to keep its leaves exposed to the sun. This cycle of burial and growth aids in the vertical rise of the dune.

Nature's forces aren't the only influences on Park Point. What was long ago a natural landscape feature was altered over the years to serve human activity. Low-lying swampy ground was filled in, and a channel was cut into the Duluth side of the point, separating it from the mainland. The cutting of the channel in the late 1800s caused a controversy between the cities of Duluth and Superior, Wisconsin—the action strongly opposed by Superior residents. Channel dredging occurred hurriedly and secretly in the middle of the night in anticipation of a court injunction against cutting the channel. The action was undertaken to keep the shipping port on the Wisconsin side where the St. Louis River flows into the lake. By the time the injunction was delivered, construction of the 300-foot-long channel was well underway.

View of Duluth, Minnesota, on the far shore of Lake Superior

Dunes are dynamic and prone to change: storms erode the sand; longshore currents bring new sediment; humans disperse the sand when walking, riding, or driving on dunes; plant life evolves; and strong winds blow on dunes. Erosion on the southeastern end of Park Point, from both natural and human impact, has caused recent concern about the point's future. As a result of a meeting between the Park Point Community Club and the U.S. Army Corps of Engineers, more than 100,000 cubic yards of clean sand dredgings were pumped onto the endangered land in the late 1990s to help alleviate the problem. Future plans include planting grasses, trees, and shrubs on the fragile dunes to help prevent further erosion; keeping people and animals off the dunes; and educating and informing the public about Park Point's unique ecology and recreational environment.

Here, on the bottom edge of Lake Superior where the St. Louis River empties its water load, birds like sanderlings, turnstones, Hudsonian godwits (rare in Minnesota), spotted sandpipers, and snowy owls delight birders visiting Park Point. Wood ducks, swans, herring gulls, ring-billed gulls, and terns are common along the shore, and the songs of countless warblers fill the woods behind the dunes. During spring and autumn migration times, Park Point is a resting spot for a variety of migrating birds, especially on foggy days when they're grounded, waiting for the weather to clear. The other sets of wings belong to small aircraft landing at and taking off from Sky Harbor Airport and Seaplane Base.

Miles and Directions

0.0 Start from the City Park parking area adjacent to the Sky Harbor Airport. Walk southeast toward a gravel road and look for a park point nature trail walk sign. The airport building will be on your right and Lake Superior on your left.

0.1 Leave the vicinity of the airport and catch a great view of Superior Bay and any activity around the airport and seaplane base.

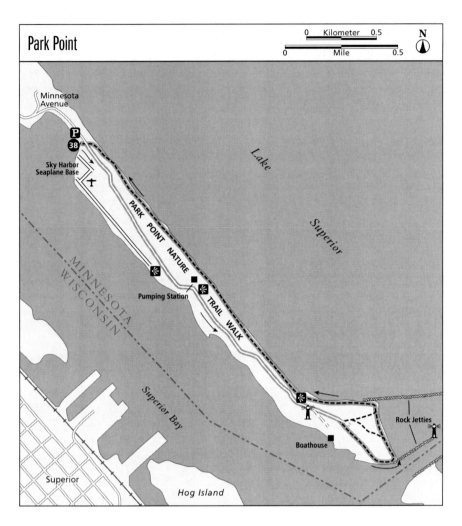

0   Kilometer   0.5

0   Mile   0.5

N

0.3   Many small trails branch off of the gravel two-track road. Stay on the road and hike past white pines, paper birch, and willow on your left. The bay is on your right.

0.6   Enjoy a view of the Superior, Wisconsin, ore loading docks, which are the largest of their kind in the world.

0.8   Walk past a pumping station and get your first view of Lake Superior. Stay on the two-track road and enter a stand of virgin white pine. Look for wild roses, raspberries, and fireweed. Beware of poison ivy all along the trail.

0.9   Walk by several small side trails to your left and stay on the main trail. The woods will open up to an area of rolling sand dunes with grasses, poison ivy, and sand cherry. Please stay on the trail and off the dunes. Dunes are a dynamic and fragile ecosystem.

1.6   Come to another picturesque view of Lake Superior and pass by the ruins of a 50-foot lighthouse built in 1855 and only used for twenty years.

1.7   Pass through a younger forest and the ruins of an old boathouse. Look for beach peas growing in the sand.

2.1 Reach the end of park point and watch the ships depart from the Superior, Wisconsin, grain and ore docks. Turn south to walk along the shore of Lake Superior with the lake to your right. The first stretch is along big rocks until you pass the rock jetty, so watch your footing. Then, enjoy a wonderful beach walk back to your car.

2.7 Pass by the end of the Minnesota breakwater protecting the mouth of the St. Louis and Nemadji Rivers. Be sure to look off in the distance to see the city of Duluth nestled into the hillside.

3.4 Pass by the pumping station on your left. This is a good spot to watch for shorebirds that live along the point. Look for an airport beacon on a large pole, turn left and follow the trail that crosses sand dunes. Be sure to stay on the trail and off the dunes.

4.2 Arrive back at the parking area.

More Information

Local Information

Duluth Area Chamber of Commerce: Duluth, MN; (218) 722-5501; www.duluthchamber.com

Duluth Convention & Visitors Bureau: Duluth, MN; (218) 722-4011 or (800) 4-DULUTH; www.visitduluth.com

Local Events/Attractions

Grandma's Marathon: Mid-June, 26.2-mile road race from Two Harbors to Duluth

Glensheen Historic Estate: Duluth, MN; (218) 726-8910 or (888) 454-GLEN; www.d.umn .edu/glen

The Depot: Duluth, MN; (218) 727-8025

Great Lakes Aquarium: Duluth, MN; (218) 740-3474; www.glaquarium.org

Lake Superior Zoological Gardens: Duluth, MN; (218) 723-3777; www.lszoo.org

SS *William A. Irvin* Ore Boat Museum: Duluth, MN; (218) 722-7876; ww.decc.org/attractions/ irvin.htm

Accommodations

Canal Park Inn: Duluth Lakeshore, Duluth, MN; (218) 727-8821 or (800) 777-8560

Hawthorn Suites at Waterfront Plaza: Duluth, MN; (218) 727-4663 or (877) 766-2665 (reservations); www.hawthornsuitesduluth.com

South Pier Inn on the Canal: Duluth, MN; (218) 786-9007 or (800) 430-7437; www.southpier inn.com

Firelight Inn: Duluth, MN; (218) 724-0272 or (888) 724-0273; www.duluth.com/firelightinn

Manor on the Creek Inn: Duluth, MN; (218) 728-3189 or (800) 428-3189; www.manoron thecreek.com

Restaurants

Bennett's on the Lake: Fitger's Complex, Duluth, MN; (218) 722-2829; www.bennetts onthelake.com

Grandma's Saloon & Grill: Duluth, MN; (218) 727-4192; www.grandmas restaurants.com

Amazing Grace Café: Duluth, MN; (218) 723-0075

Lake Avenue Café: Duluth, MN; (218) 722-2355

Bellisio's Italian Restaurant: Duluth, MN; (218) 727-4921

Little Angie's Cantina & Grill: (218) 727-6117
Taste of Saigon: (218) 727-1598

Organizations

Park Point Community Club & Minnesota Point Natural Resources Education: Duluth, MN, Beach House, City of Duluth Parks and Recreation Department; (218) 730-4300

Other Resources

Lake Superior Maritime Visitor Center: Duluth, MN; (218) 727-2497
Boat Watcher's hotline: (218) 722-6489

Local Outdoor Retailers

Duluth Pack Store: Duluth, MN; (218) 722-1707 or (800) 849-4489; www.duluthpack.com
Gander Mountain: Duluth, MN; (218) 786-9800; www.gandermountain.com
Northwest Outlet: Superior, WI; (715) 392-9838 or (800) 569-8142; www.northwestoutlet.com
Midnight Sun: 100 Lakeplace Drive; (218) 727-1330

39 Jay Cooke State Park

A 126-foot swinging suspension footbridge crosses the St. Louis River, high above the gorge with its red clay banks—clay deposited long ago by Glacial Lake Duluth, the ancient glacial lake that later became Lake Superior. This bridge, rebuilt in 1953, was the only way across the river from the Thomson Hydroelectric Station power-house in the early 1900s. Since that time, the bridge has been modified, destroyed by weather, and rebuilt. Jay Cooke State Park's 50 miles of hiking trails follow this tur-bulent portion of river for a distance, take you across the footbridge past several sce-nic overlooks, and connect with the paved Willard Munger State Trail. Silver Creek, which drains into the St. Louis, is spring fed and stocked with trout. Beaver find its running water inviting. The evidence is in the fresh cuttings lying near their dams along the creek. Silver Creek Trail is part of the Minnesota Hiking Trail system.

Start: From the park office off Highway 210
Distance: 3.5-mile loop
Approximate hiking time: 1.5 hours
Difficulty rating: Moderate due to hills
Trail surface: Dirt and rocky trails
Lay of the land: The St. Louis River valley
Other trail users: Hikers only
Canine compatibility: Leashed dogs permitted
Land status: State park
Nearest town: Carlton, MN
Fees/permits: State park vehicle permit required. Annual or day permits are available at the park office. Camping fees are separate.
Schedule: Open year-round with groomed ski trails in the winter. Hiking options offered in the winter are separate from the designated ski trails.
Maps: USGS maps: Esko, MN; state park map
Trail contacts: Jay Cooke State Park, Carlton, MN; (218) 384-4610; www.dnr.state.mn.us; Department of Natural Resources, St. Paul, MN; (651) 296-6157 or (888) 646-6367; www.dnr.state.mn.us

Finding the trailhead: From Moose Lake, drive north on Interstate 35 to Highway 210. Turn right (east) to Carlton. The park entrance is 3 miles east of Carlton on Highway 210. *DeLorme: Minnesota Atlas & Gazetteer.* Page 66 E1.

The Hike

Sandwiched within the roughly 9,000 acres that make up Jay Cooke State Park flows a river with one of the largest watersheds in Minnesota. Named after Louis IX, king of France during the Crusades, the St. Louis River is the largest tributary to Lake Superior on the American side, draining approximately 3,600 square miles, 63 of them in Wisconsin. The river begins its 160-mile journey to Lake Superior from Seven Beavers Lake—south of Babbit, Minnesota—where, in its upper reaches, it remains wild and unspoiled, cutting through miles of coniferous pine forest. Here, the river is quiet enough for canoeing. From Cloquet on, though, the St. Louis River changes its personality, dropping half of its total gradient of roughly 1,100 feet during the last 10 miles to its mouth. Its water flows through a deep gorge in a series of cascades, rapids, and whitewater. This section of the river is the park's main attraction.

Advancing and retreating glaciers and the volume of their resulting meltwater formed the Great Lakes, the St. Louis River, and its watershed. Eventually, glacial meltwater drained into the St. Louis River, accumulating enormous quantities of forceful water that eroded its lower gorge. As the glacial Great Lakes kept draining to the east, their water levels became lower, increasing the gradient of the St. Louis River into Lake Superior.

This dramatic grade explains why the lower portion of the river was considered ideal for the four hydroelectric power plants strung out along the river from Cloquet on down. In conjunction with these plants, five reservoirs were created in the Cloquet and Whiteface river watersheds in the early 1900s to regulate water flow downstream. The Thomson plant, located just upstream of Jay Cooke State Park, is the largest of the five and the one to which the park owes its existence. Jay Cooke, a wealthy Pennsylvanian, dreamed up the idea of a waterpower plant at the lower gorge of the St. Louis in the late 1860s. Extensive work went into its construction, which included a 3-mile-long canal connecting a reservoir with a forty-acre holding pond 400 feet above the powerhouse. The operating dam held back 160 million cubic feet

Suspension bridge over the St. Louis River

Looking upstream over the St. Louis River

of water—a hydropower potential second only to Niagara Falls. Because of the difficult topography at this point in the river, the dam and the powerhouse had to be constructed several miles apart, leaving idle more than 2,350 acres of Cooke's estate. This land was deeded to the state by Horace J. Harding in 1915 for the development of a state park. Harding, president of St. Louis River Water Power Company, was also executor of Jay Cooke's estate. Over the years, more land was donated until the park had grown to 9,000 acres.

Two hundred years ago, the St. Louis River was the primary waterway for trade goods headed west or south from Lake Superior. The people who transported these goods were called voyageurs, and paddling up the St. Louis River in a birch bark canoe loaded with ninety-pound packs was no small task. It was a difficult, physically exhausting life for the voyageurs, who had to make many long portages along the route. One such portage route, the Grand Portage Trail of the St. Louis River, which begins in Jay Cooke State Park, was 7 grueling miles over steep hills and wet swamps. This portage along the St. Louis River gorge began by climbing a 60- to 70-foot clay bank with hand and footholds dug into it. Ropes were often used to pull canoes up the steep bank. The voyageurs' procedure for tackling this rugged trail with heavy packs was to first shuttle their loads to the top of the hill and rest a while. They'd then pick up a load, carry it a distance to the first pose (or resting place), put it down, and then backtrack to pick up a second load. This process was repeated the length of the portage, which consisted of nineteen poses approximately a half mile apart. Depending on the weather, it could take seven days or more than a week to make the portage in this manner. In those days, this was the most efficient method for transporting goods. The dense forests, with their thick underbrush and fallen, tangled timber, made foot travel impractical. Lakes and rivers were the most efficient routes used by travelers. The voyageurs persevered in spite of their hard lives and even managed to enjoy the freedom of their rough outdoor lifestyle.

A DAY IN THE LIFE

Some have called the life of a voyageur wild and carefree, but one could question the word carefree. A voyageur had to endure treks through muddy swamps (suffering from blood-sucking insects), up steep hills, and through tangled forests. The voyageur's days were long, with little rest, and he constantly risked back injury from toting heavy loads. His daily diet consisted of a quart of dried corn or peas and an ounce of grease, supplemented by nature's provisions if he encountered them along the way. In spite of these hardships, the voyageurs embraced this rugged way of life, happy to be free of society's impositions.

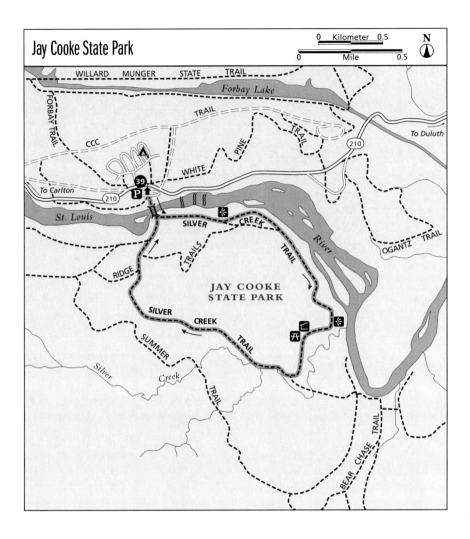

Miles and Directions

0.0   Start from the park office. Facing south, follow the trail marked to bridge. Follow Silver Creek Trail (also the Hiking Club Trail) across the bridge.

0.1   Take a left to follow Silver Creek Trail along the St. Louis, hearing the loud rush of the rapids as you walk along the bank above the river. A right goes up river on Carlton Trail.

0.3   A bench and overlook mark this spot to the left of the trail. Reach intersection 29. Take a left to remain along the river. (**Option:** A right at this intersection follows Hiking Club Trail away from the river.)

0.6   Take a left to stay on Silver Creek Trail, and continue downriver. A right loops back toward the ridge trails. The trail winds around and goes up and down gentle hills through a maple, birch, and spruce forest toward Silver Creek.

1.5 Come to an overlook of Silver Creek near where it empties into the St. Louis River. (FYI: This is a great place for a picnic, with a shelter and picnic table.)

1.8 This is intersection 37. Take a right to continue on Silver Creek Trail. A left goes south and crosses Silver Creek, connecting with some other trail loops.

3.0 At intersection 53, take a right. Here, there are several intersections within a short distance. Come to intersection 31 and continue straight ahead, then take a right at intersection 32. Finally, turn left at intersection 28.

3.4 Back at the bridge, take a left to cross the river.

3.5 Arrive back at the parking area.

More Information

Local Information
Cloquet Area Chamber of Commerce: Cloquet, MN; (218) 879-1551 or (800) 554-4350; www.cloquet.com

Local Events/Attractions
Lake Superior Zoo: Duluth, MN; (218) 733-3777
Superior Whitewater: Carlton, MN; (218) 384-4637

Accommodations
Royal Pines Motel: Carlton, MN; (218) 384-4242
Golden Gate Motel: Cloquet, MN; (218) 879-6752 or (800) 732-4241
AmericInn of Carlton: Carlton, MN; (218) 384-3535

Restaurants
The Pantry: Cloquet, MN; (218) 879-3234
River Inn Grill: Cloquet, MN; (218) 879-2760
Buffalo House: Duluth, MN; (218) 624-9901

Local Outdoor Retailers
Outdoor Advantage: Cloquet, MN; (218) 879-3185

Honorable Mentions

Compiled here is an index of great hikes in the Lake Superior and Border Lakes region that didn't make the A-list this time around but deserve recognition. Check them out and let us know what you think. You may decide that one or more of these hikes deserves higher status in future editions or, perhaps, you may have a hike of your own that merits some attention.

Bog Walk (on Highway 53)

This half-mile handicap-accessible loop on a wide, floating boardwalk gives the hiker access to six different wetland ecosystems and offers views of Pelican Lake. Unique bog plants such as the carnivorous pitcher plant and many other wetland plants are highlights that make this hike worth doing.

From the town of Virginia, drive north on U.S. Highway 53 for 29 miles. The parking area is on the left side of the road at the Tourist Information Center. *DeLorme: Minnesota Atlas and Gazetteer.* Page 87 D6

Vermilion River Gorge

This 3-mile out-and-back hike follows the rim of the dramatic, 60-foot-deep, granite Vermilion River gorge near its mouth at Crane Lake. Also a voyageur route during the fur trade, the Vermilion River is one of Minnesota's top canoeing rivers. This picturesque hike is easily accessible but remote, as it begins at the end of CR 24 deep in the Superior National Forest.

To get there from Orr, drive east on CR 23 for 14 miles. Turn left on CR 24 and proceed for 10 miles to the town of Crane Lake. Park one-tenth of a mile past U.S. customs. *DeLorme: Minnesota Atlas and Gazetteer.* Page 87 B8

North Arm Trails

The North Arm Trails provide 18 miles of hiking loop options in the wilderness setting of the Boundary Waters Canoe Area Wilderness. Also a premier ski area, the trails ascend and descend rocky ridges past small lakes and ponds through forests of large red and white pines, some more than 300 years old. A day-use wilderness permit is required and can be obtained at the trailhead.

To get there from Ely, drive east on Highway 169 one mile to CR 88. Turn left and proceed for 2 miles to CR 116 (Echo Trail) and turn right. Proceed for 9 miles to CR 644 (North Arm Road). Turn left and proceed for 3.5 miles to the parking lot and trailhead on the right side of the road. *DeLorme: Minnesota Atlas and Gazetteer.* Page 88 E3

Angleworm Lake

This 13-mile trail is a loop around Angleworm, Home, and Whiskey Jack Lakes. The trail follows rugged ridge tops and over low marsh and stream courses. Trail highlights include scenic overlooks from the high bedrock ridges of Angleworm Lake, and many old-growth pines. Most of the route is inside the BWCAW and has remote designated campsites. Because this is a remote area, the trail can be tough to find depending upon when the last trail crew was in the BWCAW with hand saws to clear the trail. So bring your map, compass/GPS, and appropriate navigational equipment.

To get there from Ely, drive east on Highway 169 1 mile to CR 88. Turn left and drive 2.5 miles to CR 116 (Echo Trail). Turn right and continue for 13 miles. The parking area is on the right marked by a U.S. Forest Service sign. *DeLorme: Minnesota Atlas and Gazetteer.* Page 88 D4

Kekekabic Trail

The Kekekabic Trail is a remote and rugged long-distance trail that traverses the BWCAW west to east between the Fernberg and Gunflint Trails for 38 miles. The hiking trail was developed on an old firefighting road originally built in the 1930s, maintained by the Kekekabic Trail Club. At its eastern edge, the Kekekabic Trail connects with the Border Route Trail, which connects to the Superior Hiking Trail.

To access the west side of the Kekekabic Trail, drive north from Ely on Highway 169 for 3 miles. At this point, the road becomes the Fernberg Trail. Proceed approximately 9 miles on Fernberg Trail to Snowbank Lake Road and take a left. The Kekekabic Trail begins on the left, across the road from the parking lot. *DeLorme: Minnesota Atlas and Gazetteer.* Page 89 E8. To access the east end of the trail, drive north on the Gunflint Trail (CR 12) from Grand Marais. Proceed for 34 miles to Loon Lake, which is on your right. The trailhead begins on the east side of Loon Lake. *DeLorme: Minnesota Atlas and Gazetteer.* Page 78 B4

Stub Lake Trail

This trail is an out-and-back 1.5-mile loop trail that begins from Fall Lake Campground about 6 miles east of Ely. From Ely, travel east for 4.5 miles on Highway 169 (Fernberg Road), which becomes CR 18. Turn left on CR 182 and continue 1.5 miles to the Fall Lake Campground. Newly constructed in 2005, most of the route is characterized by upland forest, with a 200-foot boardwalk through a cedar swamp and a bird viewing platform on the creek between Stub and Fall Lakes. A short spur trail leads to a portage between the two lakes. Reservations for the campground can be made online at www.reserveusa.com or (877) 444-6777. *DeLorme: Minnesota Atlas and Gazetteer.* Page 89 E6

Cross River Wayside

One of the North Shore's scenic rivers, the Cross River descends over a series of waterfalls through a volcanic gorge along its last few miles to Lake Superior. The 2-mile out-and-back hike begins at the state wayside and follows the edge of the river gorge past a series of waterfalls before joining the Superior Hiking Trail at a footbridge that crosses the river. Several rock ledges provide a great place to listen to the roar of the river and take in the views. Two nearby campsites make this an excellent spot for an overnight.

To get there from Two Harbors, drive north on Highway 61 for 53 miles and park at the Cross River State Wayside on the edge of the town of Schroeder. *DeLorme: Minnesota Atlas and Gazetteer.* Page 67, D8

Temperance River State Park–Carlton Peak

Views from the top of Carlton Peak include a panorama of inland forests and Lake Superior shoreline, including Taconite Harbor. Because of the extensive views, this was once the location of a fire tower. The 6.4-mile out-and-back hike to the summit of Carlton Peak is a steady uphill climb to 720 feet above Lake Superior. Carlton Peak is a prominent, erosion-resistant anorthosite knob that has also been a favorite rock-climbing area.

From Two Harbors, drive north on Highway 61 for 54 miles to Temperance River State Park. Park in the parking lot on the right side of the road. *DeLorme: Minnesota Atlas and Gazetteer:* Page 67 D8

Gooseberry Falls State Park

Gooseberry Falls State Park is the most visited state park along Lake Superior's North Shore. Many come to view the spectacular series of waterfalls along the Gooseberry River, three of which are near the visitor center. However, if you hike beyond the wayside and upriver, you can find yourself enjoying a quiet walk along the scenic Gooseberry River. The 3.1-mile Fifth Falls Trail begins at the visitor center and follows the east side of the river to Fifth Falls, then returns along the river's west side.

To get there from Two Harbors, drive north on Highway 61 for 12 miles. Park at the visitor center located on the right side of the road. *DeLorme: Minnesota Atlas and Gazetteer:* Page 67 A8

Oberg Mountain

This 1.8-mile loop circumnavigates the top of Oberg Mountain for some of the best overlooks of Lake Superior and views of Leveaux and Moose Mountains. The best times to hike this loop are when colors are at their peak in the fall and just before leaf-out in the spring when wildflowers are blooming on the maple forest floor. Be sure to take your camera and a lunch to enjoy the views from the benches and picnic table before descending back to your car.

To get to the trailhead, drive north from Two Harbors on Highway 61 for 61 miles and turn left onto Forest Road 336. Proceed 2.2 miles and park on the left side of the road. The Oberg Mountain trailhead is on the right side of the road. *DeLorme: Minnesota Atlas and Gazetteer:* Page 67 D9

Moose Mountain

A popular fall-colors "hike" is to ride the Lutsen Resort gondola to the top of Moose Mountain, taking in views 1,000 feet above Lake Superior and enjoying the 3.6-mile hike through a colorful maple forest back to your car.

To get to the trailhead, drive north from Two Harbors on Highway 61 for 65 miles and turn left onto CR 36. Follow the signs to the ski area and gondola parking. *DeLorme: Minnesota Atlas and Gazetteer*: Page 78 E4

Lookout Mountain

A favorite spot for a picnic, Lookout Mountain is located within Cascade River State Park. The 3-mile loop includes a steep climb to the summit of Lookout Mountain for views of the surrounding forested landscape and Lake Superior shoreline. The hike begins at the Trail Center and crosses the Cascade River on a footbridge overlooking the spectacular cascades for which the park and river are named. From here, follow the Superior Hiking Trail to the top of Lookout Mountain.

To get there from Grand Marais, drive south on Highway 61 for 9 miles to the park entrance, which is on the right. *DeLorme: Minnesota Atlas and Gazetteer*: Page 79 E5

Pincushion Mountain

An excellent day hike near Grand Marais, Pincushion Mountain Trail is also part of a well-used network of ski trails. The 4.4-mile loop begins at the parking area off of CR 53 and ascends Pincushion Mountain for outstanding views of Grand Marais and Lake Superior.

From Grand Marais, drive north on CR 12 (Gunflint Trail) for 2 miles and turn right on CR 53 (Pincushion Drive). Proceed for a quarter of a mile to the parking area and trailhead. *DeLorme: Minnesota Atlas and Gazetteer*: Page 79 D7

Devil's Track Canyon

Just a short distance from the parking area along the 4.8-mile out-and-back Devil Track Canyon Trail, you can view the deepest canyon in Minnesota. Several overlooks of this spectacular red-walled volcanic gorge and the rushing sound of the Devil Track River are highlights of this challenging trail. Proceed with caution, as there are many steep drop-offs along the way.

Drive north from Grand Marais on Highway 61 for 4.3 miles to CR 58. Turn left and proceed for 1 mile to the parking area and trailhead on the left side of the road. *DeLorme: Minnesota Atlas and Gazetteer*: Page 79 D7

Border Route Trail

Border Route Trail, a 95-mile trail that follows the Minnesota/Ontario border and connects the Grand Portage Trail and the Superior Hiking Trail to the east with the Kekekabic Trail, stretches to Ely and the western edge of the BWCAW. The Minnesota Rovers Outing Club in Minneapolis began to create and maintain the Border Route Trail in 1972. Nine years later, more than 75 miles were completed that linked the eastern Grand Portage Trail to the Gunflint Trail. The Border Route Trail follows high, erosion-resistant ridges some 500 feet above border lakes for spectacular views. It then descends into stream valleys and climbs back up steep ridges. The trail is almost entirely in the BWCAW, where federal regulations apply, and is maintained by the U.S. Forest Service, Minnesota Rovers Outing Club, Gunflint Lake resorts, and various groups of volunteers. The Caribou Rock and Border Route Trails are rough, remote, and some of the wildest and most primitive trails in the state. These trails aren't designed for casual day-hikes, and even accessing the trails can be a challenge. Good map and compass and backcountry skills are necessary.

To access the east end of the trail, drive north on Highway 61 18 miles past Grand Marais to Hovland. Turn left onto CR 16 (Arrowhead Trail) and proceed 4.5 miles to Jackson Lake Road. Turn right and continue for 3.1 miles to the parking area on the right. *DeLorme: Minnesota Atlas and Gazetteer.* Page 79 C10. To access the west end of the trail, drive north on the Gunflint Trail (CR 12) from Grand Marais. Proceed for 34 miles to Loon Lake, which is on your right. The trailhead begins on the east side of Loon Lake. *DeLorme: Minnesota Atlas and Gazetteer.* Page 78 B4

Mount Rose

Mount Rose overlooks Grand Portage National Monument and Lake Superior. The 1-mile steep hike climbs to 300 feet above the lake. This easily accessible hike is a great leg-stretcher after a visit to the national monument.

From Grand Marais, drive north on Highway 61 for 33 miles to CR 17. Turn right and proceed east. Follow signs to Grand Portage National Monument. Mount Rose Trail is on the left side of CR 17. *DeLorme: Minnesota Atlas and Gazetteer.* Page 79 E9

Mount Josephine

This 2-mile rugged trail to the top of Mount Josephine lies within Grand Portage Indian Reservation. Permission to use the trail is required and can be obtained at Grand Portage Lodge and Casino, which is on your right as you drive on CR 17 toward the national monument. The trail climbs 700 feet above Lake Superior and offers spectacular views of Susie Islands, Michigan's Isle Royale, and historic Hat Point, of which Mount Josephine is a part. Hat Point was the last point of land that voyageurs passed in their journey from Montreal before reaching Grand Portage. As they paddled by Hat Point, voyageurs donned their hats in order to be presentable for the summer rendezvous.

From Grand Marais, drive north on Highway 61 for 33 miles to CR 17. Turn right and proceed east. Follow signs to Grand Portage National Monument. Continue 1.5 miles past the fort. Parking is on the left. *DeLorme: Minnesota Atlas and Gazetteer.* Page 79 E9

Great Escape—
The Superior
Hiking Trail

ccording to *Backpacker* magazine, Minnesota's Superior Hiking Trail (SHT) ranks as one of the ten best hiking trails in the country and one of the top ten in the world—placing it in league with the Appalachian and John Muir Trails. This little-known treasure currently covers 270 miles of Minnesota's most rugged and spectacularly scenic terrain, paralleling the North Shore of Lake Superior and connecting public and private lands on a narrow, hand-built footpath from Two Harbors to the Canadian border (plus 39 miles through the city of Duluth). The SHT ascends and descends a series of long, volcanic ridges covered with glacial deposits along the Highland Moraine. More than two dozen rivers and streams penetrate these remote ridges of the Sawtooth Mountains, cutting through the bedrock on their journey to Lake Superior, forming spectacular waterfalls, steep canyons, and gorges. Overlooks of Lake Superior and inland lakes are numerous and breathtaking. Stands of oak and maple cover the warmer high ridges and are ablaze with color in the fall. Boreal evergreens, birch, and aspen grow throughout the area; cedar and spruce swamps thrive in cool valleys; and scattered red and white pine are prominent features of the landscape. Wildlife is rich and varied, from timber wolves, black bear, white-tailed deer, and moose to ravens, gulls, eagles, owls, hawks, and warblers. Wildflowers lure the hiker with a burst of color and aroma in spring while summertime berries abound. Fall is the most popular time for visitors as the many high ridges and overlooks afford unmatched views.

This challenging trail is unique in that it is so easily accessible via several county and Forest Service roads off of Highway 61, combined with the fact that a hiker can feel completely isolated only miles from the trailhead. The section of trail featured here is 175 miles and can be through-hiked. The SHT can be hiked in many ways, as a point-to-point, an out-and-back, or circuit hikes on 5–7 mile loops. Since we cannot cover all of the options, we include a number of great day-hike suggestions.

Created in the mid-1980s, the Superior Hiking Trail is a cooperative project of the Superior Hiking Trail Association (SHTA), the U.S. Forest Service, the Minnesota Department of Natural Resources, Lake and Cook Counties, and many private landowners. Grant money to build the trail was originally given by the Legislative Commission on Minnesota Resources. Continued trail development and maintenance is provided by the member-supported SHTA and many hardworking volunteers.

40 The Superior Hiking Trail

Start: Two Harbors, MN
End: Judge Magney State Park
Distance: Approximately 175 miles
Approximate hiking time: 14 to 18 days
Difficulty rating: Difficult due to rugged terrain and steep ascents and descents
Lay of the land: The trail ascends Minnesota's highest ridges along the North Shore of Lake

Superior and climbs in and out of more than two dozen river gorges and creek valleys.
Other trail users: Hikers only
Canine compatibility: Dogs permitted (must be in control at all times and on a leash in state parks)
Land status: National forest, state forest, state park, and private land

The Hike

Nestled along Lake Superior's North Shore 21 miles northeast of Duluth lies the iron-ore shipping and tourist town of Two Harbors. Settled in the late 1800s as a logging and commercial fishing village, the town is currently a first stop for tourists heading up the North Shore. Two Harbors is also the home of the Superior Hiking Trail Association (SHTA) office and store, where maps and trail information are available. Beginning a few miles north of the city, our featured section of the SHT ascends gently from Lake Superior to the rocky, tumbling Silver Creek Gorge through mixed woods, all previously logged. Near Silver Creek, the forest is more mature and the sense of proximity to civilization begins to fade. The 16-mile section of trail to Gooseberry River (and Gooseberry Falls State Park) crosses four major waterways, climbs to three impressive overlooks, tops off at an elevation of 1,200 feet, then gradually descends into the scenic Gooseberry River Valley. The Wolf Rock overlook offers spectacular views of Lake Superior and the steep, pine-forested Crow Creek Valley. Gooseberry, which is known for its impressive waterfalls, is the most visited state park in Minnesota. The Gooseberry River is a great place to look for agates (semi-precious gems that are banded pink and white). Agates were formed when a fine-grained quartz mineral called chalcedony was deposited in layers inside gas cavities in basalt. As ice age erosion weathered the basalts, the harder agates were exposed and transported in gravel deposits, where they are often found.

Overlook on Bean Lake

View inland from atop Mount Trudee

The next 27 miles after crossing Gooseberry River cover increasingly rugged terrain. You cross Split Rock and Beaver Rivers and two major ridges before reaching the logging and taconite processing and shipping towns of Beaver Bay and Silver Bay. Split Rock Lighthouse State Park surrounds Split Rock River Gorge with its falls and cascades, and features the historic lighthouse that was built in 1910 to warn ships of the dangerous shoreline. A side trip off the main trail to visit the lighthouse is well worth your time. A wayside on Highway 61 provides access to the river loop—one of the best day-hike loops on the SHT. From the Split Rock River Valley, you'll ascend and hike along Christmas Tree and Fault Line Ridges. Fault Line is a unique north-south ridge that was created by a vertical fault and resulted in a high, cliff-lined ridge beside a deep valley 300 feet below. A spur trail from Cove Point on Lake Superior was developed for an excellent day-hike loop to the ridge. In the vicinity of Beaver Bay and Silver Bay is one of the more developed sections of the trail, yet steep, rugged hills offer dramatic views of the lake, the inland landscape, and the towns.

Only a few miles after leaving the town of Silver Bay, the remote and rugged landscape once again envelops the hiker. The first 11 miles of the 18-mile stretch to CR 6 lies almost entirely within Tettegouche State Park, the largest of the North Shore parks. Bean and Bear Lakes are tucked into a valley surrounded by high ridges and cliffs that overlook the surrounding landscape for many miles. The trail's easy access from Silver Bay makes this a prime day hike or overnight spot—campsites are available for a one-night stay only. Erosion-resistant masses of anorthosite rock form prominent knobs and ridges that make this section challenging yet incredibly scenic. The highest concentration of these anorthosite features, rarely found anywhere else in the world, occurs between Split Rock and Tofte. Examples on this stretch include Round Mountain, Mount Trudee, and Raven Rock. A heart-pounding climb up pine-covered Mount Trudee to an elevation of more than 1,500 feet culminates in a splendid view of the Palisade Creek Valley and Lake Superior before descending into maple forest. Experience another beautiful North Shore river as the trail descends into the Baptism River Valley and crosses an impressive single cable suspension bridge above the second highest waterfall in the state. The base of the falls makes an enjoyable lunch and cooling-off stop before climbing out of the river valley to Highway 1. From here, the trail begins a long, steep climb up a 4-mile ridge that overlooks Wolf and Raven Lakes and Lake Superior. Many overlooks and ascents and descents follow, concluding with a spectacular view from Sawmill Creek Dome and a steep descent to CR 6.

Many of the overlooks on the SHT are unrivaled in their breathtaking views, especially in the fall when the sugar maples, birch, and aspen set the landscape aglow. The overlook from Section 13 offers one such view. On either side of CR 6, Section 13 and Sawmill Creek Dome are both large anorthosite domes that are well known to the local rock climbing community. From the top of Section 13 you can see an expanse of wild land for many miles, across which the next 15 miles of the SHT traverses. Completed in the fall of 2000, this section of trail is unique in that it is one of the few sections that venture inland away from Lake Superior and its bordering ridges. In addition to being relatively flat and providing a quiet respite from the dramatic relief of the previous (and following) sections, the trail offers a look at inland forests of maple, aspen, birch, and balsam, all of which are in various stages of re-growth. These diverse forests provide great habitat for deer and other wildlife. The character of rivers and streams, like the Baptism River, differs noticeably the farther inland you go. There the waterways meander slowly in contrast to their cascading final descent to Lake Superior. Dramatic relief returns at Crosby Manitou State Park where the Manitou River rushes through the park on its way to Lake Superior. George Crosby, a mining magnate, donated the land for Crosby Manitou State Park under the condition that it be a backpack-only park. It's the only one of its kind in the state. Climbing out of the river gorge onto Horseshoe Ridge is the steepest ascent on the SHT. Views of the rugged Manitou River Valley and Lake Superior unfold all along the ridge and gradual descent to the deep and scenic Caribou River Gorge.

Relatively flat and easy to hike, the next 9 miles (to CR 1) are through aspen, birch, and maple forest. Alfred's Pond is a bog type of wetland along this stretch that's worth a stop to check out the unique plants such as the carnivorous pitcher plant, sundew, sphagnum moss, and orchids. This area and the marsh near Fredenberg Creek, farther along the trail, are great places to look for moose tracks. After CR 1, the SHT crosses Fredenberg Creek and then follows along the bluff of the Cross River with a nice view of the falls. There are beautiful views of Lake Superior and campsites on either side of the river. A steep descent to the Temperance River follows, the trail winding in and out of the woods and skirting the edge of the river. The Temperance is a spectacular North Shore river. Its character changes from wide and slow in its upper stretches

Paper birch forest

High falls on the Baptism River

to a torrent as it rushes through the dramatic, deep, narrow Hidden Falls Canyon, disappearing from sight as it nears Lake Superior. A steep ascent out of the Temperance River Gorge precedes the long, gradual climb up to Carlton Peak over the next 3 miles. Carlton Peak is an anorthosite dome frequented by rock climbers and day hikers. There are spectacular views of the surrounding landscape and Lake Superior from its summit, which was also the site of a fire tower up until the 1950s. From Carlton Peak to Moose Mountain, there are several prominent hills and knobs, including Britton Peak, Leveaux Mountain, and Oberg Mountain, which have excellent overlooks and easy accessibility for day hikers. This stretch is especially popular during peak fall colors. Lutsen Resort, a popular ski and summer resort, sits at the base of Moose Mountain and offers gondola rides to its summit. Highlighted by many climbs to overlooks, this stretch culminates in a strenuous but rewarding hike up Moose Mountain, which overlooks Lake Superior and the Poplar River Valley, 1,086 feet below.

The SHT follows the Poplar River for 6 miles, beginning at its wild and raging gorge near Lake Superior. As you hike upriver through maple and mixed woods toward Lake Agnes, the Poplar widens and meanders slowly through a wide, scenic valley. This section is remote, away from the access of the previous section, and is known for its high concentration of moose. Look for tracks and mountain maple that has been heavily browsed. Lake Agnes is one of few places on the SHT with a campsite on a lake (Egge, Sonju and Bear Lakes also have campsites). Surrounded by ridges, this tiny lake has an alpine feel. From Agnes, the trail traverses a long ridge through the woods toward the Cascade River, the most photographed river on the North Shore. Take in the cascades and falls along the rugged lower section of this river, then traverse a long stretch of low, flat land all the way to Pincushion Mountain and the rugged Devil Track River. A few great views of Lake Superior and the fishing and tourist town of Grand Marais are highlights on this stretch.

Devil Track River flows through a deep and narrow volcanic canyon; the trail is steep and precipitous in places. The SHT crosses the river, climbs the steep valley, and follows the north rim of the red rhyolite canyon toward the lake. You can hear the loud roar of the river and enjoy several breathtaking overlooks along the way, including a view of Barrier Falls. Before reaching the lake, the trail continues to climb, following gentle Woods Creek to Wildflower Hill for another lake view. A long, gradual descent to Lake Superior follows, crossing the Kadunce River Gorge and crossing Highway 61 to the shore. Taking you to the lowest point on the SHT, the trail follows approximately 2 miles of cobblestone beach along the magnificent lake. Depending on the day, you may experience fog, crashing waves, or placid waters. Although it may be hard to leave the allure of this great lake, the ascent to the final highlight of the featured hike is worth the trip. The featured section of the SHT ends at Judge Magney State Park, and we recommend the 1-mile side hike up to the Devil's Kettle. The lower section of the Brule River lies within Judge Magney State Park and flows through a deep volcanic gorge. The trail alongside the river descends 180 wooden stairs as you approach the powerful Upper Falls. Upstream 0.3 mile is the unique Devils Kettle, where the Brule River splits into two channels, each falling into deep river kettles formed by the abrasive action of a rock swirling in the current and forming a depression in the softer riverbed. The kettle on the right has broken open, and the water spills into a large pool. The water on the left side disappears into the left kettle. Where this water goes remains a mystery. The SHT continues

Footbridge crossing the Caribou River

another 30 miles beyond the park and then connects with the Border Route Trail that heads west across the Boundary Waters Canoe Area Wilderness.

Getting Around

Lodge to Lodge Hiking

The Lutsen-Tofte Tourism Association offers lodging and transportation packages for the hiker who wants to hike during the day and rejuvenate in the evening at some of the finest lodges on the North Shore of Lake Superior. Lodges, inns, and B&Bs provide overnight lodging, breakfast, trail lunch, and a shuttle service as part of the package—dinner is on your own. After breakfast you drive to the trailhead where you'll end the day's hike and leave your vehicle. You're then shuttled to the trailhead to begin your hike. You can drive to your next overnight lodging at the end of the day. Reservations should be made in advance for anytime during the hiking season (May through the end of October). Lodging fills quickly beginning in July throughout the remainder of the season, especially when the fall colors appear in September and early October. Packages range from three-day to seven-day trips. Additional days can be added. Check the Web site at www.boundarycountry.com for prices.

Boundary Country Trekking: (800) 322-8327

Lutsen-Tofte Tourism Association: (218) 663-7804 or (888) 61NORTH; www.boundarycountry.com

Shuttles

The Superior Shuttle service offers options to hikers for doing one-way hikes on the Superior Hiking Trail. One option is to ride the shuttle that takes you to the trailhead where you'll begin your hike and hike back to your vehicle. Another is to drive your vehicle to the starting point of your hike and, at the end of the day, catch the shuttle back to your vehicle. This great service offers food drops and maps—additional stops at an extra charge—and they'll even shuttle pets, all for reasonable prices. The shuttle runs every Friday, Saturday, and Sunday from the third week in May to the second week in October and on Mondays over Memorial Day, Fourth of July, and Labor Day weekends. Current shuttle schedules and prices are available at www.superiorshuttle.com

Superior Shuttle: (218) 834-5511

Miles and Directions

Section 1

0.0   SHT crosses Fors Road, also known as CR 301, and enters a forest of balsam fir and spruce. The trail crosses CR 3 and descends to cross Wilson Creek.

1.1   SHT travels through a mixed forest before crossing Silver Creek Road (TR 613). Soon, it crosses a road that leads to a radio tower, climbs up over a ridge and back down, then crosses an old road and a small stream.

3.2   SHT crosses Encampment River and climbs up on a ridge for views of Silver Creek, Encampment, and Stewart River valleys.

4.7   SHT follows the base of Wolf Rock's cliffs before crossing Silver Creek Road (TR 617) and quickly climbs to the top of Wolf Rock with great views 600 feet above Lake Superior.

6.0   Pass Crow Creek Valley campsite.

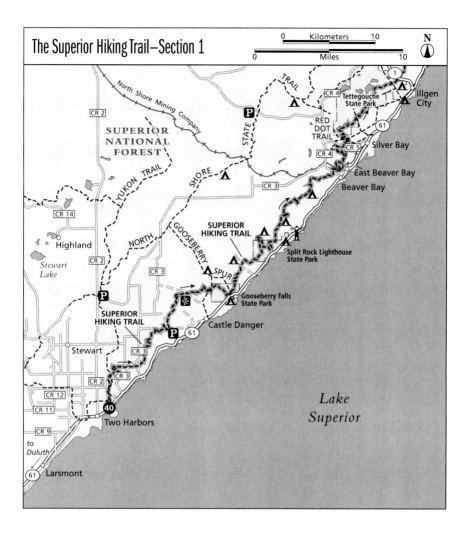

0   Kilometers   10   **N**

0   Miles   10

10.2   SHT crosses an old logging railroad grade built when logs were being moved down to Lake Superior.

10.9   The trail follows Gooseberry River and accesses three campsites over the next 1.7 miles, including a group site.

14.1   Fifth Falls bridge crosses the Gooseberry River, and then the trail passes under the bridge over Highway 61. You'll pass the Gooseberry Park Visitor Center in less than a mile.

17.9   SHT climbs out of Gooseberry Falls State Park by a well-marked network of ski trails and crosses a dirt road, then a gravel logging road. Cross a log footbridge before the Labounty Campsite.

22.1   SHT ascends to Bread Loaf overlook with views of Lake Superior and surrounding forest. Then, descend into the Split Rock River Valley where you can hear the river before you can see it.

23.2 Reach an unnamed creek and waterfall that joins the Split Rock River. At the trail junction, go left and walk upstream along the Split Rock River (see Hike 37). This is one of the most popular day hikes on the Superior Hiking Trail with its many waterfalls and gorgeous black and red basalt canyons. There are twenty-four campsites near the park headquarters down by Lake Superior, including secluded cart-in sites.

25.4 Arrive at the first of three campsites along the river. Cross over the river on a well-made bridge. The trail turns downriver from this point and heads up into the woods.

27.2 Arrive at a trail shelter and pass a series of spur trails. Take in a spectacular view of Lake Superior and the mouth of the Split Rock River. Stay left at the trail junction to follow the SHT to Beaver Bay. A right follows the spur trail down to the lake. From this point, the SHT climbs a ridge with views of Lake Superior and Split Rock Lighthouse, then descends into the Little Split Rock River valley. Cross the river and follow the old Merrill Grade railroad bed used to move timber to Lake Superior. The trail climbs Merrill Grade. Look for where the SHT departs from the grade on the right and then climbs onto a long, exposed rock ridge.

31.9 SHT crosses an ATV trail and, in less than a mile, a spur trail branches off to Christmas Tree Ridge Campsite.

37.7 SHT crosses CR 4 and, soon after, the Beaver River, also passing an accompanying campsite. The trail then turns away from the river and joins the Betzler Road for a short distance, crossing over railroad tracks and on to an intersection where the SHT goes north and on to Sulheims Overlook. Take care in this section, as trail markers may be missing or inaccurate.

39.2 Arrive at Beaver Pond Campsite and cross Fault Creek. Pass a campsite and ascend Fault Line Ridge, a north-south ridge formed by a geologic fault. Enjoy excellent views of the deep valley created by the fault. Pass two spur trails that head right and descend to Cove Point on Lake Superior. Stay left.

42.2 Cross Penn Boulevard (CR 5), ascend a stone staircase, and cross an ATV trail and gravel road. Ascend a ridge, then descend and cross another ATV trail. Ascend another ridge and cross the boundary for Tettegouche State Park. Pass a group campsite on Penn Creek. There are four more campsites within the next 3.5 miles and thirty-four campsites in the park's main campground near the Baptism River.

44.4 Enjoy breathtaking views of Bean and Bear Lakes from an overlook. The trail crosses two ATV trails and descends into a broad valley before climbing Mt. Trudee. SHT intersects the state park trail system, climbs Raven Rock, then descends rock steps for 150 feet through a feature called "the drainpipe."

52.4 Cross the Baptism River just above the High Falls. The trail follows the riverbank downstream, then cuts into the woods and ascends and descends two knobs before reaching Highway 1.

Section 2

53.3 Cross Highway 1 and, within a mile, a spur trail on the left leads to spectacular overlooks of Lake Superior and inland.

55.6 Reach Kennedy Creek campsites, one on either side of the creek. The trail then climbs a ridge that parallels Lake Superior. Upon descending this ridge, the trail turns inland and leads to a rock knob known as Sawmill Dome. From this overlook, you can view the next two day's hiking inland to the right of the abandoned Air Force radar base.

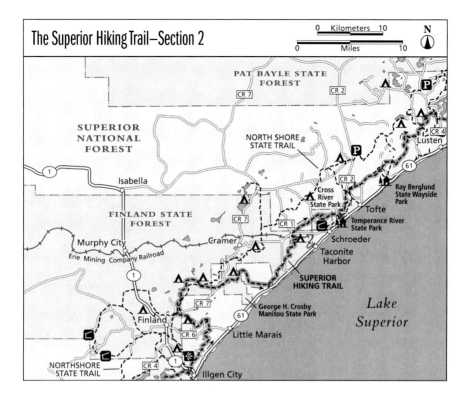

0   Kilometers   10

N

0   Miles   10

PAT BAYLE STATE
FOREST

CR 7   CR 2

SUPERIOR
NATIONAL
FOREST

NORTH SHORE
STATE TRAIL

CR 4
Lusten

61

Isabella

Cross
River
State Park

Ray Berglund
State Wayside
Park

CR 2

Tofte

FINLAND STATE
FOREST

CR 7   CR 1

Temperance River
State Park

Murphy City   Cramer

Schroeder

Erie Mining Company Railroad

Taconite
Harbor

SUPERIOR
HIKING TRAIL

CR 7

Finland

George H. Crosby
Manitou State Park

61

Lake
Superior

CR 6

Little Marais

NORTHSHORE
STATE TRAIL

CR 4

Illgen City

60.1 Descend and cross CR 6. Cross over Sawmill Creek twice and climb the steep trail to the top of a rock outcrop known locally as Section 13. The trail drops into a steep, cedar-lined valley and passes a few campsites. The terrain levels out here and you'll be entering younger, second-growth forests.

64.7 Cross Park Hill Road. Pass a campsite near the headwaters of Leskinen Creek. The trail passes over some gentle hills and then descends to cross the East Branch of the Baptism River. There are some ski trails in this area but the SHT is well marked and easy to follow. Stay right at the intersection with the spur trail leading to Finland Recreation Center.

68.1 Cross CR 7, go right, and follow the road for 0.2 mile. From here, the trail climbs steadily and crosses the North Shore State Trail.

70.1 Arrive at Egge Lake. Cross Egge Creek and pass spur trails to the Egge Lake campsites on the left. From here the trail turns north and passes the remains of Art Griffin's trappers cabin.

72.1 Arrive at Sonju Lake and pass two campsites. Follow the trail east and cross the East Branch of the Baptism River in 1 mile. Here, a spur trail leads to the Sonju Road and parking.

73.1 Pass a campsite on a peninsula of land between the East Branch of the Baptism River and a small creek. The trail crosses the North Shore State Trail and a shelter with pit toilets and a camping area. The SHT crosses two remote gravel roads in the next 2.5 miles.

77.1 SHT crosses CR 7 and Blesner Creek. Walk up the gravel road to Crosby Manitou State Park entrance. The park's twenty-one campsites are backpack-only. Follow SHT markers and descend into the Manitou River Gorge.

79.3 Cross the Manitou River, racing on its way to Lake Superior. Then ascend out of the steep river gorge. This may be the steepest section on the entire trail. Exercise caution when conditions are wet.

81.7 Pass Horseshoe Ridge camp, located on a small hill 150 yards off the SHT to the left.

83.7 Cross a logging road and Pork Bay Trail, then descend to the Caribou River Valley. You can hear the river echoing out of the gorge as you approach. Pass two campsites along the riverbank.

84.8 Cross the Caribou River. A spur trail leads to the right down to Highway 61 and Caribou wayside. Cross a logging road in 0.5 mile and 0.8 mile farther a spur trail on the right leads to Crystal Creek campsite. This is a beautiful site amidst a pure stand of birches and near a small, old, abandoned mining operation in a fault along the creek bed.

88.3 SHT skirts Alfred's Pond with its many bog plants. This is a great place to look for moose.

90.4 Pass Dyer's Creek campsite.

91.1 Cross Dyer's Lake Road, railroad tracks, CR 1, a gravel pit road, over Two Island River, and past SHT parking area.

92.9 Pass Fredenburg Creek campsite, a remote and beautiful spot.

94.4 Cross Gasco Road and an old logging road. The trail then descends into the scenic Cross River gorge.

96.8 Cross the bridge over Cross River and pass two campsites. The trail slowly climbs out of the gorge and onto a ridge, then descends to cross Temperance River Road, also known as FS 343. Here, the trail parallels the quiet, upper section of the Temperance River. Enter Temperance River State Park, with fifty campsites near Highway 61.

97.3 Climb up along the top of the spectacular Temperance River Gorge and cross over the river on a wide bridge. From here the trail heads upriver.

98.6 SHT turns away from the river and begins the long climb to Carlton Peak.

100.5 Pass the spur trail that climbs to the summit of Carlton Peak. The short climb is worth the expansive views.

102.2 Come to Britton Peak parking lot and cross CR 2. There's an extensive network of cross-country ski trails from here north to beyond Cascade River State Park.

106.3 Passing West and East Leveaux Pond campsites, the SHT skirts the backside of Leveaux Mountain and passes a spur trail that climbs to the top. Here, you get great views of Lake Superior and Carlton Peak.

107.3 Cross over Onion River and pass by the campsite.

107.9 Come to FS 336, also known as Onion River Road. There's a large parking area here for access to Oberg Mountain and the SHT. This area is very popular during the peak fall colors. SHT skirts the backside of Oberg Mountain and passes a loop trail that climbs to the top for incredible views.

109.5 Cross Rollins Creek and pass two campsites. Begin the long, gradual climb up Moose Mountain. After descending from Moose Mountain, the trail drops down into a deep valley and climbs up a high knob covered with hardwoods, then descends to the top of the Poplar River Gorge.

114.6 Cross the bridge over Poplar River. A spur trail to the right leads to Lutsen Ski Resort. Stay left and climb up into highlands overlooking quiet sections of the Poplar River.

115.6 Cross an area of many footbridges. Pass East and West Poplar River campsites and climb a high ridge for overlooks of the wide Poplar River Valley below.

118.5 Cross the bridge over the Agnes Lake outlet and pass two campsites within a half mile on the shores of Lake Agnes.

Section 3

119.9 Cross a snowmobile trail and Caribou Trail (a blacktop road) and climb a small knob. Then descend to Jonvick Creek Campsite (1.4 miles). The SHT will cross a snowmobile trail four times in the next 1.5 miles.

123.5 Come to Spruce Creek Campsite, a multi-group site. Then, climb up onto a ridge with good views inland and of Lake Superior.

125.1 SHT joins a wide snowmobile trail for 0.5 mile.

126.8 Come to Indian Creek camp, a multi-group site. In one mile SHT joins the Cascade State Park Trail network.

128.8 Enter Cascade River State Park, with thirty-seven campsites. Come to the Cascade River bank and follow SHT downstream. Cross the bridge and view a set of falls. Turn left after the bridge and walk upriver.

130.1 Come to Billy Goat campsite, and, from here, ascend to the top of the high riverbank. The trail descends back down to the river and up again.

132.7 Cross under CR 45 and walk to the left side of the parking lot. Follow SHT markers upstream (north) on the Cascade River.

133.6 Come to the North Cascade River campsite, a multi-group site. As you leave the campsite, climb a small ridge that overlooks the surrounding creek valley.

137.9 Come to the Sundling Creek campsite spur trail, a 0.7-mile trail on the left, just before an overlook of Sundling Creek and surrounding land to the north.

138.1 SHT descends to Bally Creek Road, also known as FS 158. Cross the road and come to South Beaver Pond campsite in 0.1 mile and North Beaver Pond campsite 0.2 mile farther. In another 0.5 mile you will cross nearly 200 feet of boardwalk.

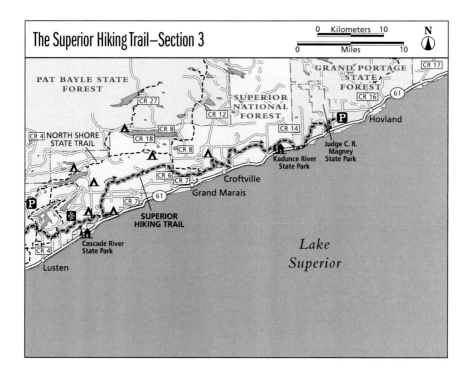

0   Kilometers   10

0   Miles   10

N

PAT BAYLE STATE
FOREST

CR 27

GRAND PORTAGE
STATE
FOREST

CR 17

CR 16   61

CR 12

SUPERIOR
NATIONAL
FOREST

CR 8

CR 14

Hovland

CR 4 NORTH SHORE
STATE TRAIL

CR 18

CR 8

Judge C. R.
Magney
State Park

Kadunce River
State Park

CR 6   CR 7

Croftville

CR 7   61

Grand Marais

P

SUPERIOR
HIKING TRAIL

Cascade River
State Park

Lake
Superior

CR 4

Lusten

140.2 Cross FS 115F. You will cross this again twice more. Within the next mile, the trail enters a large red pine plantation.

141.8 SHT crosses CR 6 (yes, again), then joins North Shore State Trail for 2.5 miles and goes on toward the city of Grand Marais.

145.4 Cross the Gunflint Trail and pass a network of ski trails. SHT is well marked here.

146.4 Come to Pincushion Mountain trailhead, which is the center for cross-country ski trails. In 0.4 mile take a left, following SHT toward the Devils Track River.

148.7 Cross an interesting bridge over Devils Track River. There are campsites on either side of the river. As you hike away from the river you may ponder how anyone managed to get that bridge there.

150.1 Cross a small stream cutting deep into bedrock and look for Barrier Falls in the steep, deep-walled canyon. Much of the canyon rim is made up of decomposed rock, so use caution. Climb out of the Devils Track River valley and eventually drop down into the Woods Creek valley and cross Woods Creek above a falls.

150.2 Cross CR 58 in 0.6 mile to Woods Creek Campsite on the left. As the trail crosses open areas, look for rock cairns.

153.2 Reach Durfee Creek Campsite and, 1.1 miles farther, Cliff Creek Campsite. Here the trail crosses many creeks, resulting in many ups and downs.

155.8 The trail descends along Kimball Creek. A campsite is on the right before crossing the creek.

157.0 Cross over Kimball Creek and then CR 14. There are good views of the lake here.

158.1 Pass Crow Creek campsite atop the steep-walled riverbanks.

159.7 Cross the Kadunce River and pass a great spur trail that leads to Highway 61 and views of a very narrow and deep gorge. Kadunce River Campsite is 0.2 mile from the bridge.

161.2 SHT crosses Highway 61 and follows a stretch of pebble beach shoreline of Lake Superior. Lakeshore camping is okay; watch for bugs.

162.8 SHT leaves Lake Superior's shoreline, crosses Highway 61 and climbs toward Little Brule River.

164.6 Pass Little Brule River campsites and climb a sandy slope. The trail then turns due east and then south as it follows the shore of Gauthier Creek.

168.0 SHT descends to Brule River and campground (with thirty-six campsites) in Judge C. R. Magney State Park. Cross the bridge, drop your pack, and walk 1 mile up the east shore to view two waterfalls and the mysterious Devils Kettle. Return to the state park parking lot.

169.0 Arrive at the parking lot. Go have dinner at Nanaboujou Lodge across from Judge Magney State Park.

Great Resources for Hiking the Superior Trail

Organizations

Superior Hiking Trail Association (SHTA): P.O. Box 4, 731 7th Avenue, Two Harbors, MN 55616; (218) 834-2700; www.shta.org. Member-supported and volunteer-maintained, SHTA offers a variety of guided hikes throughout the year that are open to the public and free of charge. Check the Web site for current schedules.

Books

Guide to the Superior Hiking Trail (Fifth Edition), edited and compiled by the SHTA—comprehensive and well-written guide to the entire trail that includes flora and fauna, geology, history, maps and trail descriptions, and directions

Maps

McKenzie maps: These maps cover all of the trail and are worth getting as they mark state trails, park boundaries, ski trails, snowmobile trails, roads, parking areas, and topography in addition to the SHT. Available at the SHTA office or at www.mckenziemaps.com.

SHTA pocket maps: Four maps cover the trail and can be purchased for 50 cents each. These maps list parking areas, roads, major landmarks, elevation profiles, and distances between trailheads. They contain no detailed mile-by-mile information. These maps can be used alone or with the Guide to the Superior Hiking Trail. Available at the SHTA office.

USGS maps: These maps don't show the SHT or any other trails and are not as useful as the McKenzie maps. They can be used in combination with the SHTA pocket maps.

NORTH COUNTRY TRAIL

Those interested in visiting some of Minnesota's choice scenic areas can do it in one long hike by picking up the continuously developing North Country Trail, along which campsites and various types of lodging are available. Authorized in 1980 and still under construction, this outstanding trail will cover approximately 4,500 miles when finished, connecting the north country of New York, Pennsylvania, Ohio, Michigan, Wisconsin, Minnesota, and North Dakota.

Development will be ongoing for a number of years as organizations, private landowners, and government entities work together to connect existing trails (such as Minnesota's Superior Hiking Trail) and to create new ones. Volunteers affiliated with organizations like the Superior Hiking Trail Association and the North Country Trail Association do the trail construction and maintenance. With so many entities involved in trail development, efforts to standardize signage have been moving slowly, and much work is yet to be done.

In Minnesota, the proposed trail begins at Jay Cooke State Park (one of several state parks in Minnesota through which the trail passes), heads north through Duluth (40 miles of the trail through Duluth is scheduled to be completed in 2006, and the trail through Duluth is complete from the Grand Portage Trailhead parking lot at Jay Cooke State Park for 39 miles to Martin Road) and up the North Shore along 250 miles of the Superior Hiking Trail, turning inland at Hovland, northeast of Grand Marais. It eventually joins the Border Route Trail, a 74-mile trail that follows the border lakes west from the Pigeon River and

connects with the Kekekabic Trail. The Kekekabic, originally built as a firefighting trail, cuts west 38 miles across the deeply forested BWCAW. The NCTA Headwaters chapter is developing a route that would reach from the western edge of the Kekekabic and connect with Paul Bunyan State Forest and Itasca State Park. There's yet a final route bringing the hiker south and west from Maplewood State Park to the North Dakota state line.

Diversity has been called the North Country Trail's most appealing quality, as the trail takes the hiker through a variety of landscapes, from flat farmland to mountains, with prairies, rolling hills, forests, lakes, marshlands, rugged shorelines, and deep river gorges in between.

Maps and other printed information are available by contacting NCTA Headquarters at 229 East Main Street, Lowell, MI 49331; or call (616) 897-5987 or (888) 454-NCTA; or visit www.northcountrytrail.org. The association is developing a multi-colored topographical trail map using computerized technology, which will be a great help to hikers in developing their routes.

The Art of Hiking

Hikers venturing into the backcountry not only expect pleasant experiences filled with adventure, discovery, and beauty, but they also are responsible for protecting the environment for the sake of wildlife inhabiting it and for future human generations who wish to experience it as well. Because of human intrusion on habitat, many species of wildlife are at risk. The following section will help you better understand what you can do to help preserve delicate ecosystems while still making the most of your hiking experience. Anyone can take a hike, but hiking safely and well is an art requiring preparation and proper equipment.

Trail Etiquette

Zero impact. Always leave an area just as you found it—if not better than you found it. Avoid camping in fragile, alpine meadows and along the banks of streams and lakes. Use a camp stove versus building a wood fire. Pack up all of your trash and extra food. Bury human waste at least 100 feet from water sources under 6 to 8 inches of topsoil. Don't bathe with soap in a lake or stream—use packaged moistened towels to wipe off sweat and dirt, or bathe in the water without soap.

Stay on the trail. Paths serve an important purpose; they limit impact on natural areas. Straying from a designated trail may seem innocent, but it can cause damage to sensitive areas—damage that may take years to recover, if it can recover at all. Even simple shortcuts can be destructive. So, please, stay on the trail.

Leave no weeds. Noxious weeds tend to overtake other plants, which in turn affects animals and birds that depend on them for food. To minimize the spread of noxious weeds, hikers should regularly clean their boots, tents, packs, and hiking poles of mud and seeds. Also brush your dog to remove any weed seeds before heading off into a new area.

Keep your dog under control. You can buy a flexi-lead that allows your dog to go exploring along the trail, while allowing you the ability to reel him in should another hiker approach or should he decide to chase a rabbit. Always obey leash laws, and be sure to bury your dog's waste, or pack it in sealable plastic bags.

Respect other trail users. With the rise in popularity of multi-use trails, you'll often find there are others using the same trail. This just means exercising the same courtesy you would expect when encountering other users. To avoid problems, first investigate whether you're on a multi-use trail, and assume the appropriate precautions. When you encounter motorized vehicles (ATVs, motorcycles, and 4WDs), be alert. Though they should always yield to the hiker, often they're going too fast or are too lost in the buzz of their engines to react to your presence. If you hear activity ahead, step off the trail just to be safe. Note that you're not likely to hear a mountain biker coming, so be prepared and know ahead of time whether you share the trail with them. Cyclists should always yield to hikers, but that's little comfort to the hiker.

Be aware. When you approach horses or pack animals on the trail, always step quietly off the trail, preferably on the downhill side, and let them pass. If you're wearing a large backpack, it's often a good idea to sit down. To some animals, a hiker wearing a large backpack might appear threatening. Many national forests allow domesticated grazing, usually for sheep and cattle. Make sure your dog doesn't harass these animals, and respect ranchers' rights while you're enjoying yours.

Getting into Shape

Unless you want to be sore—and possibly have to shorten your trip or vacation—be sure to get in shape before a big hike. If you're terribly out of shape, start a walking program early, preferably eight weeks in advance. Start with a fifteen-minute walk during your lunch hour or after work and gradually increase your walking time to an hour. You should also increase your elevation gain. Walking briskly up hills really strengthens your leg muscles and gets your heart rate up. If you work in a storied office building, take the stairs instead of the elevator. If you prefer going to a gym, walk the treadmill or use a stair machine. You can further increase your strength and endurance by walking with a loaded backpack. Stationary exercises you might consider are squats, leg lifts, sit-ups, and push-ups. Other good ways to get in shape include biking, running, aerobics, and, of course, short hikes. Stretching before and after a hike keeps muscles flexible and helps avoid injuries.

Preparedness

It's been said that failing to plan means planning to fail. So do take the necessary time to plan your trip. Whether going on a short day hike or an extended backpack trip, always prepare for the worst. Simply remembering to pack a copy of the U.S. Army Survival Manual is not preparedness. Although it's not a bad idea if you plan on entering truly wild places, it's merely the tourniquet answer to a problem. You need to do your best to prevent the problem from arising in the first place. In order to survive—and to stay reasonably comfortable—you need to concern yourself with the basics: water, food, and shelter. Don't go on a hike without having these bases covered. And don't go on a hike expecting to find these items in the woods.

Water. Even in frigid conditions, you need at least two quarts of water a day to function efficiently. Add heat and taxing terrain and you can bump that figure up to one gallon. That's simply a base to work from—your metabolism and your level of conditioning can raise or lower that amount. Unless you know your level, assume that you need one gallon of water a day. Now, where do you plan on getting the water?

Preferably not from natural water sources. These sources can be loaded with intestinal disturbers, such as bacteria, viruses, and fertilizers. *Giardia lamblia,* the most common of these disturbers, is a protozoan parasite that lives part of its life cycle as a cyst in water sources. The parasite spreads when mammals defecate in water sources. Once ingested, Giardia can induce cramping, diarrhea, vomiting, and fatigue within two days to two weeks after ingestion. Giardiasis is treatable with prescription drugs. If you believe you've contracted giardiasis, see a doctor immediately.

Treating water. The best and easiest solution to avoid polluted water is to carry your water with you. Yet, depending on the nature of your hike and the duration, this may not be an option—one gallon of water weighs eight-and-a-half pounds. In that case, you'll need to look into treating water. Regardless of which method you choose, you should always carry some water with you in case of an emergency. Save this reserve until you absolutely need it.

There are three methods of treating water: boiling, chemical treatment, and filtering. If you boil water, it's recommended that you do so for ten to fifteen minutes. This is often impractical because you're forced to exhaust a great deal of your fuel supply. You can opt for chemical treatment, which will kill Giardia but will not take care of other chemical pollutants. Another drawback to chemical treatments is the unpleasant taste of the water after it's treated. You can remedy this by adding powdered drink mix to the water. Filters are the preferred method for treating water. Many filters remove Giardia, organic and inorganic contaminants, and don't leave an aftertaste. Water filters are far from perfect as they can easily become clogged or leak if a gasket wears out. It's always a good idea to carry a backup supply of chemical treatment tablets in case your filter decides to quit on you.

Food. If we're talking about survival, you can go days without food, as long as you have water. But we're also talking about comfort. Try to avoid foods that are high in sugar and fat like candy bars and potato chips. These food types are harder to digest and are low in nutritional value. Instead, bring along foods that are easy to pack, nutritious, and high in energy (e.g., bagels, nutrition bars, dehydrated fruit, gorp, and jerky). If you are on an overnight trip, easy-to-fix dinners include rice mixes with dehydrated potatoes, corn, pasta with cheese sauce, and soup mixes. For a tasty breakfast, you can fix hot oatmeal with brown sugar and reconstituted milk powder topped off with banana chips. If you like a hot drink in the morning, bring along herbal tea bags or hot chocolate. If you are a coffee junkie, you can purchase coffee that is packaged like tea bags. You can prepackage all of your meals in heavy-duty resealable plastic bags to keep food from spilling in your pack. These bags can be reused to pack out trash.

Shelter. The type of shelter you choose depends less on the conditions than on your tolerance for discomfort. Shelter comes in many forms—tent, tarp, lean-to, bivy sack, cabin, cave, etc. If you're camping in the desert, a bivy sack may suffice, but if you're above the treeline and a storm is approaching, a better choice is a three- or four-season tent. Tents are the logical and most popular choice for most backpackers as they're lightweight and packable—and you can rest assured that you always have shelter from the elements. Before you leave on your trip, anticipate what the weather and terrain will be like, and plan for the type of shelter that will work best for your comfort level (see Equipment later in this section).

Finding a campsite. If there are established campsites, stick to those. If not, start looking for a campsite early—around 3:30 or 4:00 p.m. Stop at the first decent site you see. Depending on the area, it could be a long time before you find another suitable location. Pitch your camp in an area that's level. Make sure the area is at least 200 feet from fragile areas like lakeshores, meadows, and stream banks. And try to avoid areas thick in underbrush, as they can harbor insects and provide cover for approaching animals.

If you are camping in stormy, rainy weather, look for a rock outcrop or a shelter in the trees to keep the wind from blowing your tent all night. Be sure that you don't camp under trees with dead limbs that might break off on top of you. Also, try to find an area that has an absorbent surface, such as sandy soil or forest duff. This, in addition to camping on a surface with a slight angle, will provide better drainage. By all means, don't dig trenches to provide drainage around your tent—remember you're practicing zero-impact camping.

If you're in bear country, steer clear of creekbeds or animal paths. If you see any signs of a bear's presence (i.e., scat, footprints), relocate. You'll need to find a campsite near a tall tree where you can hang your food and other items that may attract bears such as deodorant, toothpaste, or soap. Carry a lightweight nylon rope with which to hang your food. As a rule, you should hang your food at least 20 feet from the ground and 5 feet away from the tree trunk. You can put food and other items in a waterproof stuff sack and tie one end of the rope to the stuff sack. To get the other end of the rope over the tree branch, tie a good size rock to it, and gently toss the rock over the tree branch. Pull the stuff sack up until it reaches the top of the branch and tie it off securely. Don't hang your food near your tent! If possible, hang your food at least 100 feet away from your campsite. Alternatives to hanging your food are bear-proof plastic tubes and metal bear boxes.

Lastly, think of comfort. Lie down on the ground where you intend to sleep and see if it's a good fit. For morning warmth (and a nice view to wake up to), have your tent face east.

First Aid

We know you're tough, but get 10 miles into the woods and develop a blister and you'll wish you had carried that first-aid kit. Face it, it's just plain good sense. Many companies produce lightweight, compact first-aid kits. Just make sure yours contains at least the following:

- adhesive bandages
- moleskin or duct tape
- various sterile gauze and dressings
- white surgical tape
- an Ace bandage
- an antihistamine
- aspirin
- Betadine solution
- a first-aid book
- antacid tablets

- tweezers
- scissors
- antibacterial wipes
- triple-antibiotic ointment
- plastic gloves
- sterile cotton tip applicators
- syrup of ipecac (to induce vomiting)
- thermometer
- wire splint

Here are a few tips to dealing with and hopefully preventing certain ailments.

Sunburn. Take along sunscreen or sun block, protective clothing, and a wide-brimmed hat. If you do get a sunburn, treat the area with aloe vera gel, and protect the area from further sun exposure. At higher elevations, the sun's radiation can be particularly damaging to skin. Remember that your eyes are vulnerable to this radiation as well. Sunglasses can be a good way to prevent headaches and permanent eye damage from the sun, especially in places where light-colored rock or patches of snow reflect light up in your face.

Blisters. Be prepared to take care of these hike-spoilers by carrying moleskin (a lightly padded adhesive), gauze and tape, or adhesive bandages. An effective way to apply moleskin is to cut out a circle of moleskin and remove the center—like a doughnut—and place it over the blistered area. Cutting the center out will reduce the pressure applied to the sensitive skin. Other products can help you combat blisters. Some are applied to suspicious hot spots before a blister forms to help decrease friction to that area, while others are applied to the blister after it has popped to help prevent further irritation.

Insect bites and stings. You can treat most insect bites and stings by applying hydrocortisone 1% cream topically and taking a pain medication such as ibuprofen or acetaminophen to reduce swelling. If you forgot to pack these items, a cold compress or a paste of mud and ashes can sometimes assuage the itching and discomfort. Remove any stingers by using tweezers or scraping the area with your fingernail or a knife blade. Don't pinch the area as you'll only spread the venom.

Some hikers are highly sensitive to bites and stings and may have a serious allergic reaction that can be life threatening. Symptoms of a serious allergic reaction can include wheezing, an asthmatic attack, and shock. The treatment for this severe type of reaction is epinephrine. If you know that you are sensitive to bites and stings, carry a pre-packaged kit of epinephrine, which can be obtained only by prescription from your doctor.

Ticks. Ticks can carry diseases such as Rocky Mountain spotted fever and Lyme disease. The best defense is, of course, prevention. If you know you're going to be hiking through an area littered with ticks, wear long pants and a long-sleeved shirt. You can apply a permethrin repellent to your clothing and a Deet repellent to exposed skin. At the end of your hike, do a spot check for ticks (and insects in general). If you do find a tick, coat the insect with petroleum jelly or tree sap to cut off its air supply. The tick should release its hold, but if it doesn't, grab the head of the tick firmly—with a pair of tweezers if you have them—and gently pull it away from the skin with a twisting motion. Sometimes the mouth parts linger, embedded in your skin. If this happens, try to remove them with a disinfected needle. Clean the affected area with an antibacterial cleanser, and then apply triple antibiotic ointment. Monitor the area for a few days. If irritation persists or a white spot develops, see a doctor for possible infection.

Poison ivy, oak, and sumac. These skin irritants can be found most anywhere in North America and come in the form of a bush or a vine, having leaflets in groups of three, five, seven, or nine. Learn how to spot the plants. The oil they secrete can cause an allergic reaction in the form of blisters, usually about twelve hours after exposure. The itchy rash can last from ten days to several weeks. The best defense against these irritants is to wear clothing that covers the arms, legs, and torso. For summer, zip-off cargo pants come in handy. There are also nonprescription lotions you can apply to exposed skin that guard against the effects of poison ivy/oak/sumac and can be washed off with soap and water. If you think you were in contact with the plants, after hiking (or even on the trail during longer hikes), wash with soap and water. Taking a hot shower with soap after you return home from your hike will also help to remove any lingering oil from your skin. Should you contract a rash from any of these plants, use an antihistamine to reduce the itching. If the rash is localized, create a light bleach/water wash to dry up the area. If the rash has spread, either tough it out or see your doctor about getting a dose of cortisone (available both orally and by injection).

Snakebites. Snakebites are rare in North America. Unless startled or provoked, the majority of snakes will not bite. If you are wise to their habitats and keep a careful eye on the trail, you should be just fine. When stepping over logs, first step on the log, making sure you can see what's on the other side before stepping down. Though your chances of being struck are slim, it's wise to know what to do in the event you are.

If a *nonpoisonous* snake bites you, allow the wound to bleed a small amount and then cleanse the wounded area with a Betadine solution (10% povidone iodine). Rinse the wound with clean water (preferably) or fresh urine (it might sound ugly, but it's sterile). Once the area is clean, cover it with triple antibiotic ointment and a clean bandage. Remember, most residual damage from snakebites, poisonous or otherwise, comes from infection, not the snake's venom. Keep the area as clean as possible and get medical attention immediately.

If you are bitten by a poisonous snake, remove the toxin with a suctioning device, found in a snakebite kit. If you do not have such a device, squeeze the wound—DO NOT use your mouth for suction, as the venom will enter your bloodstream through the vessels under the tongue and head straight for your heart. Then, clean the wound just as you would a nonpoisonous bite. Tie a clean band of cloth snuggly around the afflicted appendage, about an inch or so above the bite (or the rim of the swelling). This is NOT a tourniquet—you want to simply slow the blood flow, not cut it off. Loosen the band if numbness ensues. Remove the band for a minute and reapply a little higher every ten minutes.

If it is your friend who's been bitten, treat him or her for shock—make the person comfortable, have him or her lie down, elevate the legs, and keep him or her warm. Avoid applying anything cold to the bite wound. Immobilize the affected area and remove any constricting items such as rings, watches, or restrictive clothing—swelling may occur. Once your friend is stable and relatively calm, hike out to get help. The victim should get treatment within twelve hours, ideally, which usually consists of a tetanus shot, antivenin, and antibiotics.

If you are alone and struck by a poisonous snake, stay calm. Hysteria will only quicken the venom's spread. Follow the procedure above, and do your best to reach help. When hiking out, don't run—you'll only increase the flow of blood throughout your system. Instead, walk calmly.

Dehydration. Have you ever hiked in hot weather and had a roaring headache and felt fatigued after only a few miles? More than likely you were dehydrated. Symptoms of dehydration include fatigue, headache, and decreased coordination and judgment. When you are hiking, your body's rate of fluid loss depends on the outside temperature, humidity, altitude, and your activity level. On average, a hiker walking in warm weather will lose four liters of fluid a day. That fluid loss is easily replaced by normal consumption of liquids and food. However, if a hiker is walking briskly in hot, dry weather and hauling a heavy pack, he or she can lose one to three liters of water an hour. It's important to always carry plenty of water and to stop often and drink fluids regularly, even if you aren't thirsty.

Heat exhaustion is the result of a loss of large amounts of electrolytes and often occurs if a hiker is dehydrated and has been under heavy exertion. Common symptoms of heat exhaustion include cramping, exhaustion, fatigue, lightheadedness, and nausea. You can treat heat exhaustion by getting out of the sun and drinking an electrolyte solution made up of one teaspoon of salt and one tablespoon of sugar dissolved in a liter of water. Drink this solution slowly over a period of one hour. Drinking plenty of fluids (preferably an electrolyte solution/sports drink) can prevent heat exhaustion. Avoid hiking during the hottest parts of the day, and wear breathable clothing, a wide-brimmed hat, and sunglasses.

Hypothermia is one of the biggest dangers in the backcountry, especially for day hikers in the summertime. That may sound strange, but imagine starting out on a hike in midsummer when it's sunny and 80 degrees out. You're clad in nylon shorts and a cotton T-shirt. About halfway through your hike, the sky begins to cloud up, and in the next hour a light drizzle begins to fall, and the wind starts to pick up. Before you know it, you are soaking wet and shivering—the perfect recipe for hypothermia. More advanced signs include decreased coordination, slurred speech, and blurred vision. When a victim's temperature falls below 92 degrees, the blood pressure and pulse plummet, possibly leading to coma and death.

To avoid hypothermia, always bring a windproof/rainproof shell, a fleece jacket, tights made of a breathable, synthetic fiber, gloves, and hat when you are hiking in the mountains. Learn to adjust your clothing layers based on the temperature. If you are climbing uphill at a moderate pace you will stay warm, but when you stop for a break you'll become cold quickly, unless you add more layers of clothing.

If a hiker is showing advanced signs of hypothermia, dress him or her in dry clothes and make sure he or she is wearing a hat and gloves. Place the person in a sleeping bag in a tent or shelter that will protect him or her from the wind and other elements. Give the person warm fluids to drink and keep him awake.

Frostbite. When the mercury dips below 32 degrees, your extremities begin to chill. If a persistent chill attacks a localized area, say, your hands or your toes, the circulatory system reacts by cutting off blood flow to the affected area—the idea being to protect and preserve the body's overall temperature. And so it's death by attrition for the affected area. Ice crystals start to form from the water in the cells of the neglected tissue. Deprived of heat, nourishment, and now water, the tissue literally starves. This is frostbite.

Prevention is your best defense against this situation. Most prone to frostbite are your face, hands, and feet, so protect these areas well. Wool is the material of choice because it provides ample air space for insulation and draws moisture away from the skin. Synthetic fabrics, however, have recently made great strides in the cold weather clothing market. Do your research. A pair of light silk liners under your regular gloves is a good trick for keeping warm. They afford some additional warmth, but more important, they'll allow you to remove your mitts for tedious work without exposing the skin.

If your feet or hands start to feel cold or numb due to the elements, warm them as quickly as possible. Place cold hands under your armpits or bury them in your crotch. If your feet are cold, change your socks. If there's plenty of room in your boots, add another pair of socks. Do remember, though, that constricting your feet in tight boots can restrict blood flow and actually make your feet colder more quickly. Your socks need to have breathing room if they're going to be effective. Dead air provides insulation. If your face is cold, place your warm hands over your face, or simply wear a head stocking.

Should your skin go numb and start to appear white and waxy, chances are you've got or are developing frostbite. Don't try to thaw the area unless you can maintain the warmth. In other words, don't stop to warm up your frostbitten feet only to head back on the trail. You'll do more damage than good. Tests have shown that hikers who walked on thawed feet did more harm, and endured more pain, than hikers who left the affected areas alone. Do your best to get out of the cold entirely and seek medical attention—which usually consists of performing a rapid rewarming in water for twenty to thirty minutes.

The overall objective in preventing both hypothermia and frostbite is to keep the body's core warm. Protect key areas where heat escapes, like the top of the head, and maintain the proper nutrition level. Foods that are high in calories aid the body in producing heat. Never smoke or drink when you're in situations where the cold is threatening. By affecting blood flow, these activities ultimately cool the body's core temperature.

Altitude sickness (AMS). High lofty peaks, clear alpine lakes, and vast mountain views beckon hikers to the high country. But those who like to venture high may become victims of altitude sickness (also known as Acute Mountain Sickness—AMS). Altitude sickness is your body's reaction to insufficient oxygen in the blood due to decreased barometric pressure. While some hikers may feel lightheaded, nauseous, and experience shortness of breath at 7,000 feet, others may not experience these symptoms until they reach 10,000 feet or higher.

Slowing your ascent to high places and giving your body a chance to acclimatize to the higher elevations can prevent altitude sickness. For example, if you live at sea level and are planning a weeklong backpacking trip to elevations between 7,000 and 12,000 feet, start by staying below 7,000 feet for one night, then move to between 7,000 and 10,000 feet for another night or two. Avoid strenuous exertion and alcohol to give your body a chance to adjust to the new altitude. It's also important to eat light food and drink plenty of nonalcoholic fluids, preferably water. Loss of appetite at altitude is common, but you must eat!

Most hikers who experience mild to moderate AMS develop a headache and/or nausea, grow lethargic, and have problems sleeping. The treatment for AMS is simple: stop heading uphill. Keep eating and drinking water and take meds for the headache. You actually need to take more breaths at altitude than at sea level, so breathe a little faster without hyperventilating. If symptoms don't improve over twenty-four to forty-eight hours, descend. Once a victim descends about 2,000 to 3,000 feet, his signs will usually begin to diminish.

Severe AMS comes in two forms: High Altitude Pulmonary Edema (HAPE) and High Altitude Cerebral Edema (HACE). HAPE, an accumulation of fluid in the lungs, can occur above 8,000 feet. Symptoms include rapid heart rate, shortness of breath at rest, AMS symptoms, dry cough developing into a wet cough, gurgling sounds, flu-like or bronchitis symptoms, and lack of muscle coordination. HAPE is life threatening so descend immediately, at least 2,000 to 4,000 feet. HACE usually occurs above 12,000 feet but sometimes occurs above 10,000 feet. Symptoms are similar to HAPE but also include seizures, hallucinations, paralysis, and vision disturbances. Descend immediately—HACE is also life threatening.

Hantavirus Pulmonary Syndrome (HPS). Deer mice spread the virus that causes HPS, and humans contract it from breathing it in, usually when they've disturbed an area with dust and mice feces from nests or surfaces with mice droppings or urine. Exposure to large numbers of rodents and their feces or urine presents the greatest risk. As hikers, we sometimes enter old buildings, and often deer mice live in these places. We may not be around long enough to be exposed, but do be aware of this disease. About half the people who develop HPS die. Symptoms are flu-like and appear about two to three weeks after exposure. After initial symptoms, a dry cough and shortness of breath follow. Breathing is difficult. If you even think you might have HPS, see a doctor immediately!

Natural Hazards

Besides tripping over a rock or tree root on the trail, there are some real hazards to be aware of while hiking. Even if where you're hiking doesn't have the plethora of poisonous snakes and plants, insects, and grizzly bears found in other parts of the United States, there are a few weather conditions and predators you may need to take into account.

Lightning. Thunderstorms build over the mountains almost every day during the summer. Lightning is generated by thunderheads and can strike without warning, even several miles away from the nearest overhead cloud. The best rule of thumb is to start leaving exposed peaks, ridges, and canyon rims by about noon. This time can vary a little depending on storm buildup. Keep an eye on cloud formation and don't underestimate how fast a storm can build. The bigger they get, the more likely a thunderstorm will happen. Lightning takes the path of least resistance, so if you're the high point, it might choose you. Ducking under a rock overhang is dangerous as you form the shortest path between the rock and ground. If you dash below treeline, avoid standing under the only or the tallest tree. If you are caught above treeline, stay away from anything metal you might be carrying. Move down off the ridge slightly to a low, treeless point and squat until the storm passes. If you have an insulating pad, squat on it. Avoid having both your hands and feet touching the ground at once and never lie flat. If you hear a buzzing sound or feel your hair standing on end, move quickly as an electrical charge is building up.

Flash floods. On July 31, 1976, a torrential downpour unleashed by a thunderstorm dumped tons of water into the Big Thompson watershed near Estes Park. Within hours, a wall of water moved down the narrow canyon killing 139 people and causing more than $30 million in property damage. The spooky thing about flash floods, especially in western canyons, is that they can appear out of nowhere from a storm many miles away. While hiking or driving in canyons, keep an eye on the weather. Always climb to safety if danger threatens. Flash floods usually subside quickly, so be patient and don't cross a swollen stream.

Bears. Most of the United States (outside of the Pacific Northwest and parts of the Northern Rockies) does not have a grizzly bear population, although some rumors exist about sightings where there should be none. Black bears are plentiful, however. Here are some tips in case you and a bear scare each other. Most of all, avoid scaring a bear. Watch for bear tracks (five toes) and droppings (sizable with leaves, partly digested berries, seeds, and/or animal fur). Talk or sing where visibility or hearing are limited. Keep a clean camp, hang food, and don't sleep in the clothes you wore while cooking. Be especially careful in spring to avoid getting between a mother and her cubs. In late summer and fall bears are busy eating berries and acorns to fatten up for winter, so be extra careful around berry bushes and oakbrush. If you do encounter a bear, move away slowly while facing the bear, talk softly, and avoid direct eye contact. Give the bear room to escape. Since bears are very curious, it might stand upright to get a better whiff of you, and it may even charge you to try to intimidate you. Try to stay calm. If a bear does attack you, fight back with anything you have handy. Unleashed dogs have been known to come running back to their owners with a bear close behind. Keep your dog on a leash or leave it at home.

Mountain lions. Mountain lions appear to be getting more comfortable around humans as long as deer (their favorite prey) are in an area with adequate cover. Usually elusive and quiet, lions rarely attack people. If you meet a lion, give it a chance to escape. Stay calm and talk firmly to it. Back away slowly while facing the lion. If you run, you'll only encourage the curious cat to chase you. Make yourself look large by opening a jacket, if you have one, or waving your hiking poles. If the lion behaves aggressively throw stones, sticks, or whatever you can while remaining tall. If a lion does attack, fight for your life with anything you can grab.

Moose. Because moose have very few natural predators, they don't fear humans like other animals. You might find moose in sagebrush and wetter areas of willow, aspen, and pine, or in beaver habitats. Mothers with calves, as well as bulls during mating season, can be particularly aggressive. If a moose threatens you, back away slowly and talk calmly to it. Keep your pets away from moose.

Other considerations. Hunting is a popular sport in the United States, especially during rifle season in October and November. Hiking is still enjoyable in those months in many areas, so just take a few precautions. First, learn when the different hunting seasons start and end in the area in which you'll be hiking. During this time frame, be sure to wear at least a blaze orange hat, and possibly put an orange vest over your pack. Don't be surprised to see hunters in camo outfits carrying bows or muzzleloading rifles around during their season. If you would feel more comfortable without hunters around, hike in national parks and monuments, or state and local parks where hunting is not allowed.

Navigation

Whether you are going on a short hike in a familiar area or planning a weeklong backpack trip, you should always be equipped with the proper navigational equipment—at the very least, a detailed map and a sturdy compass.

Maps. There are many different types of maps available to help you find your way on the trail. Easiest to find are Forest Service maps and BLM (Bureau of Land Management) maps. These maps tend to cover large areas, so be sure they are detailed enough for your particular trip. You can also obtain National Park maps as well as high-quality maps from private companies and trail groups. These maps can be obtained either from outdoor stores or ranger stations.

U.S. Geological Survey topographic maps are particularly popular with hikers—especially serious backcountry hikers. These maps contain the standard map symbols such as roads, lakes, and rivers, as well as contour lines that show the details of the trail terrain like ridges, valleys, passes, and mountain peaks. The 7.5-minute series (1 inch on the map equals approximately 2/5 mile on the ground) provides the closest inspection available. USGS maps are available by mail (U.S. Geological Survey, Map Distribution Branch, P.O. Box 25286, Denver, CO 80225), or on-line at mapping. usgs.gov/esic/to_order.html.

If you want to check out the high-tech world of maps, you can purchase topographic maps on CD-ROM. These software-mapping programs let you select a route on your computer, print it out, then take it with you on the trail. Some software mapping programs let you insert symbols and labels, download waypoints from a GPS unit, and export the maps to other software programs.

The art of map reading is a skill that you can develop by first practicing in an area you are familiar with. To begin, orient the map so the map is lined up in the correct direction (i.e., north on the map is lined up with true north). Next, familiarize yourself with the map symbols and try and match them up with terrain features around you such as a high ridge, mountain peak, river, or lake. If you are practicing with a USGS map, notice the contour lines. On gentler terrain these contour lines are spaced farther apart, and on steeper terrain they are closer together. Pick a short loop trail, and stop frequently to check your position on the map. As you practice map reading, you'll learn how to anticipate a steep section on the trail or a good place to take a rest break, and so on.

Compasses. First off, the sun is not a substitute for a compass. So, what kind of compass should you have? Here are some characteristics you should look for: a rectangular base with detailed scales, a liquid-filled housing, protective housing, a sighting line on the mirror, luminous alignment and back-bearing arrows, a luminous north-seeking arrow, and a well-defined bezel ring.

You can learn compass basics by reading the detailed instructions included with your compass. If you want to fine-tune your compass skills, sign up for an orienteering class or purchase a book on compass reading. Once you've learned the basic skills on using a compass, remember to practice these skills before you head into the backcountry.

If you are a klutz at using a compass, you may be interested in checking out the technical wizardry of the GPS (Global Positioning System) device. The GPS was developed by the Pentagon and works off twenty-four NAVSTAR satellites, which were designed to guide missiles to their targets. A GPS device is a handheld unit that calculates your latitude and longitude with the easy press of a button. The Department of Defense used to scramble the satellite signals a bit to prevent civilians (and spies!) from getting extremely accurate readings, but that practice was discontinued in May 2000, and GPS units now provide nearly pinpoint accuracy (within 30 to 60 feet).

There are many different types of GPS units available, and they range in price from $100 to $400. In general, all GPS units have a display screen and keypad where you input information. In addition to acting as a compass, the unit allows you to plot your route, easily retrace your path, track your travelling speed, find the mileage between waypoints, and calculate the total mileage of your route.

Before you purchase a GPS unit, keep in mind that these devices don't pick up signals indoors, in heavily wooded areas, on mountain peaks, or in deep valleys.

Pedometers. A pedometer is a small, clip-on unit with a digital display that calculates your hiking distance in miles or kilometers based on your walking stride. Some units also calculate the calories you burn and your total hiking time. Pedometers are available at most large outdoor stores.

Trip Planning

Planning your hiking adventure begins with letting a friend or relative know your trip itinerary so they can call for help if you don't return at your scheduled time. Your next task is to make sure you are outfitted to experience the risks and rewards of the trail. This section highlights gear and clothing you may want to take with you to get the most out of your hike.

Day Hikes

- camera/film
- compass/GPS unit
- pedometer
- daypack
- first-aid kit
- food
- guidebook
- headlamp/flashlight with extra batteries and bulbs
- hat
- insect repellant
- knife/multipurpose tool
- map
- matches in waterproof container and fire starter
- Polar Fleece jacket
- raingear
- space blanket
- sunglasses
- sunscreen
- swimsuit
- watch
- water
- water bottles/water hydration system

Overnight Trip

- backpack and waterproof rain cover
- backpacker's trowel
- bandanna
- bear repellant spray
- bear bell
- biodegradable soap
- pot scrubber
- collapsible water container (2–3 gallon capacity)
- clothing—extra wool socks, shirt and shorts
- cook set/utensils
- ditty bags to store gear
- extra plastic resealable bags
- gaiters
- garbage bag
- ground cloth
- journal/pen
- nylon rope to hang food

continued

- long underwear
- permit (if required)
- rain jacket and pants
- sandals to wear around camp and to ford streams
- sleeping bag
- waterproof stuff sack
- sleeping pad
- small bath towel
- stove and fuel
- tent
- toiletry items
- water filter
- whistle

Equipment

With the outdoor market currently flooded with products, many of which are pure gimmickry, it seems impossible to both differentiate and choose. Do I really need a tropical-fish-lined collapsible shower? (No, you don't.) The only defense against the maddening quantity of items thrust in your face is to think practically—and to do so before you go shopping. The worst buys are impulsive buys. Since most name brands will differ only slightly in quality, it's best to know what you're looking for in terms of function. Buy only what you need. You will, don't forget, be carrying what you've bought on your back. Here are some things to keep in mind before you go shopping.

Clothes. Clothing is your armor against Mother Nature's little surprises. Hikers should be prepared for any possibility, especially when hiking in mountainous areas. Adequate rain protection and extra layers of clothing are a good idea. In summer, a wide-brimmed hat can help keep the sun at bay. In the winter months the first layer you'll want to wear is a "wicking" layer of long underwear that keeps perspiration away from your skin. Wear long underwear made from synthetic fibers that wick moisture away from the skin and draw it toward the next layer of clothing, where it then evaporates. Avoid wearing long underwear made of cotton, as it is slow to dry and keeps moisture next to your skin.

The second layer you'll wear is the "insulating" layer. Aside from keeping you warm, this layer needs to "breathe" so you stay dry while hiking. A fabric that provides insulation and dries quickly is fleece. It's interesting to note that this one-of-a-kind fabric is made out of recycled plastic. Purchasing a zip-up jacket made of this material is highly recommended.

The last line of layering defense is the "shell" layer. You'll need some type of waterproof, windproof, breathable jacket that will fit over all of your other layers. It should have a large hood that fits over a hat. You'll also need a good pair of rain pants made from a similar waterproof, breathable fabric. Some Gore-Tex jackets cost as much as $500, but you should know that there are more affordable fabrics out there that work just as well.

Now that you've learned the basics of layering, you can't forget to protect your hands and face. In cold, windy, or rainy weather you'll need a hat made of wool or fleece and insulated, waterproof gloves that will keep your hands warm and toasty. As mentioned earlier, buying an additional pair of light silk liners to wear under your regular gloves is a good idea.

Footwear. If you have any extra money to spend on your trip, put that money into boots or trail shoes. Poor shoes will bring a hike to a halt faster than anything else. To avoid this annoyance, buy shoes that provide support and are lightweight and flexible. A light weight hiking boot is better than a heavy leather mountaineering boot for most day hikes and backpacking. Trail running shoes provide a little extra cushion and are made in a high-top style that many people wear for hiking. These running shoes are lighter, more flexible, and more breathable than hiking boots. If you know you'll be hiking in wet weather often, purchase boots or shoes with a Gore-Tex liner, which will help keep your feet dry.

When buying your boots, be sure to wear the same type of socks you'll be wearing on the trail. If the boots you're buying are for cold weather hiking, try the boots on while wearing two pairs of socks. Speaking of socks, a good cold weather sock combination is to wear a thinner sock made of wool or polypropylene covered by a heavier outer sock made of wool. The inner sock protects the foot from the rubbing effects of the outer sock and prevents blisters. Many outdoor stores have some type of ramp to simulate hiking uphill and downhill. Be sure to take advantage of this test, as toe-jamming boot fronts can be very painful and debilitating on the downhill trek.

Once you've purchased your footwear, be sure to break them in before you hit the trail. New footwear is often stiff and needs to be stretched and molded to your foot.

Hiking poles. Hiking poles help with balance, and more important, take pressure off your knees. The ones with shock absorbers are easier on your elbows and knees. Some poles even come with a camera attachment to be used as a monopod. And heaven forbid you meet a mountain lion, bear, or unfriendly dog, the poles can make you look a lot bigger.

Backpacks. No matter what type of hiking you do, you'll need a pack of some sort to carry the basic trail essentials. There are a variety of backpacks on the market, but let's first discuss what you intend to use it for. Day hikes or overnight trips?

If you plan on doing a day hike, a daypack should have some of the following characteristics: a padded hip belt that's at least 2 inches in diameter (avoid packs with only a small nylon piece of webbing for a hip belt); a chest strap (the chest strap helps stabilize the pack against your body); external pockets to carry water and other items that you want easy access to; an internal pocket to hold keys, a knife, a wallet, and other miscellaneous items; an external lashing system to hold a jacket; and a hydration pocket for carrying a hydration system (which consists of a water bladder with an attachable drinking hose).

For short hikes, some hikers like to use a fanny pack to store just a camera, food, a compass, a map, and other trail essentials. Most fanny packs have pockets for two water bottles, and a padded hip belt.

If you intend to do an extended, overnight trip, there are multiple considerations. First off, you need to decide what kind of framed pack you want. There are two backpack types for backpacking: the internal frame and the external frame. An internal frame pack rests closer to your body, making it more stable and easier to balance when hiking over rough terrain. An external frame pack is just that, an aluminum frame attached to the exterior of the pack. An external frame pack is better for long backpack trips because it distributes the pack weight better, and you can carry heavier loads. It's easier to pack, and your gear is more accessible. It also offers better back ventilation in hot weather.

The most critical measurement for fitting a pack is torso length. The pack needs to rest evenly on your hips without sagging. A good pack will come in two or three sizes and have straps and hip belts that are adjustable according to your body size and characteristics.

When you purchase a backpack, go to an outdoor store with salespeople who are knowledgeable in how to properly fit a pack. Once the pack is fitted for you, load the pack with the amount of weight you plan on taking on the trail. The weight of the pack should be distributed evenly and you should be able to swing your arms and walk briskly without feeling out of balance. Another good technique for evaluating a pack is to walk up and down stairs and make quick turns to the right and to the left to be sure the pack doesn't feel out of balance. Other features that are nice to have on a backpack include a removable day pack or fanny pack, external pockets for extra water, and extra lash points to attach a jacket or other items.

Sleeping bags and pads. Sleeping bags are rated by temperature. You can purchase a bag made of synthetic fiber, or you can buy a goosedown bag. Goosedown bags are more expensive, but they have a higher insulating capacity by weight and will keep their loft longer. You'll want to purchase a bag with a temperature rating that fits the time of year and conditions you are most likely to camp in. One caveat: The techno-standard for temperature ratings is far from perfect. Ratings vary from manufacturer to manufacturer, so to protect yourself you should purchase a bag rated 10 to 15 degrees below the temperature you expect to be camping in. Synthetic bags are more resistant to water than down bags, but many down bags are now made with a Gore-Tex shell that helps to repel water. Down bags are also more compressible than synthetic bags and take up less room in your pack, which is an important consideration if you are planning a multi-day backpack trip. Features to look for in a sleeping bag include a mummy style bag, a hood you can cinch down around your head in cold weather, and draft tubes along the zippers that help keep heat in and drafts out.

You'll also want a sleeping pad to provide insulation and padding from the cold ground. There are different types of sleeping pads available, from the more expensive self-inflating air mattresses to the less expensive closed-cell foam pads. Self-inflating air mattresses are usually heavier than closed-cell foam mattresses and are prone to punctures.

Tents. The tent is your home away from home while on the trail. It provides protection from wind, snow, rain, and insects. A three-season tent is a good choice for backpacking and can range in price from $100 to $500. These lightweight and versatile tents provide protection in all types of weather, except heavy snowstorms or high winds, and range in weight from four to eight pounds. Look for a tent that's easy to set up and will easily fit two people with gear. Dome type tents usually offer more headroom and places to store gear. Other tent designs include a vestibule where you can store wet boots and backpacks. Some nice-to-have items in a tent include interior pockets to store small items, and lashing points to hang a clothesline. Most three-season tents also come with stakes so you can secure the tent in high winds. Before you purchase a tent, set it up and take it down a few times to be sure it is easy to handle. Also, sit inside the tent and make sure it has enough room for you and your gear.

Cell phones. Many hikers are carrying their cell phones into the backcountry these days in case of emergency. That's fine and good, but please know that cell phone coverage is often poor to nonexistent in valleys, canyons, and thick forest. More important, people have started to call for help because they're tired or lost. Let's go back to being prepared. You are responsible for yourself in the backcountry. Use your brain to avoid problems, and if you do encounter one, first use your brain to try to correct the situation. Only use your cell phone, if it works, in true emergencies.

Hiking with Children

Hiking with children isn't a matter of how many miles you can cover or how much elevation gain you make in a day; it's about seeing and experiencing nature through their eyes.

Kids like to explore and have fun. They like to stop and point out bugs and plants, look under rocks, jump in puddles, and throw sticks. If you're taking a toddler or young child on a hike, start with a trail that you're familiar with. Trails that have interesting things for kids, like piles of leaves to play in or a small stream to wade through during the summer, will make the hike much more enjoyable for them and will keep them from getting bored.

You can keep your child's attention if you have a strategy before starting on the trail. Using games is not only an effective way to keep a child's attention, it's also a great way to teach him or her about nature. Play hide and seek, where your child is the mouse and you are the hawk. Quiz children on the names of plants and animals. If your children are old enough, let them carry their own daypack filled with snacks and water. So that you are sure to go at their pace and not yours, let them lead the way. Playing follow the leader works particularly well when you have a group of children. Have each child take a turn at being the leader.

With children, a lot of clothing is key. The only thing predictable about weather is that it will change. Especially in mountainous areas, weather can change dramatically in a very short time. Always bring extra clothing for children, regardless of the season. In the winter, have your children wear wool socks, and warm layers such as long underwear, a fleece jacket and hat, wool mittens, and good rain gear. It's not a bad idea to have these along in late fall and early spring as well. Good footwear is also important. A sturdy pair of high top tennis shoes or lightweight hiking boots are the best bet for little ones. If you're hiking in the summer near a lake or stream, bring along a pair of old sneakers that your child can put on when he wants to go exploring in the water. Remember when you're near any type of water, always watch your child at all times. Also, keep a close eye on teething toddlers who may decide a rock or leaf of poison oak is an interesting item to put in their mouth.

From spring through fall, you'll want your child to wear a wide-brimmed hat to keep his or her face, head, and ears protected from the hot sun. Also, make sure your children wear sunscreen at all times. Choose a brand without Paba—children have sensitive skin and may have an allergic reaction to sunscreen that contains Paba. If you are hiking with a child younger than six months, don't use sunscreen or insect repellent. Instead, be sure all skin exposed to the sun is protected with the appropriate clothing.

Remember that food is fun. Kids like snacks so it's important to bring a lot of munchies for the trail. Stopping often for snack breaks is a fun way to keep the trail interesting. Raisins, apples, granola bars, crackers and cheese, cereal, and trail mix all make great snacks. If your child is old enough to carry her own backpack, fill it with treats before you leave. If your kids don't like drinking water, you can bring boxes of fruit juice.

Avoid poorly designed child-carrying packs—you don't want to break your back carrying your child. Most child-carrying backpacks designed to hold a forty-pound child will contain a large carrying pocket to hold diapers and other items. Some have an optional rain/sun hood.

Hiking with Your Dog

Bringing your furry friend with you is always more fun than leaving him behind. Our canine pals make great trail buddies because they never complain and always make good company. Hiking with your dog can be a rewarding experience, especially if you plan ahead.

Getting your dog in shape. Before you plan outdoor adventures with your dog, make sure he's in shape for the trail. Getting your dog into shape takes the same discipline as getting yourself into shape, but luckily, your dog can get in shape with you. Take your dog with you on your daily runs or walks. If there is a park near your house, hit a tennis ball or play Frisbee with your dog.

Swimming is also an excellent way to get your dog into shape. If there is a lake or river near where you live and your dog likes the water, have him retrieve a tennis ball or stick. Gradually build your dog's stamina up over a two- to three-month period. A good rule of thumb is to assume that your dog will travel twice as far as you will on the trail. If you plan on doing a 5-mile hike, be sure your dog is in shape for a 10-mile hike.

Training your dog for the trail. Before you go on your first hiking adventure with your dog, be sure he has a firm grasp on the basics of canine etiquette and behavior. Make sure he can sit, lie down, stay, and come. One of the most important commands you can teach your canine pal is to "come" under any situation. It's easy for your friend's nose to lead him astray or possibly get lost. Another helpful command is the "get behind" command. When you're on a hiking trail that's narrow, you can have your dog follow behind you when other trail users approach. Nothing is more bothersome than an enthusiastic dog that runs back and forth on the trail and disrupts the peace of the trail for others. When you see other trail users approaching you on the trail, give them the right of way by quietly stepping off the trail and making your dog lie down and stay until they pass.

Equipment. The most critical pieces of equipment you can invest in for your dog are proper identification and a sturdy leash. Flexi-leads work well for hiking because they give your dog more freedom to explore but still leave you in control. Make sure your dog has identification that includes your name and address and a number for your veterinarian. Other forms of identification for your dog include a tattoo or a microchip. You should consult your veterinarian for more information on these last two options.

The next piece of equipment you'll want to consider is a pack for your dog. By no means should you hold all of your dog's essentials in your pack—let him carry his own gear! Dogs that are in good shape can carry 30 to 40 percent of their own weight.

Most packs are fitted by a dog's weight and girth measurement. Companies that make dog packs generally include guidelines to help you pick out the size that's right for your dog. Some characteristics to look for when purchasing a pack for your dog include a harness that contains two padded girth straps, a padded chest strap, leash attachments, removable saddlebags, internal water bladders, and external gear cords.

You can introduce your dog to the pack by first placing the empty pack on his back and letting him wear it around the yard. Keep an eye on him during this first introduction. He may decide to chew through the straps if you aren't watching him closely. Once he learns to treat the pack as an object of fun and not a foreign enemy, fill the pack evenly on both sides with a few ounces of dog food in resealable plastic bags. Have your dog wear his pack on your daily walks for a period of two to three weeks. Each week add a little more weight to the pack until your dog will accept carrying the maximum amount of weight he can carry.

You can also purchase collapsible water and dog food bowls for your dog. These bowls are lightweight and can easily be stashed into your pack or your dog's. If you are hiking on rocky terrain or in the snow, you can purchase footwear for your dog that will protect his feet from cuts and bruises.

Always carry plastic bags to remove feces from the trail. It is a courtesy to other trail users and helps protect local wildlife.

The following is a list of items to bring when you take your dog hiking: collapsible water bowls, a comb, a collar and a leash, dog food, plastic bags for feces, a dog pack, flea/tick powder, paw protection, water, and a first-aid kit that contains eye ointment, tweezers, scissors, stretchy foot wrap, gauze, antibacterial wash, sterile cotton tip applicators, antibiotic ointment, and cotton wrap.

First aid for your dog. Your dog is just as prone—if not more prone—to getting in trouble on the trail as you are, so be prepared. Here's a rundown of the more likely misfortunes that might befall your little friend.

Bees and wasps. If a bee or wasp stings your dog, remove the stinger with a pair of tweezers and place a mudpack or a cloth dipped in cold water over the affected area.

Porcupines. One good reason to keep your dog on a leash is to prevent it from getting a nose full of porcupine quills. You may be able to remove the quills with pliers, but a veterinarian is the best person to do this nasty job because most dogs need to be sedated.

Heat stroke. Avoid hiking with your dog in really hot weather. Dogs with heat stroke will pant excessively, lie down and refuse to get up, and become lethargic and disoriented. If your dog shows any of these signs on the trail, have him lie down in the shade. If you are near a stream, pour cool water over your dog's entire body to help bring his body temperature back to normal.

Heartworm. Dogs get heartworms from mosquitoes that carry the disease in the prime mosquito months of July and August. Giving your dog a monthly pill prescribed by your veterinarian easily prevents this condition.

Plant pitfalls. One of the biggest plant hazards for dogs on the trail are foxtails. Foxtails are pointed grass seed heads that bury themselves in your friend's fur, between his toes, and even get in his ear canal. If left unattended, these nasty seeds can work their way under the skin and cause abscesses and other problems. If you have a long-haired dog, consider trimming the hair between his toes and giving him a summer haircut to help prevent foxtails from attaching to his fur. After every hike, always look over your dog for these seeds—especially between his toes and his ears.

Other plant hazards include burrs, thorns, thistles, and poison oak. If you find any burrs or thistles on your dog, remove them as soon as possible before they become an unmanageable mat. Thorns can pierce a dog's foot and cause a great deal of pain. If you see that your dog is lame, stop and check his feet for thorns. Dogs are immune to poison oak but they can pick up the sticky, oily substance from the plant and transfer it to you.

Protect those paws. Be sure to keep your dog's nails trimmed so he avoids getting soft tissue or joint injuries. If your dog slows and refuses to go on, check to see that his paws aren't torn or worn. You can protect your dog's paws from trail hazards such as sharp gravel, foxtails, lava scree, and thorns by purchasing dog boots.

Sunburn. If your dog has light skin, he is an easy target for sunburn on his nose and other exposed skin areas. You can apply a nontoxic sunscreen to exposed skin areas that will help protect him from overexposure to the sun.

Ticks and fleas. Ticks can easily give your dog Lyme disease, as well as other diseases. Before you hit the trail, treat your dog with a flea and tick spray or powder. You can also ask your veterinarian about a once-a-month pour-on treatment that repels fleas and ticks.

Mosquitoes and deer flies. These little flying machines can do a job on your dog's snout and ears. Best bet is to spray your dog with fly repellent for horses to discourage both pests.

Giardia. Dogs can get giardia, which results in diarrhea. It is usually not debilitating, but it's definitely messy. A vaccine against giardia is available.

Mushrooms. Make sure your dog doesn't sample mushrooms along the trail. They could be poisonous to him, but he doesn't know that.

When you are finally ready to hit the trail with your dog, keep in mind that national parks and many wilderness areas do not allow dogs on trails. Your best bet is to hike in national forests, BLM lands, and state parks. Always call ahead to see what the restrictions are.

About the Authors

Mary Jo Mosher is a freelance writer and retired journalist, with an undergraduate degree in journalism and a master's degree in communication management. She is also the author of *One Man Against the Mountain,* published in 2008. She and her husband, Robert Dingmann, are volunteers for the USDA Forest Service and have ridden horseback in many of Minnesota's state parks, national forests, and other parks. Their favorite trails in Minnesota are Pillsbury State Forest and the rugged Tamarack in St. Croix State Forest. They live in Becker, Minnesota.

Kristine Mosher (center, with her husband, Evan Faltesek, and their daughter, Maarja) grew up in Minnesota. She spent many years as a wilderness instructor/outdoor educator and worked with the Voyageur Outward Bound School in Minnesota and Texas, and Prescott College in Arizona. She has hiked extensively throughout the United States, Canada, and Mexico, yet Minnesota remains one of her favorite places to explore. Kristine lives in Ely, Minnesota.

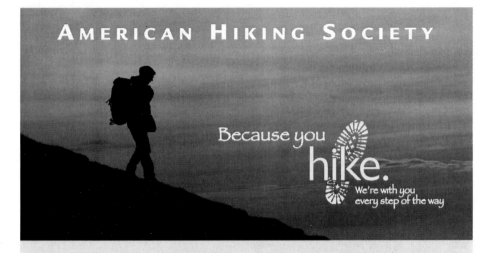